Mission Possible

Paul Williscroft's Epic Struggle Against Nazi & Communist Oppression

The young Paul Williscroft in 1937

Praise for *Mission Possible*

Reads like a novel

From the secure life of a rural pastor in Montana to the shadow of the Iron Curtain, the life of Paul Williscroft reads like a novel. There is no fiction, however, in the fact that through personal risk and sacrifice he found ways to penetrate political and military barriers with the gospel of peace. Paul and Gladys Williscroft had a mission in life; to offer faith, hope and love to people who did not and could not know. Their mission was made possible by the ingenuity of those who persevere in love.

— Paul Goodman, Superintendent Montana
District Council of the Assemblies of God

A Reminder of How Much One Person Can Change History

Paul and Gladys Williscroft watched Hitler kidnap an entire generation of children and bend their minds and made a promise to their God to devote the rest of their lives to leading children to Christ and teaching them to live for God.

As newlyweds in prewar Europe, the Williscrofts got on the last train out of Poland and then the last train out of Danzig on the eve of the Nazi invasion. There were narrow escapes from Denmark and Norway as well. They returned almost as refugees to the United States, yet they lived for the time when they could return to Germany and pursue their mission.

I had the privilege of working with the Williscrofts near the end of their ministry. Paul Williscroft was a teacher, soul winner and prayer warrior till the day he died.

Read this story of an amazing unsung hero in the battle to bring the Gospel behind the Iron Curtain and be inspired to pursue the passions God has given you.

— A Kindle Reader

With God's Help

Skilfully written account of young husband and wife missionaries in Europe before WWII and their danger-filled escape. In God's will they pastor a church in Montana for many years before returning to the mission field. A great book that will intrigue and interest Christian and non-Christian alike.

— *Richard D. Ellis*

Love this book!!!

This is a great book - Paul & Gladys Williscroft dedicated their lives to bringing the gospel and the message of God's love to the world. It is a book definitely worth reading and sharing with your friends.

— *Randolyn Wallace*

A passion for world missions

To read this is to sense passion for world missions. This is a story of submission, sacrifice, and joy that is found only in a life that is truly dedicated to Christ.

— *Harley Allen, Senior Pastor*
Calvary Temple Church

Mission Possible

Paul Williscroft's Epic Struggle
Against Nazi & Communist
Oppression

Gladys L. Williscroft

STARMAN
PRESS
Centennial, Colorado

Mission Possible

First Edition
Published 2000 by
Biography Press
Enterprise, Oregon
ISBN 0-915214-37-7

eBook edition
Starman Press 2013
ISBN 978-0-982166-22-2

eBook & Softcover
Starman Press 2025
Email: rgw@RobertWilliscroft.com
Website: RobertWilliscroft.com

Cover art by Robert G. Williscroft
Photos by Paul Williscroft
Book design by David Hiatt

BISAC Subject Headings:
BIO018000 BIOGRAPHY & AUTOBIOGRAPHY / Religious
BIO019000 BIOGRAPHY & AUTOBIOGRAPHY / Educators
BIO000000 BIOGRAPHY & AUTOBIOGRAPHY / General

Library of Congress Control Number: 2025921104
ISBN-13: 978-1-968367-54-1 Softcover
ISBN-13: 978-1-968367-56-5 Ebooks

Dedication

To the memory of my loving husband, Paul.

TABLE OF CONTENTS

Mission Possible

Paul Williscroft's Epic Struggle
Against Nazi & Communist
Oppression

CHAPTER ONE

Paul and I watched excitedly through the open window as our train pulled into the Polish Corridor station.

We were fleeing from Poland. God had helped us thus far. We had heard on shortwave radio of the Russian-German pact and the impending invasion of Poland. We had spent the summer there after a busy term of teaching at the small Bible School in what was then the Free City of Danzig, or *Freistadt Danzig*. Paul had been able to inform our fellow missionaries of political developments and of the danger of war breaking out in the next few days. In spite of obstacles, we made it to the railway station. A train was just leaving for the Polish Corridor border. There it would be necessary to change to another train to take us on to Danzig. With a prayer in our hearts, we hurried to the ticket window. To our joy, we were actually given tickets, no questions asked.

Now we were at the Polish Corridor. It was interesting watching the people milling about the station platform in the warm, late-summer sunshine. We stepped onto the platform with a thrill of relief, knowing that after a short local run we would be safe in Danzig.

3

A friendly Polish customs official came smiling toward us and directed us to separate rooms for baggage inspection and a body search. I was soon released, apparently because my luggage appeared to be merely personal.

It was a beautiful day. I had nothing else to do, so I found a crude, splintery bench on the station platform and sat down to wait for Paul. It was almost time for our train, and I expected him to show up any minute. The time dragged by, but Paul didn't come. The train came and went. Still no sign of Paul.

I was becoming more and more uneasy. What could have happened to him? A ripple of fear took possession of me. Nagging questions for which I had no answer kept hammering away in my thoughts. *Why hasn't Paul come? Where was he? What could be hindering him? Is he in some terrible kind of trouble?*

Right in the middle of these disturbing thoughts, a distraught official came rushing out, hastily grabbing a colleague by the shoulder and dragging him along as he hurried toward me. "Search the lady's luggage again, and thoroughly this time," he shouted. "Don't miss a thing! These people are German spies!"

It seemed to me my heart literally stood still. Chills ran up and down my spine and my teeth began to chatter in spite of the warm afternoon. Spies! That was a dreaded word in those tense days in the late, prewar summer of 1939. A strange sense of foreboding overcame me. I struggled to decipher what had brought about this dreadful turn of events. Did Paul have something in his luggage that triggered it, something I didn't know about? What could it be? And why? Spies! Ridiculous! Of course he didn't have anything he shouldn't.

Paul was always correct and above reproach in everything. Then what was wrong? Couldn't everyone see we were just two carefree young people returning to our Bible School in Danzig after a summer of practical work in Poland? We were friends of Poland and thoroughly despised the terrible Nazi system. Spies indeed! What an outrageous mistake!

The customs official, fully aroused now and terribly upset, grabbed my bags, snapped them open, and proceeded to dump the contents unceremoniously onto the rough, dusty platform, hate and hostility in every gesture. There lay dainty lingerie, pretty summer dresses, silk stockings, various other articles of clothing, rolls of developed movie film, souvenirs, everything scattered in sickening disarray at my feet.

I watched, helpless and desperate, trembling uncontrollably. There lay our film in its neat little round tins, very conspicuous among my other baggage. Our precious film, taken in Nazi Danzig, film we planned to show friends and churches, schools, and other interested groups. It contained all kinds of Nazi propaganda, Blackshirts marching, Brownshirted men and boys goose-stepping to militant music, anti-Jewish activities of all sortspfrom hate posters to *Kristall Nacht*. There were pictures of waving swastikas, vast crowds saluting Hitler, decorated shop windows featuring Hitler, sometimes with candles burning before him as though he were divine. All this and more. If the Polish officials looked at our film, they would conclude that we had to be Nazi spies, or at least Nazi sympathizers or fellow travelers. It could condemn us to years in prison or even death before a firing squad.

Oh, Father God, my spirit cried out from the depth of my being. You are our Father. You love us and have promised to be with us always. Please close the eyes of the officials that they don't notice our film. Guide them away from it, oh Father, and protect your children who are only here to work for you. Thank you! My confidence is in you and I know you will help us.

Suddenly, to my joy and relief, the official looked disgustedly at me for a minute or two, then at the untidy disarray on the platform and began to kick my scattered belongings into a pile, glancing quickly now and then at some item that caught his eye. He overlooked completely the very conspicuous film. I stood glued to the spot, amazed and thrilled at my heavenly Father's intervention and revelation of His love and protection. I was so lost in God's goodness I almost forgot the irate gentleman glaring at me. Then his angry voice broke into my reverie.

"Hey, you, get that junk of yours packed up again! We can't have it here all day, cluttering our platform. Get going! On the double!"

I started picking up my belongings, stuffing them hurriedly back into my suitcases. Still trembling, but with an inner sense of precaution, I unobtrusively locked my luggage and dropped the keys into a secret compartment of my large travel handbag, hardly daring to believe that the official had not investigated my personal effects more thoroughly.

Breathing a prayer of gratitude that all my things, especially our telltale film, were safely packed, locked up, and out of sight, I wandered back to my bench, settled myself as comfortably as possible, and waited anxiously to see what would happen next. I was tired. It had been a long, harrowing day. The suspense-filled hours had taken their toll. Now all the disquieting questions kept crowding back into my weary brain. There were no answers as far as I knew.

My head throbbed and an unbidden sob caught in my throat when a sudden calm, a peace, a quietness, flowed through my being. A verse from the Bible I hadn't thought of for a long time seemed to sing in my heart. It was Isaiah 41:10: "Fear thou not; for I am with thee: be not dismayed; for I am thy God: I will strengthen thee; yea, I will help thee; yea, I will uphold thee with the right hand of my righteousness." I bowed my head and softly breathed, "Thank you, Lord!"

Meanwhile, in the other dressing room, angry officials were shouting threats as poor Paul cringed before their verbal abuse. He felt resigned, defeated, and totally at the mercy of his accusers.

"Stand still, you Nazi swine! Not a move out of you, pig!" they shouted.

On the table lay a small, wrinkled Nazi flag, the swastika, which the officials had discovered as they searched Paul. It had the same effect on the customs men that waving a red flag has on a bull. They were infuriated. The further search became a wild frenzy. Now, beside the swastika, glittering in the late afternoon sunlight, lay a small gold pin. It was the insignia of the dreaded Blackshirts, the most feared order of the Nazi party.

"My God!" escaped from Paul's white lips. "They found the evidence they've been looking for. Only a miracle can save us now. I surrender this problem to you, Lord!"

What had gone wrong? We were innocent of any wrongdoing, although the evidence was condemning. The truth was really quite simple and not unusual for young travelers in a foreign land.

Paul was walking down a Danzig street one day when his attention was drawn to something shiny in a crack in the sidewalk. He stooped to look and was excited to discover a Blackshirt pin some Nazi dignitary had lost. He picked it up, thinking it would be a wonderful souvenir or conversation piece when we got back to America. He slipped it into his inner breast pocket and forgot all about it.

We had been given the Nazi flags at a church conference we attended in Sweden just before we went to Poland. Many language groups were represented at the conference. Each language group received flags representing its language. We were working in a Germanspeaking area so were given the swastika, which was the official German flag during the Nazi era. We wore them while at the conference, but as soon as possible, we wanted to get rid of them. I must have thrown mine away, but Paul, always a saver and lover of souvenirs, stuck his under his lapel to get it out of sight. He probably planned to put it in a safe place later, for posterity. He forgot to remove it from under his lapel, not thinking of the dire consequences of wearing a concealed German flag in a land like Poland, where the Germans were passionately hated, especially in those tense days. Now, like two evil witnesses, the pin and the flag condemned us to possible imprisonment or even death before a firing squad.

I was still sitting nervously on my rough bench, trying to control my shaking knees, when I heard running footsteps behind a tall barrier that separated the incoming and outgoing trains. I rushed as close as possible to the barrier. I could see Paul's drawn face as he hurried past me, so near and yet so far. How I hated that tall fence between us! I almost fell in my desire to get as near to him as possible.

"Oh, honey, what in the world has happened? Where are you going? Please, please, don't leave me here alone!"

He swung around and faced me, his finger on his lips, signaling me to silence. Quickly, in low tones, he told me all that had happened since he left me at the dressing room.

"And I don't know what lies ahead of us. We are in a very critical and dangerous situation. All of our currency has been confiscated and our last mission check must be handed over to the officials or sent back to Poland. I think we should send it back to the missionaries who haven't left yet and may have great difficulties getting out now. What do you think?"

Of course I agreed. He had the envelope in his hand and was allowed to take it to the station letter box. He told me he had to report right back to the officials, so he didn't know when he would see me again.

"But, darling," he added, "I've put us and this whole mess in God's hands. He is in control now, and He never fails. Are you trusting Him with me?"

Was I? What a question! I watched silently as Paul, without another word, turned and walked quickly toward the letter box. Would I ever see him again? What would become of us?

Oh, Father, my aching heart cried, please lay it on the hearts of dear Christian friends at home to pray for us. Give them a spirit of intercession right now and keep them praying until we are out of danger.

As I made my way back to the bench, I kept mulling over what Paul had related of his grueling experiences. I realized now how extremely serious our situation was, but the peace of God in my heart never wavered. Now I understood why the officials were so disturbed. One could hardly expect these poor, harassed Poles to believe such a bizarre tale as we had to tell.

The vast German army was camped along the Vistula River at their doorstep. The Germans were equipped with the most modern weaponry available. They were ready to move in and make hash of the spunky but poorly equipped Poles, who feared for their lives, their families, and their homeland.

Then here comes a couple of unconcerned, happy-go-lucky young Americans who should rightfully be their allies but appear to support their enemies. I could actually identify with their anger and dismay, though I knew we were in real trouble. The possibility of our being released seemed bleak. As I waited alone on my bench, one thing was crystal clear to me: Our fate lay in God's hands.

My thoughts were suddenly interrupted by the harsh voice of an official. "Hey, you, get up and get moving!"

I rose to obey, but felt repelled and humiliated when he laid his hand on my back and shoved me ahead of him until we reached a room

I hadn't seen before. On a couch across the room sat Paul, the strain of the last hours showing in his drooping shoulders and ashen face. I was shoved unceremoniously to a place beside him and the officer stomped out, shouting for us to wait until he returned. We looked at each other wonderingly. Were we really together again? We hardly dared breath, let alone say anything, but silently our hands touched as we waited and prayed.

We came to attention with a start as the door softly opened. There before us stood the most beautiful woman we had ever seen. Her golden hair was arranged in a soft roll at the nape of her neck. Tall and stately, she had deep blue eyes that fixed warmly upon us. She waited a moment in the doorway, then stepped lightly into the dingy room. It actually seemed to brighten with her presence. In fact, prickles ran up and down my spine as I looked at her. Had God sent an angel to help us as He had done so long ago for Peter when he was in prison? Paul shared my excitement as we gazed at her. Was she really there? Could she possibly be only a figment of our tortured imaginations? Had God sent a heavenly visitor to us?

As we continued to gaze at her in wonder, she quietly closed the door. With steps as light and graceful as a gazelle, she drew up a chair and seated herself before us. Then she smiled a radiantly beautiful smile. She gave no name, no introduction, nor did she ask any questions; just that lovely smile. We felt ourselves relaxing. The tensions of that long, awful day seemed to drain away. Shyly we smiled back at her.

At last she spoke, and in perfect English said, "Don't be afraid. Please tell me your story."

How eagerly we did just that, our words tumbling over each other as we both tried together to tell what had happened – the pin, the flag, our reason for being in Danzig, our work in Poland. She listened intently, nodding now and then.

As our long story ended, she rose, smiled her winsome smile, and left the room, saying gently as she went just two words: "Wait, please."

When she was gone we exchanged wondering glances, our hearts pounding. Had an angel of the Lord really appeared to a very ordinary young couple like us? What would happen next? We hadn't long to wait.

Our good angel was back in a few minutes with a new official in tow. Apparently he was someone of importance. He nodded with a friendly grin and beckoned us to follow him. To our joy, our angel came in just behind him and went along with us. They led us through a long corridor, past several rooms, to a final door. We blinked as we were led out into the blazing sunlight of the station platform. Before us waited a puffing locomotive with a long train of cars. One car door stood open. A redcap appeared, his cart loaded with luggage – *ours!* Excitement bordering on ecstasy flooded our hearts, as well as joy and thankfulness beyond words to express. God had indeed sent a deliverer, be it heavenly or earthly, to save us from our dilemma.

The luggage was soon loaded into the compartment and we were hustled to our place in the car without even an opportunity to bid our benefactress farewell or to express our gratitude. The car door was locked securely behind us as though we were common criminals, and we were alone together at last. We looked out the open window for a last glance, and there was the precious lady, standing alone on the platform, waving a good-bye and calling after us, "Don't be afraid."

The train pulled out of the station in the direction of Danzig. We looked at each other with tear-filled eyes and hearts full of gratitude and amazement – and questions, too. What had really happened? Could this person actually have been an angel? Were we really so important to God that he would send a heavenly visitor to old planet Earth to help two of His "kids" who were in trouble? After all, did it really matter how it happened? The fact remained, God had intervened and saved us from a very desperate and dangerous situation.

We were on our way at last, headed for safety and home. We rejoiced and praised God that the horror lay behind us. We were even more thankful when we learned that ours was the last train to leave Poland before World War II broke out.

CHAPTER TWO

The summer of 1913 was long and hot n the Big Bend country of eastern Washington state. The tiny settlement of Trinidad was situated atop a bluff overlooking the mighty Columbia River. The builders of the Great Northern Railroad made their headquarters there in the early days. Beginning late in the nineteenth century, many German emigrants traveled over land and sea, lured by the rumor of free farmland on the Columbia. This was lonely, dusty, unfriendly country, but the diehard settlers dreamed of the day when golden grain would wave triumphantly in the ever-blowing winds of their new homeland.

Among the many German settlers who came to this area at the turn of the century was the Krenz family. They were sturdy, hard-working people. Their first home in the New World was in the Midwest. Later they heard about wonderful opportunities out West, where good farmland was to be had just for improving it. The reports that drifted eastward were exciting and almost irresistible to these land-hungry people whose dream had always been to own a farm and gain independence. They had been serfs to wealthy landowners in Europe. When they arrived in the land of unlimited opportunity, they were ready to endure almost any hardship to make their dream come true.

The Krenz family realized its dream. Michael Krenz, the family head, staked a large land claim near Wilbur, a vital, growing town and trading post. They were frugal, hardworking people. They put all their time, strength, and effort into their precious land and were eventually rewarded. Their dream became a reality. Acres and acres of golden grain waved triumphantly in the summer breeze. Crops were good and prices were high. The future looked bright and golden as the grain. They saved every penny they could spare for the fine home they dreamed of building some day.

That day finally came. The Krenz family was able to start the lovely home they had always wanted. It was a large, square house, typical of the architecture of that period. By this time the family consisted of three boys and two girls. The middle child was Martha, with an older brother and sister and two younger brothers. It is said that the middle child in a family is often different from the others. This was the case with Martha. When the new house was being built she was in her middle teens, and a bit chubby, which was quite acceptable with these rugged farmers. Her twinkling brown eyes and rosy cheeks made many a lad's heart beat faster.

The great day arrived when Michael Krenz planned to have a crew from Wilbur come and start painting the wonderful house. They wanted it to be a dazzling white. The painters came with all their paraphernalia, and the excited family gathered around to watch. Martha was there with the rest, and her bright eyes and glowing cheeks did not go unnoticed.

A young man, recently arrived from Wisconsin, had found a job with a painting firm in Wilbur. He was part of the crew painting the Krenz house. He just couldn't take his eyes off pretty little Martha, and she found excuses to remain outside while the painting went on. It was a perfect "boy meets girl" situation. They spent many beautiful hours getting to know each other before the painting was finished. She was a tiny five feet tall; he, a good six feet. She was chubby; he, a beanpole. She was a little chatterbox; he, the strong, silent type. If it is true that opposites attract, they must have really banged together.

On the twenty-first of February, 1908, Grover Cleveland Williscroft and Martha Krenz were married. Grover had always wanted to farm in the West. He obtained a piece of land near Trinidad on a bluff overlooking the Columbia. He put up a small, two-room shanty with a tar roof where the young couple set up housekeeping.

It wasn't an easy life, trying to carve a farm and make a living out of that uncooperative desert. The hours were long and hard, the yield inadequate. For Martha and Grover, however, it was all a grand adventure. They were young and strong. They pitched in with a will. Those were busy, happy years for them, despite disappointments. Sometimes crops failed due to drought, floods, or insect pests. Grain prices fell or farm machinery broke down. Despite these problems, though, they carried bravely on, always hoping that better times lay just ahead.

Several years went by. The tiny shanty now rang with the laughter of two lively boys. Lloyd, the older, was more quiet and serious. John, the younger, was eager for fun and adventure. With two more mouths to feed, Grover worked harder than ever. He had never done much farming, however, and the good times they both dreamed of never materialized.

Fortunately, consumer goods didn't cost much in those days. A little peek at a grocery list from that early time in Trinidad brings a smile to our lips today: 16 lbs. of sugar, $1.00; 10 lbs. of cornmeal, 25¢; 10 lbs. of cracked wheat, 28¢; 10 lbs. of rolled oats, 35¢; 1 lb. butter, 25¢; 1 can condensed milk, 10¢.

Despite low prices and hard work, farming in Trinidad was a struggle for existence. Grover rented a second farm nearby and worked them both. Another little Williscroft was on the way, and every penny he could muster would help.

It was the summer of 1913, August 20. In that rustic little farmhouse on the desert, great excitement reigned. Martha lay exhausted in the tiny bedroom. Her face was radiant as she hugged an infant boy to her breast, looking him over to see if all was well.

"Oh, he's so perfect, so beautiful!" she sighed. "And, I think his name should be Paul – Paul Aden. I wonder what he will be

when he grows up. He is somehow so special. I don't quite understand it myself, but he is…well…different." Was this a prophecy?
Our son, after Paul's death, asked Paul's older brothers why they
were not as close to him as they were to each other. They looked
at one another a moment and answered. "It's hard to say, but he
was… well…different." And so he was. Paul went through life
being different.

Paul and his father, Grover Williscroft, 1914

Baby Paul nursed happily, warm and secure in his mother's loving
arms. What was the future to him? He was just a little baby, a part of
the Grover Williscroft family, with nothing more important on his
mind than the next feeding time.

Now there were three boys in the little house. It was bursting at
the seams. Paul grew rapidly and was soon a lively little boy. He tried
hard to do all the things his clever big brothers did, getting into all
kinds of trouble in the process.

There were not many other children in the neighborhood so the
Williscroft boys made their own fun. One winter, when Paul was still
quite small, Grover made sleds for the boys and even little Paul joined
in, though he spent most of the time crying and running to Martha

when he fell from his sled or was teased by the older boys. Perhaps the slope looked too long or too steep from his small-boy perspective. Whatever caused all those tears, the crying really irritated the older brothers, resulting in even more teasing.

Paul and his brothers, John and Lloyd, 1915

Paul's brothers were not to blame for everything that happened to him. He was just too small for some of the things he tried, and that was to be the set of his sails for the rest of his life, with one variation: As an adult his rule of life was, "I can do all things through Christ which strengtheneth me." (Philippians 4:13)

Lloyd likes to tell about an old horse Paul was allowed to ride when he was still quite small. The animal was so slow and harmless he couldn't possibly hurt anybody. Paul loved that horse, and felt like a big boy whenever he rode him around the yard. As Paul rode bareback round and round the yard, poor old Pointer finally got tired of the game. He knew exactly what to do to get rid of that pest on his back. He simply walked under the clothesline, raking Paul off onto the hard, dusty ground. The big boy who had sat so proudly on his mount a few seconds ago wasn't big and brave anymore. He was only a humble little five-year-old, running to mommy's comforting arms.

The older boys went to school every day. When they were gone, little Paul could ride his old slow horse all he wanted to. He could even fall off and run crying to mother. There were no clever, capable, big brothers there to make fun of him. He missed those rascals when they were away, however, and was always happy to see them come home from that mysterious place called school. He often fantasized about that awesome, far-off day when he would be big enough and lucky enough to go to school.

School days finally did arrive for Paul. The three boys were bussed from their farm to a two-room school in Trinidad. At the beginning of Paul's first year, he began having awful tummy aches about five minutes before the bus arrived. Yet, he always got better as soon as the bus disappeared over the hill. It was well over a month before unsuspecting Martha and Grover understood frightened little Paul's problem – he just wasn't ready for school yet. They made him leave with his brothers now when they ran to catch the bus, tummy ache or not. To everyone's relief, he began to like school and to show signs of fine learning ability.

The years flew by. The family moved from the Big Bend country to the Yakima Valley. What a contrast it was to the arid desert where the family had lived so long. Everywhere were luscious orchards, green fields of melons, vegetables, and many varieties of good things to eat. In springtime the air was filled with the fragrance of blossoming orchards. In the fall it was like heady wine with the tang of many varieties of ripening fruit. It was a land of "milk and honey." The Williscrofts loved their new home.

The boys went to different schools in the valley. They were no longer the little fellows from Trinidad. The older boys were fine, tall lads. Lloyd attended high school in the little town of Wapato, and John soon joined him. Paul was going on fourteen, not quite as tall as the others yet, but showing promise of becoming an unusually attractive young man. He had a good head on his shoulders, even though it was sometimes a rather stubborn one.

In 1927 the Williscrofts moved to Yakima, queen of the Yakima Valley, with its pretty homes, well-kept lawns and gardens, and wide, tree-shaded streets.

Grover soon found a job as manager of a prestigious apartment complex with a nice manager's apartment. The older boys were in high school now, and Paul attended a large junior high near his home. He was a good student with an insatiable thirst for knowledge. He eagerly discovered the new world about him, the world of books, of people (especially girls), and of faraway places. Most of all, he was beginning to discover himself.

The beautiful summer of 1927 was beginning to have the feel of autumn. School started and Martha took a job. One day a letter came from Grover's mother, a refined, soft-spoken lady of the old school, with her own strong ideas and convictions. She was planning to visit Grover and his family in Yakima.

The family loved Grandmother, and what an exciting time it was getting everything ready for this big event. Windows had to be washed, carpets cleaned, furniture polished. Even the bedding had to be hung out to air. Paul gave up his room for the special visitor, and everyone had a part in making it look cozy and inviting for Grandmother. One of the boys put a pretty bouquet of flowers on the little round table by her bedside. Another arranged an attractive basket of fruit with a paring knife for her convenience. Paul looked through his books and picked out some that he thought might appeal to a lady as clever and intelligent as Grandmother. Then, with Grover's help, he put up a little shelf near her bed and carefully arranged the books. Paul may have been thinking how nice it would be, when he was back in his room again, to have this neat shelf for his books.

The long-awaited day finally arrived. The whole family drove to the railway station to welcome their guest. They were excited about bringing her home to the shiny house and the pretty room with its flowers, fruit, and books, to the beautifully set table groaning under piles of crisp fried chicken, creamy, buttery mashed potatoes, several vegetables and salads, fresh rolls, and Martha's specialties in cakes and pies.

As the train rolled into the station, everybody was anxious to be the first to see Grandmother. They all ran out onto the station platform, crowding as close to the cars as they dared. They eagerly watched as the passengers stepped onto the platform. Happy cries of "Grandmother! Grandmother!" greeted her the moment she appeared. The whole family crowded in to welcome the dear lady.

She and her luggage were soon packed in with the family and they were on their way home. Ahead lay a great time of sharing all that happened since they last saw each other. As for Paul, he was about to face his greatest life-changing experience.

CHAPTER THREE

During that special time the family and Grandmother learned to know each other all over again. This dear lady's love, as well as her gentleness and total acceptance of them, was a benediction in the home. Grandmother Williscroft loved God and her family deeply, but it troubled her that her precious grandsons were growing up with little benefit of either church or Sunday school. They had been a busy, hard-working family, burdened with keeping body and soul together. Like many other pioneer families around them, they had never gotten around to doing much about spiritual matters.

Talking with fourteen-year-old Paul one day, Grandmother was shocked to discover he didn't know that such a book as the Bible existed. He also knew little, if anything, about God or Jesus or the Holy Spirit. Grandmothers are special people, though, who know how to fix things up. Grand mother Williscroft was determined to do something about this situation. She did so, not by preaching, scolding, or criticizing. Nor did she quote scripture by the yard. Grandmother had her own ways of doing things, and they usually worked. "Everything in its time," must have been her motto. She waited and prayed and kept right on loving them all.

One day she heard of special meetings being held at a church in town. Grandmother had been waiting and praying for this opportunity. She took the opened newspaper, showing the announcement in bold type with the picture of the church clearly displayed, and walked into the living room where the family sat. Smiling broadly, she suggested an early dinner, after which they could all attend the meeting that evening. Dishes could wait until later.

No one declined the invitation or made excuses to do something else. After dinner everyone hurried away to get ready, and they soon were on their way to the church.

When they arrived, the door stood open. The choir sang the beautiful refrain of the best-loved hymn in America, "The Old Rugged Cross." Perhaps only Grandmother had heard it sung before. Paul thought it was the loveliest song he had ever heard.

Grandmother Williscroft led the way down the long aisle almost to the very front of the sanctuary. The others followed, Paul close behind Grandmother. They almost filled the long pew, from which they could hear and see everything with very little distraction. For Paul, with his eager mind and his thirst for knowledge, a whole new dimension was opening. There was heart-lifting congregational singing, stirring anthems by the choir, and just before the sermon, a thrilling baritone solo sung by a young man whose radiant face and sparkling personality deeply impressed Paul.

The music all seemed to be about Jesus and how much he loves us. Paul's heart was moved as he listened. He longed to know more. He listened intently to the sermon, trying his best to follow the thread of the message. It was really very simple and clear for one better versed in the scriptures: God loved the world, a world lost through Adam's disobedience. He sent His Son to this lost world to take the punishment that sinful humans should have suffered, the punishment of eternal separation from God. He died in our place, and when we believe in him and confess our lostness and our need to him, he forgives us and makes us one of his children. It's as simple as that!

The minister also spoke of the Resurrection and how Jesus is alive in heaven, seated at God's right hand. He is there like our attorney, taking our part and interceding for us and our mistakes to his Father, who is now our father, too. It was all strange and wonderful, but confusing, too, for Paul. He wanted to believe it, but he couldn't understand it well enough to grasp what it meant for him personally.

As they walked home under the summer stars, everyone was unusually quiet, each wrapped in his own thoughts. Grandmother was walking on air because her loved ones had heard such a clear gospel message, but she kept her thoughts to herself. Paul was deeply touched and impressed, too. He knew he had felt what must be God in that church. Maybe, just maybe, that man's sermon was what life is all about. Could he find out? He would try.

When the family reached home, everybody got busy doing dishes, cleaning up the kitchen, and putting things away. Paul was with the others physically, but his thoughts were still on the meeting, the songs, the happy people, and most of all, the sermon. Could it possibly be true?

When he finally got to bed he couldn't sleep. There was a battle raging in him. His mind kept saying, *It can't be true. No dead person can come back to life.* Then his heart would respond, *But maybe it is true. If there is a God, he should be able to do anything. Why don't I challenge him and see what happens?*

Burying his face in the pillow, he began to pray. He couldn't remember if he ever heard anyone pray. He wasn't sure how to go about talking to someone he couldn't see and whose very existence was doubtful. It was worth a try, though, so he timidly began speaking softly into the pillow.

"Hello, God! Are you there? Do you hear me? If you are there and you are listening, will you please let me know? Will you make yourself so real that I can't doubt you any more? I will give my life to you if I can only know for sure. Thank you very much, Sir."

As he lay very still and listened, he did not know what to expect. Then a warm current seemed to flow over and through him. A deep, quiet peace filled his whole being and somehow he knew that God is. It was a vast, unexplainable knowing: *God is and He is right here in this room.* No voice or vision, no flashing lights or anything else visible, but an absolute, total confidence in, and assurance of, God's reality. This was the turning point in Paul's young life.

A few evenings later the family attended the church again. Paul, pleading that a friend was there whom he wished to greet, stayed for a while after the others left. He marched down to the front where people had gathered to pray and commit their lives to the Savior who gave himself for them. Paul made a total commitment of all that he was and all that he ever would be to the One he knew was there. He had truly stayed behind to meet a Friend.

This was a solemn surrender that Paul never revoked as long as he lived. Sometimes family and friends asked, "Why is Paul different? Why isn't he like the rest of the family?" He couldn't be, for he had found the King, who was now Lord of his life.

All through his life, Paul's faith never wavered. He never doubted God's will or his plan.

Once I asked him, as we were going through a great trial of our faith, "Don't you ever have doubts about God's being in all that happens to us, honey?"

He gave me a look he often wore when his decisions or judgment were questioned. It was an expression of tenderness, love, and compassion. "No, darling, I never do. It's not because I'm so spiritual or anything like that. It's because I met God one day and gave Him my life for time and eternity and He has never let me down. I've proven Him time and time again. He is faithful!"

Yes! Paul's surrender was complete.

CHAPTER FOUR

Paul's new life was exciting and satisfying. He loved the church and took an active part in everything. The youth group welcomed him into their circle. That active crowd had fun as well as a good balance of unselfish Christian involvement. They sang in rest homes and jail meetings, and visited hospitals and shut-ins. This gave Paul an enormous sense of fulfillment. Sharing Jesus with others became one of his favorite pastimes, even though he wasn't very skilled or diplomatic in his approach at first. He did, however, improve with time and experience.

There was one event early in Paul's association with the church that helped lay a solid foundation for his future life. A Bible teacher held a seminar of concentrated Bible teaching at the church for several weeks. He made it very interesting with charts, maps, and other visuals. Paul enrolled, was fascinated, and never missed a session. He had an insatiable hunger and thirst to learn all he could about this wonderful book that so recently he hadn't known existed.

During the seminar, the subject of the believer's baptism came up. Jesus' baptism in Matthew 3:13 and 14 was discussed, as well as Jesus' "Great Commission" to His disciples and to us – Matthew, 28:19, 20. Paul saw that Jesus' baptism was an example for us, for he was sinless and didn't need it himself. Then, in Jesus' commission to his disciples, He told them to make disciples of people, true believers, and then to baptize them. The teacher explained that the word baptize means to immerse, or put down under the water, in the original Greek, the language of the New Testament. He went on to explain the importance of baptism as an outward sign to the world of the cleansing and inward experience we have had with God.

Now Paul knew that his next step in Christian growth would have to be baptism. He could hardly wait for the next baptismal service.

When the day finally arrived, he invited his family to attend, too. He just couldn't see taking a big step like that without them there to support him. For his family, who knew only infant baptism, it must have been a mind-boggling experience to see their son and brother let right down under the water in the baptistry. For Paul, it was one of the highlights of his life, and he cherished every second.

This seminar was responsible for another lifechanging event in Paul's life: the "baptism in the Holy Spirit." He had heard this expression in sermons and Bible classes in the short time he had been going to church, but he had yet to find out what it was all about. Now it was explained and carefully shown from God's Word to be true and an important experience in the life of a Christian. He learned, too, that this is a "promise of the Father" and is for all peoples of all time who love and serve God. (Acts 2:38-39)

Not long after his water baptism, Paul went to the prayer room in the church to pray. Other friends soon joined him, and they all had a grand, old-fashioned prayer meeting. In this time of praying and waiting before God, Paul suddenly felt totally and gloriously engulfed in the Holy Spirit. It was beyond words to describe. He just felt, to quote him, "full to the bursting point."

Then it happened! Something seemed to give way, and as waves of heavenly joy flooded his being, a beautiful language he had never learned flowed like a river from his lips. Losing all sense of time, he knelt for hours in God's presence. The friends watching called it one of the most beautiful sights they ever witnessed. His face literally glowed as he communed with God in his heavenly language. The precious Promise of the Father, the blessed Holy Spirit, came upon him. He received the Baptism in the Holy Spirit and was never the same again.

Paul loved to share Jesus with hurting, troubled people. He lost his fear of talking about the Lord with school friends or anyone else who would listen. He was often called "Sunshine" because of his sunny smile and loving way of answering when people asked him about his faith.

Sometimes, after this beautiful experience, the Holy Spirit would tell him in that still, inner voice to speak to this one, or to go and see that one, or perhaps to stop everything and pray for a missionary or a sick or needy person somewhere.

In one instance, the Holy Spirit awakened him in the middle of the night and told him to get up and dress and walk down Yakima Avenue. It was a strange order. Why? Who would be walking along the main street of a small city at that late hour? And how does one approach a stranger after midnight on a deserted street?

Paul knew the Voice. It was the Holy Spirit who had given him orders before. He got up, dressed warmly, and went out into the chilly night. Walking briskly down Yakima Avenue, he saw a man crossing and coming toward him, slouched down, shoulders drooping, head bent low in despair. Paul noticed how shabby and untidy his clothes were. As he slowly lifted his head, Paul knew why the Spirit had sent him on this mission.

Paul went to him, and with an arm about his shoulders, asked what his problem was and how he could help. It was the usual sad story of the Depression era. He was out of work and had a family. In his discouragement he had started drinking, until before long alcohol was his master. His wife took the children and went to her mother. He had failed them miserably. Now he was on his way to the river to end it all.

Paul, with his arm still over his shoulder and speaking words of encouragement to him, led the desperate man to the church, which wasn't far away. After hearing him out, he shared the way to his Father's house, and the brokenhearted man cried out to God for mercy and forgiveness. A brand-new life began for him. People from the church helped him find a job. Loving, caring women from the church visited his wife at her mother's, told her about her husband's new life, and were able to lead her and her older children to the Lord. There was great rejoicing as the family was reunited and later became happy, active members of the church, the parents leading their children by word and example to their Savior and to the church.

Paul loved the many outreach activities and opportunities for service in this fine, growing church. He never missed a meeting and was a special delight to the older people of the church. They couldn't remember ever seeing such dedication and such zeal for the work of the Lord in one so young. His peers were less enthusiastic. They liked him well enough but felt irritated when their parents were forever asking why they couldn't be more like dear Paul. "He is so consecrated and Christlike!"

They sometimes teased him good-naturedly, but he never retaliated and was always ready to do things with them or to fill in for someone who couldn't be there. He was also recognized as dependable and faithful in the responsibilities given to him.

I imagine his family often despaired of him, too. "Paul, why do you have to be so different? Couldn't you, sometimes at least, be a little more like other people?" was a question I'm sure everyone in the family often asked him. But Paul couldn't be like other people and never wanted to be. He had to be himself and that self was a "bond slave" of Jesus Christ.

Paul was no saint, though. He still liked girls and cars and fun. He loved to tease and could be really annoying when he felt like it.

As the "baby" of the family he expected to have his own way. He was never belligerent about it, but very, very insistent, wearing everybody down until he got what he wanted.

Paul also tended to feel he was always right. He loved to correct people, even his elders, on almost any subject. That didn't add to his popularity. Yet he never really wanted to hurt anyone and was so sincerely sorry and surprised when a person took exception to his criticism that one could not stay provoked with him.

The Bible college dream became more and more vivid as his high school years passed. It was Depression time, though, and money was hard to come by. In the cities, one saw long soup or bread lines everywhere. People sold apples on street corners, trying to raise a little money. Many were on relief. Others refused to accept what they termed charity and managed to exist on whatever they could earn from odd jobs or peddling fruit, vegetables, or even firewood, from house to house.

Paul's brothers had married in the meantime and started families of their own. Somehow they were able to make it, and that was a challenge to Paul. If they could raise enough money to take care of their families, he certainly should be able to find a way to get funds for Bible College. Friends and family tried their best to dissuade him, not unkindly, but for his own good. College seemed like an impossible dream, but if other young people were going, so could he.

That persistence, so typical of Paul, stood him in good stead. Weren't there apples to pick all around Yakima? What if many fruit growers left their apples to rot on the trees because of prices so low it didn't pay to hire pickers? Some farmers were getting their apple crops harvested. If anyone was hiring apple pickers, he would get a job. And he did. In fact, every summer through his high school years, Paul found various small jobs besides work in the fruit harvests. He delivered papers in the morning and after school. He worked on a road-building crew one summer, doing all the dirty and rough jobs for the builders. Whenever he saw a group of men working and was out of a job, he swallowed his pride and asked if they needed a good man. Usually he got hired.

Paul had a dream he couldn't forget. He didn't share his dream so often with family and friends now. It was somehow too personal and private. It was his future and God's hand upon his life.

After graduating from high school, Paul decided that a business course would help in his future ministry. He dipped into his precious savings and went to Seattle to business college after his busy summer work. This meant postponing college for a year, but he felt very strongly that this was what he should do, and it was confirmed many times in the years to come. God doesn't make mistakes.

Paul enjoyed business college. He was a "natural" in it. A new job as busboy kept him hopping every second of his waking hours outside school. A job was important to him since too much of his precious savings went for his business course, room and board, and other living expenses.

The months in Seattle flew by. Soon summer jobs and a busy vacation again beckoned him. Raising money began to seem less of a hurdle. He went to work with a will, earning more than before. He took on many hard tasks. He was going to make it to college. The struggle was long and hard, but now he could see the dream just ahead and he was excited.

After much prayer and consultation with his pastor and friends, Paul decided God's place for him was at Southern California College, or Bible School, as it was known then. Paul could scarcely believe it was happening as he mailed his application. He could hardly eat or sleep as he waited and watched for an answer.

Finally he received the answer he had been waiting for.

Dear Mr. Williscroft,

I am very happy to inform you that we have gone over your application carefully. We have also contacted your Pastor as well as the other references you gave us. We are satisfied that you will fit very well into our college life and program. Herewith, we wish to inform you that you have been accepted.

Waving the letter, cheeks flushed and eyes bright with unshed tears, Paul dashed into the kitchen where his mother was just putting dinner on the table and his dad was coming in, newspaper in hand, to see what was going on.

"Look, look!" he shouted, as his surprised parents stopped everything to see what in the world had happened to their usually grave and mild-mannered son. "I've been accepted! I've been accepted! I'm going to SCC! I just can't believe it! I've actually been accepted!"

It seemed as though everybody wanted to do something nice for Paul before he left. There were parties, picnics, hikes, swimming, and a farewell service held in his honor at the church. There were mixed feelings as it began to dawn on people that Paul was actually leaving them.

On his day of departure Paul was excited, but he felt a sadness, too, over leaving everything and everybody he had known and loved. Nothing would ever be the same again, but there was no more time, now, for reminiscing. People were already gathering at the bus station. He looked around at high school friends, church friends, friends he had made at the various places where he worked, and even some business people he knew who had come to say good-bye. There, among the others, was his own dear family. They were proud of him. One of their sons was going to college, and he had earned it by himself. He would make good, too. He had already proven himself through hard work and self-denial.

A long, loud horn blast announced that the bus was ready to leave. A scramble of last good-byes, hugs, kisses, and slaps on the back, another horn blast, people stepping aside, a last hug for his mother, handshakes all around for his dad and brothers, a hasty jump into the bus just as the door was closing, and Paul was off on his first big adventure, waving and smiling at everybody until the bus turned the corner.

He was on his way at last, his dream becoming a reality.

CHAPTER FIVE

Paul spent a busy, happy year at SCC. He loved his classes, and his beloved Bible became more meaningful to him than ever. He thoroughly enjoyed the related subjects, too, which gave new perspective to the Bible itself: church history, Bible geography, apologetics, and much, much more.

He made new friends and enjoyed leisure times with them. The practical assignments were a delight. The students visited city missions, jails, hospitals, detention homes, churches, and youth groups, sharing Jesus with hurting, lost, and lonely people wherever they were found.

This was truly living for Paul. Now he longed for the time when he would finish college and get out and do his work full time. He had glimpsed the broken hearts, shattered dreams, and vanished hopes in the world of make-believe, which so many called the real world. Now he could hardly wait to plunge in and do his part.

The college year flew by. It was summer again. Yakima seemed like a quiet, sleepy, little place after the hustle and bustle of the greater Los Angeles area. Paul appreciated being there, however, with family and friends. He enjoyed church activities and was a good recruiter for Southern California College. Perhaps he thought it would be great to have a gang of Yakima young people to keep him company. However it was, he rounded up several who were excited about going to California with him.

His next business was to find a job. He did road work again with his uncle and spent another busy three months earning his college expenses for the next term.

In the meantime another college of his denomination had opened in Seattle. It was much nearer home and the tuition and housing were far less costly than in Pasadena. There were also more job opportunities in Seattle, enabling students to earn their way while attending college. This appealed to Paul. From Seattle he could even go home for Thanksgiving and Christmas. As he thought it over, talked about it with his pastor and others, and prayed earnestly for guidance, he felt that Seattle was God's choice for him.

It was exciting to be going to college in his own state just across the mountains from his home. Northwest College, or Northwest Bible Institute, as it was called in those days, seemed to touch just the right note in Paul's heart. This was going to be a special year for him. He felt it in his bones.

September came at last and Paul was enrolled in Northwest Bible Institute. At first he found the school disappointing, for there was no campus. There wasn't even a school building. Classes were held in a church that kindly opened its doors to the fledgling school. It was hard not to compare it to SCC with its fine old buildings and lovely grounds. Academically, the new school left much to be desired. This was the hardest drawback for Paul to accept. NBI had one big plus, however. A warm atmosphere of Christian love and fellowship overshadowed its disadvantages. The eagerness and excitement among the students was contagious. Paul found himself beginning to enjoy it as the days went by.

Like most fellows, Paul looked around to see if there were any pretty girls who interested him. And here is where I entered Paul's life.

I was born in Everett, Washington, but spent most of my school years in the sleepy little town of Snohomish, about nine miles away.

After high school, a girlfriend and I found jobs in Everett. Times were hard but we were making good money, so we rented a little apartment in Everett, attended the Assembly of God church there, and felt we had it made, until Northwest Bible Institute was founded. My friend, Iola, felt she was in the place where she belonged and was content. On the other hand, I felt that God wanted me in some type of Christian ministry. Until I got my job, I intended to prepare myself for whatever God wanted me to do. I had sent for and studied several different college brochures but hadn't decided it was God's time for me yet.

The young Gladys Buck, 1936

Now here was a school almost on my doorstep and I didn't want to give up my good job. Work was scarce. Dare I leave it to go off to college? I began to bargain with God. "My brother is going to college and it is so hard for boys to get jobs; why don't I keep my job and put George through? You need men in your service more than women anyway, don't you?"

Thus, I tried to reason with God, but He remained silent. I took His silence for consent, and to George's joy, I paid his college expenses that year. God had given me my desire but, as the Bible says about the Israelites in the Old Testament, He gave me leanness in my soul.

What a horrible, barren year that was. I *never* want to experience such an inner dearth again.

God doesn't give up easily on His children. My mother and a family friend felt a burden on their hearts to unite in prayer for me until I found God's will for my life. For months they prayed without knowing the wilderness experience I was going through. I didn't understand what was going on, but little by little, I began to hate my job, which had once seemed so perfect. I became so bored that I could hardly bear to get up and go to work in the morning.

One day while I was trying to concentrate on what I was doing, a thought occurred to me: *What are you doing here, Gladys? Why aren't you in Bible School where you belong?* The thought would not leave me when I was finished for the day. It nagged at me, tormented me, tore me apart. I couldn't sleep. I lost my appetite. I was utterly miserable. One day I told the Lord, "I'll do anything you want me to do, Father. Just make it clear to me. Is it Bible School?" That was all. Surrender.

A quiet peace filled me. I wanted to sing and laugh and share my joy with someone. My dear mother was the logical person. As I told her about my experience, she rejoiced with me and then revealed her prayer pact for me. I loved her and appreciated her faithfulness in holding on with her prayer partner until the answer came.

At last I was going to Bible School. I felt I was burning my bridges behind me the day before I left for college. I had made a dedication that was to last as long as I live. With this consecration I also experienced a taste of God's delicious humor. I loved the Lord with all my heart after my conversion, but I loved a lot of other things, too, that I needed to relinquish. I made a little bonfire of all my old love letters, souvenirs of dates and romantic occasions, and even pictures of men I had dated at one time or another. As I left for Seattle the next day, I felt that my past was behind me. From now on I was going to be a very serious Christian. No more frivolous relationships for me. I was going to college to prepare myself for the work of the Lord. I wouldn't even look at a man romantically anymore. I was through with all that sort of thing. The past lay in a little heap of ashes back in Everett.

✳

It was my first night in Seattle as a student. My two roommates and I unpacked and settled into the little cottage we were to share. Then, dressed in our best, we went to a big youth rally in one of the large Seattle churches. It was Saturday night. The place was packed. There was a feeling of expectancy in the air. We were excited. We would probably see a number of students at church tomorrow who were from our hometown. Then, on Monday, classes would begin. That was what we were waiting for.

The rally began. A large youth choir marched in and took its place. In marched an orchestra, composed of young people carrying different instruments. They took their seats and began to tune their instruments. I saw him then, seated on the front row in the second place to the right – the most handsome man I had ever seen! All my noble resolutions seemed to take wing and float away. The orchestra began to play and that special young man lifted his violin and began to play with the rest. A strange, almost prophetic something inside me seemed to whisper, "There is the man you are going to marry someday." Strangely, it seemed quite natural to me. It never crossed my mind that such thoughts were contrary to what I had promised God before I came to Seattle.

I said nothing about this experience to the other girls as we laughingly caught our bus just in the nick of time and enjoyed the long ride through the brightly lit streets of the city. The other girls laughed and chatted while we rode, but I was busy with my thoughts. *Who is this young man? Is he a student at the Bible School? Will I ever see him again, and if so, will we like each other?* Of one thing I was certain. I wasn't going to do anything about this situation. If God was in it, He would work everything out. At this point I placed the whole thing completely and absolutely in His hands and left it there.

We enjoyed a wonderful Sunday, meeting old friends and making new ones. The church where the college was housed was packed. Not only were the regular attendants there, but many of the students, too. I glanced casually around. He wasn't there. No matter. God was in charge. He knew what He was doing.

Next day classes began. The last session was an assembly where we were to get acquainted. The students were to stand and give their names, tell from where they came, their home church, and why they had enrolled in Bible School. I gave a quick look around the room as I sat down. There was the young man! He was, indeed, a student at Northwest. My heart gave a joyful flip-flop when I saw him. I listened carefully as he gave his name. "Paul Williscroft, Yakima, Stone Church."

He must be English, I thought as I heard his name. That pleased me since I have a British background. He sat quite far behind me, so I had to twist a bit to see him. He was even more handsome now that I saw him closer. He had a high, intellectual forehead, hazel eyes and wavy brown hair. He wore a serious expression, but when he smiled, his whole face lit up. He seemed so special. Could he really be the one God had picked out for me?

I saw Paul often in the days ahead, though we were in different classes. I was a warm, outgoing girl, who enjoyed people and made friends easily. With Paul, however, a strange shyness kept me from talking much with him or even from trying to know him better. I prayed often about it, and my vow to leave everything in God's hands always came back to me. I thanked the Lord for His faithfulness. He was in charge of my life. All I needed to do was carry on as natural and normal as ever. I saw Paul every day. We exchanged a casual, "Hello," or a "How are you?" now and then, and I was perfectly content with that. God held the reins.

I loved NBI. The studies were a delight. I made many friends and enjoyed my housemates. Most of the students were dedicated Christians, which helped create an almost heavenly atmosphere. Each day brought new surprises. I was given the pleasant task of tutoring students who had trouble with some of the subjects. I was chosen to be in charge of Friday afternoon activities and often gave makeup tests to students who were behind. I enjoyed doing these things and was glad that others loved and trusted me.

On Friday evenings we went on special assignments with our practical work groups. We would scatter over different areas of the city to sing, play, or give our testimonies. Some of the more advanced students would often speak. Some of them did well, and God used them to touch the hearts of people in many congregations. Many of these experienced precious conversions to Christ. That was always a special time for us.

We always came back from these field trips rejoicing. They were rich learning experiences for us, not only on how to handle ourselves and present our program, but we learned to love and appreciate the others on our team. It was a terrific experience for young people.

As days and weeks went by, I began to notice a pattern emerging. Paul was in charge of putting these teams together every week and posting them on the bulletin board. He also led one of the teams. The idea was to change the people on the teams constantly so each student could have a stint in each group, thus broadening horizons and experiences.

I looked at the bulletin board expectantly each week to see what I would be doing Friday evening. I found myself more and more often on Paul's team, especially as winter gave way to spring. It was a beautiful drive to what was then the little city of Renton, not too far from Seattle. With trees turning a soft green, flowers blooming everywhere, and the air sweet with the scent of apple blossoms and lilacs, it was a romantic drive. In those days Bible Schools were very sternly controlled with rules segregating the sexes that were like an iron fence. We could talk with each other only about lessons, assignments, work schedules, and other necessary but mundane things. It was interesting to observe how much students found to discuss about these topics.

Paul and I learned to know each other better through this team work. One day I got up the courage to ask him why I couldn't be on other teams more often, since this was one of the main reasons for dividing up like we did. He studied me thoughtfully for a moment, apparently trying to decide just how he should word his answer. Then, in his rather slow, grave manner he looked me square in the eye and said, "I guess it is because you bring something special into our team. Do you really mind helping us out? I can make a change if that's what you want. Do you?" How could I turn him down as I stood there looking into those gentle, questioning, hazel eyes? Besides, he had paid me a beautiful compliment I would remember as long as I lived. I stayed in his group.

Paul and I knew one another better now. We were never alone, but that was normal at NBI. We both took part in a group piano class organized by Delbert Cox, our fine music teacher. We sometimes chatted there, but mostly about music.

As time went on I became more and more involved in college activities. I had a job taking care of two children in the afternoons, so I had to do homework burning the midnight oil. I hardly took time to eat, and due to pressure and stress, my sleep was fitful and restless. I began losing weight and felt miserable. Dr. Ness, our school president, called me to his office one day, forbade all extracurricular activities, and sent me home for a week of complete rest. It was just what I needed. Under Mother's tender loving care and with the fun and frolic of my younger brothers and sisters, to say nothing of Dad's jokes, my spirits lifted. My father's long, weighty discussions about the beast of Revelation accelerated my recovery. I could take only so much of that heavy diet. The following week found me back at NBI.

It was good to be back again. Everyone was kind and gave me a royal welcome. Paul was among those who came to give me special greetings. He took my hands in his and, looking deep into my eyes, said, "I've missed you, Gladys. You don't know how much. Will I see you in piano class today?"

I stood like an idiot, staring back at him, as he continued gazing into my eyes and, I feared, into my heart. Could he see what I felt? It seemed so obvious to me. Did he just possibly feel a tiny bit like I did? It was a very special moment. Then the spell was broken as I gently drew away my hands, looking now more at his tie than into his shining eyes.

"No, Paul, I haven't planned to. The spring semester will soon be over and I've gotten so far behind because of the time at home that I can't handle it now. Maybe next year." As I looked at his crestfallen face, I almost changed my mind, but I couldn't afford to. I added gently, "I'm so sorry!"

A naughty little twinkle suddenly replaced the disappointment in his eyes as he remarked a bit tauntingly and with vague sarcasm, "How will you ever make a good preacher's wife if you don't play the piano?"

Possibly because of the sarcastic note in his voice, or maybe because he had touched a tender spot in my armor, I felt defensive. I had been put on the spot. I could pay him back in like coin. Tossing my head saucily and giving him a withering look, I answered smartly, "I don't plan on being a preacher's wife. I intend to be a preacher!"

In 1937 roles were more clearly defined. There was men's work and there was women's work, and though there were sometimes women preachers, the ministry was definitely for men and that was that. Paul looked at me a moment in stunned silence and shocked disbelief, then turned on his heel and stalked away, muttering half under his breath, "So that's how it is! I'm glad I found out!"

I stood glued to the spot, watching him walk away from me. My merry mood vanished. I felt like the sun had hid its face behind a cloud. The balmy spring air felt chilly. I shivered as I tried to recall our conversation and just why it went sour.

Why couldn't I ever learn to keep my mouth shut? What a nitwit thing to say to a man studying for the ministry. Today a girl would feel smart and comfortable about herself saying what I said and consider the man nothing but a loud mouth, a male chauvinist who was welcome to go on his way.

At that time, though, it was the most natural thing in the world for a ministerial student to react as he did. It was too bad Paul didn't just think his remark and let it go. It would have saved months of near estrangement and an almost shattered romance – -a romance that was still too fragile on both sides to stand much pressure.

The spring term at NBI closed. There were tears and laughter, sad and loving good-byes. There was even a rash of engagements. I don't know how the concerned parties ever arranged it with so little time together. Perhaps even Bible students cheated a little bit on what they discussed during the few moments they found together.

Summer vacation began with little more said between Paul and me than, "Bye-bye. Have a good summer. See you in September."

CHAPTER SIX

Home again, and for the whole summer. Back in my dear old home church, too. What fun things the young people had planned for the Bible students from Everett. It was good to be home!

The large family camp would be held in June at the fairgrounds in Centralia. Any students who had time and cared to go were invited to help at the camp. We got only our room and board out of it, but the fun and fellowship of being together again was worth it. My job was in the cafeteria, checking trays as the people came by me, then placing the price slip on the trays to be picked up by the cashier.

One Sunday noon as I was busy checking trays for an endless line of Sunday visitors, who should come smiling up to my stand but Paul Williscroft. Both our faces lit up as we saw each other. As I made out his bill, he leaned over and whispered in my ear, "Gladys, would you be free this afternoon to take a little drive with me in my dad's Hupmobile?" Hupmobile! Wow! That was a beautiful luxury car for that time.

I was free, and we went for the drive, stopping here and there at a pretty spot to take pictures and just chat and catch up on all that happened since we told each other that curt good-bye at the Bible School. Paul brought his camera with him and took a lot of pictures, promising to send me copies or even bring them, since Yakima wasn't the end of the world. Why, if he could use his dad's car, he could make it in three hours.

It was a beautiful afternoon together. All the tension and strain of our last time together seemed to have melted into thin air. We were both natural and relaxed. It was amazing all the things we found to talk about. We discovered we both wanted Christ to be Lord of our lives. We felt a burden on our hearts for missions and thought we would undoubtedly end up somewhere on foreign soil, though neither of us was quite sure where. We shared much about our childhood. It was a beautiful afternoon, one that meant a lot to each of us.

Then it was time to drive back to camp. Paul had to go on to Yakima and I needed to be at camp in time for the evening rush in the cafeteria. We parted as good friends, promising to keep in touch. Paul had his jobs in Yakima and I planned to return to Everett, find a job, and earn my expenses for the next school year.

Then something happened to change my plans. A very dear aunt and uncle from Pasadena visited us only a day or two after I got home from camp. They were special people, Christians, and eager to do something nice for one of their nieces. When they were ready to go home, they decided it would be something special for me to go to Pasadena and spend the rest of the summer with them. I was just starting to teach in vacation Bible School so didn't feel I should leave. They were very persuasive and persistent people. They did their best to change my mind. Perhaps I symbolized the daughter they never had. My mother thought I should go too. She felt the experience would be good for me. In the end I let myself be persuaded against my better judgment. I had a nagging feeling deep inside that should have warned me, but I didn't listen. Almost before I knew it, I found myself on my way to California.

It was a lovely drive down the coastal route. I had never visited California before and should have loved every minute of it, but that uneasy feeling wouldn't go away. I thought of the kids in the vacation Bible School I'd left in the lurch. I thought of the job I needed to find so I could earn enough to attend NBI next fall. I thought of Paul, his dedication, the Lordship of Jesus in his life, his quiet determination to give God first place in all he did. I had failed on all points. What would he think of me now? Worst of all, what would Jesus think?

Sitting quietly in the back seat of the car, I wept softly as I asked the Lord to forgive me, and He did. I knew it. I felt forgiven. The peace of God came back into my heart. I had made a choice – the wrong one – but I was forgiven. I couldn't go back. I didn't have the money. I had to stay here until school started. With God's help, though, I would make the rest of the summer really count for Him.

My aunt was sweet to me and my uncle accepted me as one of the family. We did many exciting things together. They took me to Mt. Wilson, to the seashore, to visit old friends. It was fun and some things were educational, others entertaining. In all of it, I tried to keep God in focus. It was a time of learning and maturing.

My aunt had a younger sister, Elise, just a few years older than I. She was a devout Christian and a help and an inspiration to me as I tried to honor the Lord with my life. How I loved her. She seemed to have an inborn sense of just what people needed. I noticed it in her relationship with her father and her brothers. With her sister and brother-in-law she also showed that gentle, caring spirit.

One day we were talking together and I shared my financial plight with Elise. I told her about my plans to go back to NBI when the fall term began, but I could see no earthly way I could even get my fare together for the trip to Seattle, let alone tuition and other college expenses. It was then that Elise told me about SCC. I had heard about it from Paul but had not thought much about it because of my plans for NBI. Her idea appealed to me, though. If they accepted me on such short notice, I could still probably get a job without too much trouble and I would be all set up.

We went and visited SCC and I liked what I saw. I filled out my application there and was accepted on the spot. The dean of women made a few phone calls, and the next thing I knew, I had a job as governess for a little girl in a wealthy Jewish family. I started work right away and God helped me to win the hearts of this family. They loved me and I loved them. All through my school year they were staunch friends and supporters. Many were the golden opportunities to share my faith with them, and they listened and wondered. I didn't have the joy of seeing them surrender to the claims of Christ while I was with them, but I believe they did eventually.

My days at SCC began. I met a girl I knew from Everett who already knew some of the students at SCC and was attending there herself. She showed me around and introduced me to many of the students. I was soon right in the middle of everything and busy with lessons, assignments, and friends. It was all interesting and fun. One of the men students lived not far from where I was working. He suggested that I ride back and forth with him to help me with expenses. That was a kind and thoughtful gesture, as bus fare took quite a lot of my tiny salary. We became good friends and enjoyed many pleasant times together.

I was beginning to feel quite at home at SCC. I laughed and socialized and enjoyed myself. I studied and worked and counted pennies. I made friends with some of the upperclassmen and learned to know and appreciate the fine faculty. I had made it. I was doing all right. I should have been happy, but deep in my heart was a sad, strange loneliness as though I didn't quite belong.

One day I received a letter from my brother George. At the end were greetings from Paul Williscroft. I was thrilled and excited. I had been so busy with studies, my job, and trying to be one of the "in" crowd on campus, that I hadn't thought of him much lately. I was surprised at how glad I was just to know he hadn't forgotten me. When I wrote to George, I sent greetings to Paul and asked how the pictures turned out taken on that drive the previous summer.

Soon a thick, typewritten letter arrived from Paul. It was a long letter with copies of all the pictures we had taken. I was on cloud nine the rest of the week. Friends at college said I looked like a cat who had just gotten into the cream. I don't know exactly how that looks, but my friends thought I looked and acted like a different person. I felt like one, too.

I wrote to Paul and he wrote back. Soon a brisk correspondence was going on between us, each letter revealing a little more of the persons we really were. I lived for those letters. We could write things we would have been too shy or self-conscious to express in person. We were very careful not to give the impression that we had a romantic interest in each other.

Our relationship remained that of good friends all during that school year. It was a good time for both of us. Each earned the respect and admiration of the other as we shared our thoughts, our insights into God's Word, and our longing to do God's will and to be used by Him. Without realizing it, we were growing closer to the Lord, and to each other.

CHAPTER SEVEN

My girlfriend from Everett was driving home in her old car that had faithfully served us through the whole school year. We called her "Shasta," because she hasta have gas, she hasta have oil, she hasta have a new tire, or she hasta have something or other all the time. Shasta strained our pocketbooks to the limit, but we just couldn't have made it without her. We were really fond of that car.

Several of us girls who lived in or around Seattle were invited to go along with Dorothy in Shasta. What a time we had in spite of a few flat tires and pouring rain all the way through Northern California, Oregon, and most of Washington.

We drove north on the inland route this time. It was interesting and beautiful. We visited Indian missions where Dorothy had ministered before she went to SCC. We chatted for hours in homes of missionaries to the Indians, trying to get the feel of serving in such a different culture. I was enthralled! I almost wanted to leave everything and minister to the Indian people we met along the way.

We were getting hungry, too, traveling along in the pouring rain with little in our purses and less in our tummies. We didn't tell anyone about our financial plight, but those terrific missionaries hadn't worked among needy, hungry people all those years without learning to sniff out the exact problem of those God led their way.

No food ever tasted better than the crisp, brown waffles, floating in a pool of golden syrup, that these dear missionaries so lovingly served us. Beautiful wild berry pies were often on the menu. The berries grew everywhere in the forest around the mission stations. It might be venison steak or elk roast brought in by grateful Indians. Their lives were given purpose and meaning through the selfless efforts of those dedicated missionaries. They couldn't do enough to show their gratitude.

It was a red-letter day for us when we crossed the Oregon state line, the rain still coming down in sheets with faithful old Shasta about to gasp her last. We were almost home. All of us were getting excited and restless. Shasta went so slow! We felt like getting out and pushing her. We were driving through familiar territory now. There was a town where one of us spent a vacation. Here was a store where someone had done some shopping. Now we were driving through beautiful Olympia, the state capital. The rain suddenly stopped and sunshine broke through the dark clouds. It felt like a warm caress welcoming us home. The clouds rolled away as we drove north, until, as we arrived in Everett, the sky was blue and the sun was warm. We drove into my street and there stood our familiar old white house with its rain-washed lawn and dripping shrubs, sparkling in the afternoon sunlight. It all looked dear and familiar.

The girls let me out and drove on. I rushed into the house. Doors were seldom locked in those days in my little city. To my great disappointment, no one was home. I felt very much let down, but how could anyone have known I would arrive on that day and just at that time? I took a shower, put on a dainty summer dress, fixed my hair, and went to the phone to see if I could find where everybody was.

Before I could make my call, however, there was a knock at the front door. I ran to open it and there was Paul. I felt an urge to throw myself into his arms as he stood there smiling down at me. We shook hands, instead, and I led him into the living room, directing him to an easy chair, while I went to the kitchen to make lemonade.

Sitting in the sunny living room, we sipped our lemonade and proceeded to catch up on all that had happened since we heard from each other. My first question was, "How in the world did you ever manage to guess, almost to the minute, when I would be arriving home? Even my parents didn't know that. I didn't know myself." I wrote them and Paul, too, the approximate time of my leaving SCC. I also mentioned we would be making a number of stopovers along the way; they shouldn't expect me until they saw me.

Paul grinned and then, suddenly serious, said, "I don't exactly know myself. I felt you might have gotten home today and couldn't resist the temptation to drive over and see. Is that okay?"

It was very much okay, but I only smiled and let him know I thought it was nice he came. "Why don't you tell me all about your graduation, Paul?" was my next question. He had written so enthusiastically about this big event in his life that I just wanted to hear about it.

He told about the last busy weeks when he, as one of the year-book team, worked day and night to get it out on time. Then, since he was business manager, came the horrendous task of selling enough of them to meet expenses and, hopefully, make a little profit. They scored on both counts.

With glowing eyes, he described the graduation exercises. Trying hard to sound modest, he told how he graduated with honors, one of the top in his class. Then came the big news at which he had vaguely hinted in a recent letter.

He told about being invited, by the leader of the Russian and Eastern European Mission, to teach in a small Bible college in the Free City of Danzig. He shared with me how the Holy Spirit had impressed him to have a talk with Paul Peterson, leader of the mission, who was lecturing at the college. He had no idea what to say or even why he should talk with him. He was only a student and Mr. Peterson was a well-known speaker and missionary leader. Paul had learned to obey this still, small voice, so he went.

They talked a long time. Mr. Peterson literally picked his brains, searched his heart, made sure of his motives, and studied him through and through. He must have liked what he saw and heard, because there, on the spot, he asked Paul if he would be interested in coming to the college in Danzig to teach and also to help encourage and counsel the students. It was an important assignment for a young man just out of college. Paul felt he needed to do a lot of praying before he could be sure this was God's plan for him. Mr. Peterson was satisfied with this and would wait for his answer. He assured Paul of his prayers as he went on his way.

After graduation, Paul received a formal invitation in writing to come to the college and assist in teaching and other areas. Now the ball was in Paul's court. He must let Mr. Peterson know as soon as possible what his intentions were.

Then the battle began for Paul to decide what he should do. There were many factors to consider. I didn't know then that I was the main one. He shared with me how difficult it was to decide. I assured him of my prayers for guidance and also that the most important thing was to do God's will. I knew this was Paul's main concern, too. I wondered why it was so hard for him to make up his mind when he seemed so sure earlier.

As we talked together about many things, I was having my own battle inside. My heart was aching. Had we at last found one another, only to lose each other again? But I wouldn't be sad. Paul was in my home for the first time, and I would do what I could to see that we both enjoyed an unforgettable afternoon.

We were still busy catching up on the news when my parents came home. What a happy time of getting acquainted they had. The two men started a lively discussion over some theological topic, so Mother and I went to the kitchen to plan dinner. Mother fried a chicken she had on hand, while I prepared a salad. Mother made a family favorite, a yellow layer cake with thick chocolate frosting. While she was doing the last minute things in the kitchen, I set a pretty table in the dining area.

A door slammed and in came my three younger brothers, George, Roland, and Walter. They all cleaned up and were soon joining heartily in conversation with Dad and Paul. Mother called us to dinner and my little sister Margaret, a lively teenager, as sweet as she was pretty, came bouncing in from somewhere and we gathered around the table.

Dad prayed as we bowed our heads. I looked around the table at the happy faces. What a precious family they were. How I loved them! If only the missing two could be with us. Al Buck, later of Buck Knife fame, was far away in California, and my sister, Dorothy, an attractive young mother of two, couldn't always pick up and leave on such short notice.

The brothers and Margaret were excited to find big sister Gladys home at last. What chattering, sharing, laughing, and teasing there was! My brothers enjoyed teasing me about the boyfriend who got there almost before I did. We had a good laugh over it, and Paul didn't seem to mind a bit. In fact, I think he rather enjoyed it. I was glad to see he liked my family and they totally accepted him.

After dinner, Mother and Margaret went in the kitchen to do dishes and tidy up. Dad and the boys vanished. Paul and I were alone again. We were grateful to them for being so thoughtful and appreciated every minute of that perfect evening. We made a date to drive together to camp meeting the following weekend in Paul's little Austin. It would be our first real date, and we were both excited about it.

The evening passed too quickly. It was time for Paul to leave. He had gotten a good job after graduation at Bank and Office Equipment Co. in Seattle and had to be there early. We shook hands rather formally but our hearts were singing as we parted. We would see each other again soon. It wasn't like most of our previous partings.

That precious evening lives in my heart today, as fresh as when it happened over fifty years ago. Some who were with us then have gone on. My dear parents, my brother Roland, and dear Paul. Others may leave before this book is finished, bute haven't lost them, for we know where they are and will see them again – our hope as Christians.

Paul was now on the horns of a dilemma. Should he accept this exciting opportunity to go to the old medieval Hansa Stadt of Danzig? He prayed, he fasted, he read all he could find about famous missionaries and how they were led to leave all that was dear, to go out into the unknown. He felt, deep in his heart, he should go. God had made His will clear. The real problem wasn't if it were God's will for him to accept this wonderful invitation. It was more private and personal.

He told me later what his thoughts were. What about Gladys? How can I leave her now, just when we have found each other? Does she love me enough to wait? Or does she even love me? I think she does, but I don't really know. Some days his heart was so filled with anguish and uncertainty, he was almost ready to give up the whole idea of Danzig.

Then it was camp meeting weekend. We had a lovely time talking and sharing our thoughts and ideas as we drove along. On the way, he confessed his indecision about making the plunge and writing his letter of consent to the mission. He didn't mention my role in his troubles, and I didn't even dream of the possibility of going with him. We weren't even engaged and I didn't feel that God was leading me to Europe anyway. I was sure, though, that this once-in-a-lifetime opportunity had to be God's plan for Paul. I told him how I felt about it and encouraged him to just put it all in God's hands and leave it there; and then to write the mission that he would be coming.

I'll never forget the loving expression on his face or the warm hand clasp, as he said, "You are a gem, Gladys, a real gem."

Paul sent his letter of acceptance not long after our camp meeting weekend, and God's peace filled his heart once more.

Those summer days were golden with joy and young love. We saw each other several times a week. Paul drove up from Seattle in his little Austin. We went on picnics, to young people's meetings, took a trip to Paradise Park at Mt. Rainier, and went on a moonlight cruise on beautiful Puget Sound with the Bethany Temple young people. We took long walks around the countryside, talking, sharing, exploring one another's minds and hearts.

One night, as Paul left me at my door, he lifted my hand gently to his lips and kissed it. We usually held hands as we walked along or sat in church, but this was his first kiss. It was very different from anything I ever experienced. *Boys of today just don't kiss a girl's hand*, I thought, but it suited Paul. It was characteristic of the quiet dignity and respect he always showed. I was very impressed. Every date with him was full of fresh surprises.

One Sunday evening Paul went to my church with me. I usually sang in the choir on Sunday nights. This time I decided to sit in the congregation with him. As I took my place at his side, slipping my hand in his, he pressed it lovingly, his face lighting up in the way I'd learned to love. Then he leaned over and whispered in my ear, "Don't you think it is your service to God to sing in the choir and do your part?"

In that quiet moment before the service began, I suddenly saw him for the man he was, and would be, always. God first. "Not my will, but His be done" was his watchword as long as he lived.

I withdrew my hand, gave him a warm smile, and made my way to the choir loft with a singing heart. This was a man I could respect as well as love. He would lead and I would gladly follow because he knew and I knew just where he stood. I was a proud and happy girl as I sat with the choir and sang with the others, peeking now and then at Paul's serene and tender face looking up at me.

One Sunday night, before Paul went back to Seattle, we sat in the car for a long time talking. That was the night he drew me to him and kissed my lips for the first time. He told me he loved me and had for a long time, but he didn't know if I loved him. I'll never forget that evening. I loved him so much. I cried on his shoulder as I poured out my uncertainties and fears.

I didn't feel I had a call to Europe – couldn't even think of a life's work there without clear guidance – and yet how could I stay home without him? What would I do when he left? How could he not leave, though, when God had so wonderfully opened this door of ministry for him?

There was a sob in his voice as he held me close, whispering, "Darling, my darling! How can I ever leave you? Oh, God, give me the strength to be obedient to your call!"

We sat quietly in the tiny Austin for a few minutes, our hearts too full of sorrow and joy even to talk. Sorrow because of parting, joy in the mutual love we shared. Then Paul took my tearstained face in both hands, looked me deep in the eyes, and whispered again, "My Sweetheart, how will we ever get together and how can we ever exist apart?"

My feelings, exactly.

We promised each other to pray very, very earnestly about it, reassuring one another that, if God was in our love and had brought us together, He would work it all out.

It was hard to say good night and let Paul escort me to my door, but he had to work the next day, so finally we parted, almost dizzy with mingled joy and pain. I watched as he strode resolutely to the car, turned for a last wave, and was off into the night. I never felt so sad and so glad all at one time as I did that night.

Before I got into bed, I dropped to my knees as usual for my evening prayers. I gave us both afresh to God, for Him to do with as He wished. My heart filled with a sweet, quiet peace, and I felt almost happy as I drifted off to sleep.

The next week was one of praying and trusting God to make clear His way for us both. I was so sure that Europe wasn't where God wanted me, though, that I wasn't open to listen for His voice or receive His directions. I was determined to do what I felt God wanted, regardless of the pain and loss it might cost us both.

When Paul came on Wednesday afternoon, I felt I was strong and sure and ready for him. I told him I didn't have a call to Europe, so didn't feel I should make any plans to go with him to Danzig unless I knew, without the shadow of a doubt, that this was what God wanted me to do.

Poor Paul just stared at me, his face ashen.

"Oh, Paul," I sobbed, "I really do love you. I love you enough to give you up, if that is God's will for us. We wouldn't be happy if I went with you, feeling I was pleasing myself instead of God. I would probably make you miserable, always feeling out of God's will. Don't you see? I just can't go with you until the Lord gives me a clear yes. You do understand, don't you? Just pray for me and I will keep on praying, too. I feel so sure God is in our love, I believe He will work it all out for us in some way that we can't see now."

All the time that I was trying to make my position clear to Paul, he kept gazing at me with a look of total disbelief on his face.

"I've been praying, too," he finally answered. "And that isn't the answer I got. God doesn't have two wills for us, so one of us made a mistake. Forgive me for putting the blame on you, darling, but I know what I know. That is, we should go to Danzig together and stay together as long as we live. Of course I'll pray for you, but you must put aside any preconceived ideas you might have and listen very carefully to that still, small voice of the Holy Spirit. I had to learn to know that voice very well as a teenager trying to live for God in a family that couldn't understand me at all, and He never failed me. He won't fail you, either. Listen for Him. Now, cheer up. Everything is going to be all right."

I felt comforted and encouraged as I snuggled down in his arms. Maybe I had been too sure I already knew what God wanted. Yes, I would pray and pray and pray, and this time I would really listen to what God wanted to tell me. Paul was right.

Then he shared something he had on his mind. He wanted to write to the mission right away and let them know about me and ask if it would be possible for us to go together to Danzig and share in the teaching and other activities. I urged him to wait until I was completely satisfied about going before he wrote, and he agreed to do that. I could see, though, he had no doubts at all about the final outcome of our dilemma. For him it was no dilemma, just another chance to prove God's faithfulness.

As we parted that night, the situation was no different than at the beginning of the evening, but I was different. God was in charge of our affairs, and He would bring it to pass. Our love seemed even sweeter and purer when we parted at my door. Our love went through fire and stood the test.

Whatever could be wrong with my bed that night? It felt lumpy and hot and very uncomfortable. I couldn't fall asleep no matter how many sheep I counted, or how many times I recited the Twenty-third Psalm. I tossed restlessly, trying to find a comfortable spot. Useless. There wasn't one. All of a sudden the thought flashed through my mind. *This is a good time to pray. Why waste all these wonderful hours tossing about on this horrible bed? I have a lot to pray about and there is no better time than now.* I wasn't even happy about praying because I was so disgusted at that bed.

As I lay quietly praying, I thought of what Paul said about listening for the still, small voice and laying aside all my own ideas of what I should do. I tried to do that, repeating over and over, "Not my will, but Thine be done." The result was rather interesting. I began to get drowsy.

As I lay in a sort of half sleep, I seemed to sense Jesus near me. Then He spoke, gently, lovingly, "Gladys, did I ever tell you to go to Africa?"

"No, Lord," I answered, "but I just thought you wanted me to go, because of the deep love you had put in my heart for the people there." Then Jesus spoke again.

"Did I ever forbid you to go to Europe? Did you never weep over the spiritual darkness that is creeping over that continent?"

"No, Lord. You didn't tell me not to go, but neither did you tell me to go. Forgive me, Lord, but I didn't realize Europe is a mission field, too. I'm so sorry." I truly was. "What do you want me to do, Lord?" I asked.

"Gladys, I speak in many ways. Does an open door not help reveal my plan? Does the deep, true love of a good man, whom I'm sending to Europe, not show you my plan for you? It's by his side. Now stop trying to be more spiritual than I am and get on with my plan."

I lay trembling. Did it really happen or was I dreaming? Would Jesus actually come down and talk to one of His silly kids who could not make up her mind?

The air around me seemed pulsating with the presence of God, and the pieces of my life seemed suddenly to fall into place. I still didn't know if I had been dreaming or if I really heard the still, small voice Paul talked about. I don't know to this day what actually happened. Was it a dream or the Lord talking to me personally? Whatever it was, it changed my life. I found myself singing softly into my pillow, "My stubborn will at last hath yielded." Then I fell into a sweet, refreshing sleep, that lovely song still echoing in my heart.

What a joy it was to write Paul the next morning. He read the letter the following day and called asking me to meet him in Seattle for lunch. I could hardly wait. We were as excited as a couple of kids at Christmas as we sat in the restaurant talking. We planned what we would do and how we would do it. Then we went downtown to shop for a ring. We chose a small but perfect diamond in a beautiful setting.

Later, on our way to Everett, Paul stopped at a quiet lakeside spot and tenderly put the ring on my finger, sealing the little ceremony with a kiss. We were engaged. There would be later celebrations among his friends and mine, but this was our moment.

Now it was time to write the mission and introduce another missionary candidate. They responded immediately and very positively, telling us they preferred sending couples, rather than single people. It proved more satisfactory for both the missionaries and the nationals. So our door was opened, our pathway cleared to get on with God's purpose for us.

CHAPTER EIGHT

It was time now to plan our wedding. We wanted it to be nice but weren't quite sure how we could arrange it. We were as poor as church mice. Our mission arranged for us to have a monthly salary of seventy-five dollars when we started our work in Danzig. It wasn't much, but food and rent and other things were cheaper in Danzig than in the States, and we felt we could manage on that amount when we got there, but that didn't help us now.

Paul still had his job, for which we were thankful, but we had college debts to pay and we needed to put a missionary outfit together for Danzig. We did visit a few churches where we told about the mission and what we hoped to do there. We were young and inexperienced in presenting a missionary program, so the offerings were often small. We also felt that all monies raised in our meetings should be used for missionary purposes, not for our wedding.

All well and good, but we needed money *now*. We talked with our parents, and they agreed to help us as much as they could. They were very understanding and helpful, which gave us new courage to go on with our plans. Young people from my church volunteered to take care of decorating the sanctuary and fellowship hall. The local florist provided the flowers and candelabra, for the tremendous price of eight dollars. My pastor, Dr. Butterfield, offered to let the marriage ceremony be his gift to us. The ladies of the church took care of cakes and sandwiches. The men bought the ice cream. Several of my aunties provided finger foods.

We were reminded of the children of Israel bringing contributions for the tabernacle. Finally, Moses had to order them to stop; they brought more than enough. It was exactly like that in our wedding planning. We had to tell our friends they could stop now. We had more than enough. We felt rich beyond words with friends like these!

We visited churches in the Seattle-Everett area on behalf of the Russian and Eastern European Mission whenever we had a free evening or weekend. We learned a lot about each other on these trips. We discovered our glaring lack of speaking experience, our immaturity when it came to working things out with pastors or appealing for funds from congregations, and many other things. Each could observe the other's talents and abilities, or lack of them.

At that period in his ministry, Paul had a hard time expressing himself before an audience. He would make long pauses while he tried to collect his thoughts. His words refused to flow smoothly. Often they were interspersed with verbal pauses: an "ahhhhh…" or an "errrrrr…or, maybe, an "ummmmmm…." I loved him so much I would writhe in agony for him as he tried so desperately to express himself in a way that would inspire his audience, but somehow it wouldn't come out right.

What about me, though? Did I pull any booboos? Paul, in his systematic way, always kept a little notebook in his breast pocket. As I talked to the people, Paul would pull it out and begin writing. I got so nervous when he did this I would stutter and stammer and forget what I wanted to say. Of course that all went into the notebook. I knew that, in his precise way, all my blunders and weaknesses of manner or speech were written down in that horrid little book. I dreaded it when we were back in the car and he opened his little black book and read the riot act. It usually went something like this: "Too many gestures. You smile too much. Remember, this is serious business. Don't raise and lower your voice so often; it is distracting." And on and on.

I would be seething by this time, but usually only promised to try to do better. A few times I tried defending myself or reminded him that he wasn't so hot himself. However, his loving, "Darling, I only wanted to help you," silenced me promptly. Then I told him things I thought would improve his presentation. He never defended himself or showed resentment over my comments. Instead, after my barrage of "constructive criticisms," he would take me in his arms and lovingly confess how much he needed my help and cooperation in trying to improve his platform manner and delivery. I felt like a first-class worm!

I don't know if either of us were really helped by this method, unless it relieved tensions after a meeting that taxed everything in us to capacity. In later years we learned how to handle these delicate matters more diplomatically and were often blessed through each other's observations.

Between meetings, visits, and fun times, we went shopping for our wedding and the forthcoming trip. One day my girlfriend, Iola Christenson, and I went shopping in Seattle for my wedding dress. We shopped at almost every store in the city except the Bon Marche. Everything we saw was either unsatisfactory or it was too expensive. We finally decided it wouldn't do any harm to try the Bon. A gracious saleslady greeted us. We told her we were looking for a wedding gown, the prettiest we could get, and named a price. She smiled, hurried away beaming, and soon returned with a dress made of the palest ivory slipper satin on graceful princess lines, with a beaded yoke of tiny seed pearls. It was *the* gown.

When I tried it on. I felt transformed from an ordinary girl into a beautiful bride. It was *my* dress! But could I have it? In a tiny voice, I asked the price. The lady smiled. I'm sure she knew what was going on in my mind.

"This particular dress is on sale today. You are the lucky one. It has been marked down to seven dollars. Is that all right for you?"

✳

Iola was wonderful about helping with our wedding plans. I was so in love and so excited about the future and our ministry in Europe that I couldn't seem to get very wrapped up in the wedding itself. One day as we were talking about various possibilities for making the wedding new and impressive, Iola came up with a marvelous idea.

"Gladys, why don't you have a white wedding?" she asked. Well, that was what we were already planning. That was nothing new, I reminded her.

"Gladys, you don't know what I mean," she went on. "I was thinking about an *all* white affair. You, of course, will wear white, but how about the maid of honor, the bridesmaids, and the flower girl, all wearing white, too. All the flowers could be white, those for decoration and those we wear or carry. You and Paul will be in the Lord's service, so white would be very appropriate and charming, don't you think? You and all of us girls could carry white Bibles decorated with white or light pink flowers. The boutonnieres for the men and the corsages for the mothers and those who pour and serve could be white, too. What do you think?"

Her face glowed with love and enthusiasm. It was contagious. I fell right into the spirit of the thing with her.

"Yes, and we could have a tall white cross covered with evergreen boughs and entwined with snowy calla lilies. On either side of it could be the candelabra and on either side of those tall vases or urns of white gladioli. Gladioli would be special, because everyone calls the pair of us 'Gladioli' anyway, don't they, and you are my maid of honor, so that would make it just perfect! Paul and I would stand in front of the cross, but on a lower level, while his friend, Hilding Halvorson sings, 'Beneath the Cross of Jesus.' Doesn't that sound wonderful?"

Our wedding day finally arrived – a clear, cool, sunny autumn day: October 2, 1937. We were so busy all week with last-minute arrangements we scarcely had time for each other. We missed the sweet times of sharing, praying, teasing, and enjoying being together. It was Saturday, and there were still things to look after at the church, so I went down early to see what I could do.

As we were laughing and talking and sometimes working, my father dropped by with a letter for me. It had just arrived and was from Paul. He had to work that day. I dashed off to a quiet spot to enjoy it alone.

To my own Sweetheart,

Honey, I'm just going to write you a brief note tonight to tell you I love you with all my heart. Our letters this week seem to have been so cold and businesslike. There has been just too much on our minds, hasn't there? Tomorrow at this time we will belong to each other for ever and ever. I'm sooo glad!

That's all I have to say – everything is arranged at this end, and I hope you haven't worn yourself to a frazzle in Everett. Be seeing you tomorrow as early as possible.

With lots of love,

Paul

This little note, short, written in haste on a company letterhead, somehow expressed Paul's deep, inner feelings, his tenderness and caring for his bride-to-be, who might feel lonely or neglected because of our busy week. I loved him so much. His little note made my day, my wedding day, our wedding day. I've kept and cherished it for over fifty years.

*

The ceremony was beautiful. We were both so unspeakably happy as we stood before that cross and let the beautiful words Hilding sang fill our hearts.

"Beneath the cross of Jesus, I feign would take my stand. The shadow of a mighty rock, within a weary land. A home within the wilderness, a rest upon the way, from the burning of the noontime heat, and the burden of the day." How often the memory of this lovely hymn has comforted and sustained us in times of danger, loneliness, or sorrow.

I wrote these lines in our wedding book not long after the wedding.

Eighty-five guests were present. Henry Fenstra presided as toastmaster. Speeches, songs, and games filled the evening. Many dear friends and relatives were present. The reception broke up around midnight.

I draw a rosy, silken curtain over the rest of that beautiful day. It was too precious, too intimate, too personal to share. It was ours alone, to cherish and treasure as long as we lived.

On Sunday, after church, we drove to a little cabin near Lake Tipso on the Yakima side of Mt. Rainier. Already the trees were attired in robes of gold and crimson. A wee mountain stream babbled its way over the pebbles, almost at our doorstep. The music of the brook, mingled with the sleepy twitter of birds, blended into our nighttime dreams. It was a story-book experience. We knelt together that first night in our little retreat and thanked God for each other and for this beautiful place of refuge and quiet after the busy weeks we'd just gone through. We thanked Him most of all for His love to us and for His presence in our lives which made our human love more divine.

Newlyweds Paul and Gladys Williscroft, October 1937

This is how the *Everett Daily Herald* reported our Christian wedding:

> Bethany Temple was the scene of an impressive and beautiful wedding Saturday evening when Miss Gladys L. Buck, daughter of Mr. and Mrs. H. Buck of Everett, became the bride of Paul Williscroft, son of Mr. and Mrs. G. Williscroft of Yakima. The candlelight service was performed by the Rev. C. E. Butterfield, before a tall white cross entwined with calla lilies in a setting of autumn leaves, evergreens, and white flowers. Preceding the ceremony, Professor Delbert Cox of Seattle, accompanied by Mrs. E. Carlson, played "To a Wild Rose" as a violin solo, during which the tapers were lighted by Miss Gladys Rodland and Miss Verna Bohnstedt, who were gowned in white. This was followed by a solo, "I Love You Truly," sung by Mrs. A. Arnivick. The wedding march was played by Mrs. Yaden of Yakima. After the wedding party reached the altar, Hilding Halvorson of Seattle sang "Beneath the Cross of Jesus."
>
> The bride, given in marriage by her father, wore a white satin gown made on fitted princess lines. Her long veil was banded with wide lace, which was fashioned bonnet-style with a coronet of beaded seed pearls. She carried a white Bible showered with gardenias and swansonia. Miss Iola Christenson, maid of honor, wore white taffeta and carried a white Bible with Cecil Brunner roses, and bridesmaids were Miss Bernice Brown, in white lace, and Miss Margaret Buck, sister of the bride, wore white organza. They also carried white Bibles with Cecil Brunner roses. Little Yvonne Butterfield, in white moiré with a basket of pink rose petals, was flower girl. Earl Wilkie was best man and Harold Rhodes and Walter Wheeler were groomsmen. At the close of the ceremony, Hilding Halvorson sang "At Dawning."
>
> A reception for eighty-five guests was held at the Grace Methodist Episcopal Church. Assisting were the Misses Ruth and Ethel Ingelstadt, Clarice Christenson, Dorothy Dalton, and Marjorie Butterfield.

The Paul Williscrofts left on a short wedding trip, after which they will leave for Danzig in Europe, where they will teach in the Russian Eastern European Bible Institute. For traveling Mrs. Williscroft wore a currant-red knit dress with a brown coat and matching accessories.

(*The Everett Daily Herald,* October 4 or 5, 1937, by permission.)

CHAPTER NINE

The big day of our departure finally arrived. Our trunks were packed and ready to send ahead to the ship. Our hand luggage was ready to take with us. Our farewell notes had been written and sent. We had paid our respects to relatives and friends in the vicinity. With pounding hearts, we were ready to take our little Austin, that had served us so well, to Seattle and leave it with our best man, Earl Wilkie, to be sold.

It was a bone-chilling, dismal January day. The leaden sky threatened snow. Our train was to leave Seattle at seven thirty that evening, so we had the whole day to wind up things in Everett and take a leisurely drive to Seattle. The faculty and students of NBI arranged a farewell gathering for us at the station. We adjusted our schedule to get there in plenty of time before the train left.

Since the train would pass through Everett to pick up passengers after leaving Seattle, Bethany Temple arranged a station farewell for us there. The train stop would be long enough to allow for that. It was all very exciting, but we had mixed emotions as well. We thought of the long, long distance between Everett and Danzig. We remembered the critical political situation in Europe, brought on by Nazi Germany and her busy preparation for war. It might be a very long time before we saw our home and loved ones again. Though neither of us voiced it, we both realized we might never see them again.

Home, in the light of these bleak possibilities, looked very precious, and our families and friends never seemed more dear. We packed the two overseas trunks that the Stone Church in Yakima gave us as a going-away present with a strange mixture of joy and sorrow. We could hardly pack because of unbidden tears that dribbled down our cheeks. The neatly folded linens and other things in our trunks got a salty bath.

My parents gave us a wardrobe trunk with many drawers. They were perfect for organizing smaller articles. The wardrobe area was just right for hanging clothing that wouldn't be needed right away. This loving gift had also touched a soft spot in our hearts. Paul's parents, too, did many thoughtful things for us. The young people in both our churches gave going-away parties. They loaded us with things for future use in Danzig or for the trip. Our home churches held formal farewell services where the whole church prayed and committed us into God's hands.

These were all beautiful and caring tributes. We felt surrounded with love. No wonder, when we were actually leaving, that the anticipation and excitement were a bit dampened. We realized we would probably never again know the selfless love and unconditional support that these loved ones from our youth were showering upon us.

As we gathered on the station platform in Seattle, there were songs, speeches, a short word from the college president, Henry Ness, and a closing prayer. It was almost drowned out, though, by the clatter of the train pulling in with a puff of steam and a whistle blast. Passengers poured out and new ones vied with one another to get in. We were all busy hugging, kissing, and back-slapping, mingled with tears. Paul and I were torn between laughter and tears the whole evening.

The deep-throated voice of the whistle sounded again – -that nostalgic, lonely sound that we loved to hear as children, snug in our beds, quivering with delight as the midnight express rumbled through town. Its mournful whistle always seemed to be calling out to us in the night.

This time, though, we were going to be on that train. We stood on the steps until the last passenger had clambered aboard. With a stentorian "All aboard," the trainman began closing doors. Friends grabbed our hands and held on until a last blast of the whistle and the impatient gesture of the trainman let them know it was time for us to get in the coach so the door could be closed.

We opened the window at our seat and watched until we rounded a curve, whereupon station and people vanished into the misty darkness. We were on our way at last.

Paul reached over and took my cold hand in his warm one, grinning down at me with a twinkle in his eye.

"Well, honey, what do you know? We are actually alone at last and on our way. Let me wipe away those tears glistening on your eyelashes. No time for them now. We've burned our bridges behind us and before us shine the promises of God. We are on our way to do what we were born to do. It's time for rejoicing, don't you think?"

All the while he was speaking, he was gently wiping my tears away with his clean pocket handkerchief. I saw that sparkle of excitement in his eyes and sensed the tug of his commitment, urging him on. All at once my loneliness and sorrow of parting vanished. I felt as inspired as he looked. I tingled all over with expectation and eagerness to be up and doing. We hugged each other out of pure exuberance as we flew through the night to our appointment with destiny.

Our joy was so great and the pull of our calling so intense, we had completely forgotten we were to make a stop in Everett and go through the agonies of good-bye all over again. The speeding train slowed coming to a grinding halt at the Everett station. The church people, young and old, were gathered, as well as some of my friends from work. Among them I could see my family smiling bravely at me, while holding back tears.

The young people sang and Pastor Butterfield spoke a few kind and encouraging words. The stopover was short. Before we knew it, in the middle of the beautiful old hymn, "God Be with You Till We

Meet Again," the cry, "All aboard" rang out. The whistle blew, we hurried up the steps into the train and were on our way once more.

The lovely strains of "God Will Take Care of You" wafted through the open window where we sat. We looked out for a last glimpse of these dear ones. They were waving their handkerchiefs as they sang. I'll never forget my teenage brother, Walter, as he raced along the platform beside the moving train. All the way he was waving and shouting, "So long, Glad and Paul! So long, Glad and Paul! So long! So long!"

The train was too fast for Walter. He had to stop while we rushed away from him. We looked until the last faint glimpse of him and the others, faded into the winter night.

The day was long and emotion-packed. We were bone tired as we took our seats and stared into the darkness outside our window. There was nothing to see but steam and an occasional spark from the locomotive, so we decided it was time to try out the accommodations in the sleeping car. It was our first experience in a pullman, and we thought it would be difficult to sleep. We were weary, though, and before we knew it, we were in dreamland. Our train sped into the night, ever eastward on the first leg of our long journey.

※

The trip across the snow-covered landscape was unforgettable. The glorious Cascade Range, the magnificent Rockies, the rolling plains, stretching out into infinity – so vast, so varied, so endless. As we crossed Montana, a man in our car who had never made this trip before slept a lot. Whenever he awoke he would ask at random, "Where are we now?"

Someone would answer, "Montana."

Then he would go back to sleep for awhile. When he woke up again he would make the same inquiry.

Again the answer, "Montana."

This went on for the two or three days it took to cross this endless state.

The poor fellow finally decided there was no end to Montana. He had resigned himself to this, when someone shouted noisily,

"North Dakota!" The man jumped up, looked out the window, sighed, and sat down again, murmuring to himself, "No difference. No difference."

At Rochester, New York, we made a stopover to visit Paul's former pastor, Arnie Vick. He was pastoring in Rochester at that time. Pastor Vick and his wife received us warmly and did all they could to show us a good time. One day we went with them to see the winter wonderland of Niagara Falls. It was our first visit to this American and Canadian marvel. I don't have words to describe our impressions as we gazed on this fairyland of ice and snow. Its lacy, glittering splendor was awe inspiring. Our hearts and minds, already so full of the wonder, grandeur, and greatness of America, could hardly take in anymore. *This must be the crowning feature,* we thought. *This is the icing on the cake.*

We loved the few days in Rochester, but it was time to go. We were headed for the Big Apple, New York City, another first for us. I don't know if I can properly describe our impressions of this behemoth. It dwarfed everything. Even half a century ago the streets seemed like tunnels between towering skyscrapers. How does the first glimpse of this great city affect people today, I wonder?

Most of the people on the street gave the impression of racing, glassy-eyed, to some earth-shaking event. If we stopped to inquire the way, they would give us an impatient stare, wave a hand in one direction or the other, mumbling "Uptown" or "Downtown," leaving us utterly bewildered.

The sights and sounds and smells excited us. The irresistible aroma of fresh buttered popcorn from a street vendor's stand tickled our nostrils. The old flower woman, with cheeks like withered apples, held out a bunch of fragrant purple violets, coaxing me to sniff them. They were a delight to eyes and nose alike. For a few cents we traveled all over the city by subway. It was very exciting for us two small-town kids. We took bus tours to different places of interest. We visited the big, well-known stores like Macys and Gimbels, which was fun, even though we didn't have much money to spend. We went to Times Square and listened to soap-box orators. We laughed when two of them, quite near each other, did their best to make fools of each other.

We loved it all and were amazed at how much we were able to see and do in the short time we had in the world's biggest city.

New York was a wonderful, exciting, exhilarating place to visit, but we decided we preferred the quiet serenity of Puget Sound or fruitful Yakima Valley as a place to call home.

Our last day in New York was busy, but we had lots of time to take care of the remaining details. We didn't have to board ship until eleven that evening. She was due to pull out at midnight. We wanted to visit the dock to see if our luggage had arrived and to check on our mail. We hadn't heard from home since we left. We stayed in a missionary home in the city not too far from the subway and bus lines, so it was easy to get around. We were booked to sail on the *SS Bremen* of the North German Lloyd Line. We were awestruck at the immensity and beauty of the magnificent vessel that was designed to carry us across the vast expanse of water.

Other matters relating to the voyage needed our attention, so we spent all morning and part of the afternoon winding things up and wandering along the docks. It was a treat for me, having spent my life on the coast where I loved watching the ships come and go. We saw passenger liners from all over the world. It seemed one would come in and another steam out every minute or two. Besides the great ocean liners, there were freighters and tankers, large and small. Tug boats darted about like water bugs. All the waterfront activity was exciting.

I kept a log of our voyage. The following passages convey the freshness and thrill we were feeling when I wrote it so many years ago.

We boarded the boat last night about eleven o'clock. What excitement on the pier just before we embarked. It was like a carnival. Toys, balloons, gadgets, and other junk were everywhere on display. Flower vendors shouted their wares. As a big bunch of delicious violets was thrust into my hands, Paul took one look at my enraptured face and bought them for me. They are in our stateroom now and bring the fragrance of spring with them.

There were crowds of people on the pier. Some had come to see friends or loved ones off. Others were just curious onlookers, but most of them were happy, excited passengers like ourselves, waiting impatiently to board ship. It was easy to spot them by the look of expectancy on their faces. It formed a delightful picture: the warm good-byes, and the sad ones; the fond embraces of friends and relatives. Who knew what could happen? They might not meet again for months or years; perhaps never in the critical temper of our time.

We watched it all with mingled emotions. No one was there to wish us even one *au revoir*. We didn't feel that it was really important, however, because our best friend was with us. He always would be, no matter where in the world we went. At last the call went out to board ship. Passports came out, hand luggage was gathered together, and the passengers began lining up at the ribboned-off gangplank. An officer stood at the bottom and top of the gangplank to check our papers, passports, and possibly other things.

We stayed on deck, watching the pageant going on around us, until a booming voice sounded over the megaphone, "All ashore that's goin' ashore!" People began a final round of hugs, kisses, and tearful good-byes, as friends and well-wishers started back down the gangplank. We went down to our stateroom for a few minutes to warm up, then, just before the whistle announced our departure, we hurried up to the deck again, to watch our boat pull out.

The deep tones of the whistle rumbled through the ship. It was twelve thirty a.m., thirty minutes late. With an easy, gentle motion we moved out from the pier. Little tugboats heaved and chugged as they turned the huge vessel around so her nose pointed down river. We stood fascinated, watching every move. The sailors on a lower deck were hauling enormous ropes and doing all sorts of important jobs that we didn't understand. They sang and shouted lustily as they worked. What fun to watch them.

As we continued on down the river, the beautiful skyline of New York, skyscraper upon skyscraper gleaming against the dark blue velvet of the midnight sky, gradually faded farther and farther into the mist. We were very tired after the long, busy day, but didn't dream of going to our stateroom until we passed the Statue of Liberty. Standing with several others in a protected spot between two large ventilators, we watched and waited, straining our eyes to see a light in the darkness. Finally, through the gloom, a faint gleam shone out across the dark water, the beams of a torch held bravely aloft in the outstretched hand of Liberty.

It was so dark we could only faintly discern the outlines of the famous monument. We looked as long as there was the vaguest shadow to be seen. Then, cold and tired, we made our way to our cabin. It was cozy and warm. Our beds were turned invitingly down so we could jump right in. We were ready to do just that, too.

First, though, we read a psalm and had our evening prayers together. We thanked our Heavenly Father for all His loving care thus far on our long journey. We slipped between the clean white sheets and were gently rocked to sleep in the cradle of the deep.

January 22, 1938

We were pleasantly awakened this morning by the soft, bell-like tones of a gong in the hands of a passing steward. With a stretch and a hasty rub of sleepy eyes, we jumped out of bed and before long were following the crowd to the lovely dining room. The appetizing aroma of bacon and eggs, good German coffee, toast, and all sorts of German goodies greeted us. A typical American breakfast was always served, no matter what European delicacies might be on the menu.

A courteous steward showed us to our table and we proceeded to order a hearty meal. Paul ate two omelettes and informed me that I would have to learn to make them like that. After breakfast we strolled out on the deck where we watched the waves and enjoyed trying to identify passing steamers. We met two nice German girls who told us a lot about the country, its customs and traditions, as well as conditions under the Nazis. They seemed quite satisfied under that system, which caused us to wonder.

We found a lot of mail in our stateroom last night, so found a sunny, sheltered spot on deck and went through it. There are twenty-nine steamer letters, eight telegrams, one cable, and a lot of cards. It is fun going through them, but they often bring a tear to our eyes, they are all so loving and sweet.

A strong wind came up this afternoon and almost blew us away as we walked on the deck. It is customary to dress for dinner, so we slipped into something nice and found they were serving a beautiful buffet. It looked like a picture, spread out on the gleaming white cloth. There was so much to eat we couldn't possibly sample even a part of it. We managed to eat our share, though, and everything was simply delicious. There are many night-time activities, but I don't think we care to take part in all of them, but there are still plenty of things we can enjoy. It's late now and we are tired from last night's excitement and late hours, so we bid you all, good night.

CHAPTER TEN

We enjoyed the first night. It was exciting, romantic, and fun. The first day was pleasant. When we got up the second morning, Paul was bright and chipper as usual, but I had a queer feeling in the pit of my stomach that wouldn't go away. Paul suggested a brisk walk on the deck might help my queasy tummy, so we went topside to the high, breezy upper deck for our promenade. As we opened the doors to go out, a strong gust of wind and a sudden long roll of the ship almost threw me to the deck, but Paul caught me in time. I felt very dizzy and nauseated then. Without warning, my whole world turned upside down.

"Paul, Paul, I think I'm dying! Help me to the rail, please!" I gasped.

Paul took one look at my greenish face and terrified eyes and rushed me to the railing as fast as he could. In spite of my awful feeling, there wasn't much for the fish. All I could do was gag, retch, and cough, feeling worse every second. I can smile now, but there was certainly nothing to smile about then. Paul gaped at me, his face a mixture of concern and mischief, sympathy and amusement.

I hated for him to see me in this condition, and I hated myself, the daughter of seafaring people as far back as our British history reached, for succumbing to that most unromantic, ugly, and utterly horrible malady, seasickness.

Paul thought a little food in my stomach might help, and against my better judgment, I allowed him practically to drag me down to the dining room. He opened the door and as the scent of food poured out, a literal barrage, a hurricane of indescribable nausea swept over me. Paul, food, and everything else was forgotten. I turned and ran to a nearby powder room. I felt awful. I just wanted to die! I didn't think I could stand any more, but neither could I die. I just had to stand it.

Paul was waiting for me outside the powder room as I reeled out. He helped me to our stateroom, got me ready for bed, tucked me in, and went to get some breakfast.

I was glad to be back in bed, but felt sick and miserable. I was sorry for Paul, too. We had looked forward for a long time to this romantic voyage together, and now I had ruined it all by my stupid seasickness. There was nothing to do but bear it, or so I thought.

After Paul had a little breakfast, he came back to our room with a hot cup of tea and a plate of zwieback for me. I took one look, and the dreadful nausea began again. I could only lie back down, murmur a weak thank you, and wave it away. Paul looked so helpless and disappointed I felt sorry for him. He wanted to stay with me, but I felt he needed the fresh air and a chance to take advantage of the bright sunny day. I urged him to go on up and enjoy the glass-enclosed promenade deck. There were plenty of deck chairs, blankets, and pillows to help make one comfortable. That was the place where passengers liked to gather, drink hot bouillon, and get acquainted. Paul decided to do that. There was nothing much he could do for me anyway, so with a kiss and a wave of the hand, he was gone.

I lay, weak, exhausted, and miserable, wondering how long this siege would last. Suddenly there was a knock on the door, and our room steward poked his head in. He wanted to see if we had gone up on deck yet so he could make up our room. He looked surprised to see me in bed, but one look let him know what the trouble was.

He evidently had a lot of experience with passengers like me. He mumbled something in German, that I didn't understand, and hurried away.

A few minutes later he returned with a cup of steaming bouillon and a package of seasickness bags. I took one look at the soup and knew I couldn't drink it. He went ahead and made Paul's bed and tried to straighten mine a little, while he pleaded with me to at least try the bouillon. Just to humor him I did take a sip. That was all it took. My stomach felt as if it would jump right out of my body. Wave after awful wave of nausea rolled over me again and again. I motioned wildly for one of the bags. He brought it and watched sympathetically while I made good use of it. Finally he gathered up dishes and bag, gave me an understanding nod, and was gone.

Around noon Paul came to get ready for lunch and see how I was. He grinned as he said he had some heartening information for me. "Seasickness is all in your mind. Yes, ma'am. That's what I just heard on deck. You are a big baby, honey, who hasn't yet learned to think positively." I stared at him through bleary eyes, my stomach rolling and pitching with the ship.

"Who said that?" I asked feebly. Paul's answer made me so angry I could only gasp, "That's a lie! I was hoping and praying you wouldn't get sick, too, but now I wish you would. Then let's see if it is only in the mind!"

Paul's answer to my question had been just one word, "Inge." Paul had never seen me angry, but now he did! I'm sure I was a weird sight with my pea-green complexion, tousled hair, and swollen eyes. I could see surprise on his face, but what infuriated me was a twinkle of fun in his eyes and the suggestion of a smile on his lips as he looked at me.

One thing was impossible for me, though. That was to be angry with Paul for more than a minute or two. His gentleness and love always won out. I realized I must look a fright and, answering him as I did, with my swollen eyes flashing angrily, I must have been rather amusing. I tried to smile and assure him I wouldn't wish my condition on my worst enemy, let alone the dearest one in the world to me. That did it. He hugged me tight, sick and ugly as I felt, telling me I was beautiful to him and always would be. He dipped a cloth in warm water and washed my face and hands, murmuring sweet nothings all the while. Then he got my brush and tidied my hair, brushing it into a neat, if not too becoming, pony tail. He helped me slip into a clean nighty and soon, refreshed and contented, I snuggled back on the pillow.

I had a headache and the nausea was still with me, but it was good to have Paul there. I missed him during the morning hours, but he needed to get up to the dining room if he wanted lunch. I slept a little while he was out and felt a bit better when he came back. I prepared to listen as he sat on his bed to tell me about his morning.

He had gone on deck, found a chair, and was just settling down for his morning devotions, when Inge, one of the German girls we met the day before, came and snuggled down beside him. They spent the whole morning together. With face aglow and sparkling eyes, he told me she was going to give him German lessons every day for the rest of the voyage. He seemed very innocent and appreciative of her offer. He was serious about his German and wanted to master it, though try as he would, he never did really accomplish that goal. His German was always a source of good-natured ribbing throughout his long missionary career.

Inge was a beautiful young woman about my age. I noticed the day before, as we were all walking up and down the deck together, how she clung to Paul every time the ship rolled a little. It was hard to stay on one's feet though, with nothing to hang on to, so I never gave it another thought. I held on to him, too. Now, though, as I looked at him, so boyish and happy because he had found a good teacher, I knew Inge was a force to be reckoned with. She clearly excluded me from the German study. It was to be a twosome just for them. She was cleverly arranging it for her own reasons.

I prayed in my heart for wisdom. To talk about the situation with Paul could be a help to him or it could be utterly devastating. I knew he had no romantic thoughts about her. I could see that in his openness and obvious pleasure. He would probably have been careful and secretive if he had had any other motive. Gently I broached the subject of Inge, reminding him of the freedom Hitler was allowing pure Aryan girls like Inge. He encouraged them even to bear children for him, making sure the father was as pure-blooded as the girl. They could entice the men, beguile them, trick them, or anything else. Their marital status meant nothing. This was happening all the time in Nazi Germany. It was no secret.

Paul listened to what I said, and agreed it was true, but felt we should give Inge the benefit of the doubt without more evidence. Paul was right, of course, and I agreed with him. We hugged each other and mentioned how beautiful it was we could talk about a sensitive subject like this without hurting one another or being unduly critical. He told me, very simply, that any motive on Inge's part, except wanting to help another human being, never entered his mind, and I believed him. There we left the matter, and he went back on deck.

I was glad we talked the matter over, but I was still somewhat uneasy. I thought it was probably because I felt so ill and tried not to worry, but that strange feeling wouldn't go away. I trusted Paul completely, but I distrusted Inge. I hurt all over, but more in spirit now, than in body. I prayed that God would keep Paul from all danger.

I was startled from my prayers and thoughts by a loud knock on the door. I called a faint "Enter," and the steward came in with a glass of orange juice and a few tiny white pills. I drank a little juice which decided to come right back up. Then he suggested a few swallows of water and a couple of the pills. He insisted I really needed them. They should help me feel better in a hurry. Dutifully I took the water and swallowed the pills. The steward bowed out just as Paul crept in, looking sicker than I'd ever seen him. His face had a peculiar greenish look, while his eyes were glazed and feverish.

He flopped down on his bed muttering, "I'm sick! I couldn't get away from that awful Inge. She talked and talked and talked. She wouldn't stop, and I was getting sicker every minute. I just couldn't shake that witch loose! All she could talk about was Nazi propaganda; how wonderful Hitler is and how the people love him. She delighted in informing me how much sexual freedom they have in Germany and what good times she and I would have together. She didn't once mention studying German. You were right, honey; she has something furtive up her sleeve. I didn't want to be rude, but I felt so sick I just couldn't put up with her any longer. I got up and walked out."

I felt really sorry for the poor guy. I couldn't even say what I wished to tell him earlier, "Never mind, dear. You are just seasick and that's only in your mind, remember?"

Seasick he was! No more studying German with Inge even if he wanted to. I hated to see Paul so sick, but I did thank God for showing him the evidence against her.

Neither of us wanted to go to dinner that evening, but the steward brought us tea and zwieback with more pills. They had already helped me. I almost felt like living again. We both took a couple before we went to sleep, and Paul began to feel better, too. They were a real wonder drug at that time. Now no one ever travels by land, sea, or air, without having a supply of Dramamine or a similar medicine on hand.

The next morning we were both well enough to go to breakfast. Our tummies were still a bit queasy, and I was wobbly on my feet because of the long fast, but it was good to be with the others again.

The breakfast guests clapped us a hearty welcome, and we smiled our thanks. We didn't feel like eating much and soon went out on the sunny, breezy deck. We pulled two chairs together and studied German.

It later came out that Inge and her friend were being deported from the United States together with a couple of German men we met on the boat. They were classified as unwanted aliens. So that was that, and God protected us from getting into a net that might have proven disastrous.

The journey from New York to Southampton took five days. We both felt better and enjoyed the remaining days to the full. There were lots of interesting things to do. We especially enjoyed playing shuffleboard out on deck. Paul loved Ping-Pong, and I was very proud when he was voted ship's champion of a Ping-Pong tournament. We loved promenading the decks when the weather allowed it. There was swimming, too, and a good library for bookworms. Many table games, like chess, Chinese checkers, regular checkers, and others were available. Evenings were gala times with dancing, movies, and other activities. We loved to walk on the glass-enclosed deck and watch the stars as we talked about home or our future and our plans and dreams. The stars were big and bright in the clear winter sky.

We were excited about our stopover in England. Paul's fraternal family originally came from England, and my mother had come from Liverpool as a young woman. My father's people stemmed from Scotland and his mother was part English. We felt we were going back to the land of our roots and wondered how everything would work out when we met all these unknown relatives.

Paul and Gladys cross the Atlantic to Europe, 1938

Sunday aboard ship was very special. It was our only Sunday on the voyage. Paul, probably the only clergyman aboard, was invited to hold Sunday services in the first-class salon. That was a fabulous room. It was like some of the grand salons we saw later in several German palaces. Paul looked young and boyish, standing before a great fireplace, a small gold-and-glass table set in front of him as a pulpit. I prayed quietly for him, knowing what a great responsibility this was.

The beautiful room was full and overflowing. We sang some of the old hymns of faith and inspiration that everyone knows, then Paul preached a beautiful and dignified message of hope and trust in Christ, our Lord and Savior. Some people told me they never heard anything like this before. I wondered what their pastors preached about if the people had never heard the simple gospel of the saving grace of Christ. Some of the listeners talked with Paul later, and he was able to point them to Jesus who loved them and gave Himself for them. It was a wonderful Sunday for two young, inexperienced missionaries. We were made to realize God could use us anywhere so long as we let Him work through us.

We were nearing Southampton now. Early the next morning we were to go through British customs on the boat. Then we would be taken ashore by motor launch. A delectable buffet was served that last evening. Whole pig heads with cranberry eyes and red apples in their mouths rested on a beds of greens. They made a different and impressive decoration for the long table. Everyone was in evening clothes, looking very elegant for this last big event of the voyage.

The food was delicious and displayed most temptingly. We were glad we felt like eating again and enjoyed the evening as much as anyone. There were songs and toasts, skits and German folk dances. A really good German band played many of the old ballads of Germany. We almost felt like we were there already and began to get excited about this culture we were soon to partake of. All good things must have an end, though. We had to process through customs early the next morning and catch our launch. Quite a few of us were debarking in Southampton, so we left the festivities early to pack and get ready for departure the next morning.

It had been a good voyage despite our bout with seasickness and the problem of Inge. We saw her a few times at a distance, but she made no effort to come nearer. We were glad to leave it that way, thankful that everything turned out well. We made many new friends on the trip and were sorry to leave them, but the thrill of new experiences and adventures lured us on. We said good night in a jovial atmosphere, and went to our room.

It was a good voyage. We thought about the good friends, the good times, the good food, the good everything. We packed our luggage, then the steward came to see if we needed anything. He turned down our beds, set a pitcher of ice water and two fresh glasses on our dresser, and wished us a cheery good night.

We were spoiled and pampered and treated like kings during four story-book days on the wide, winter Atlantic. A new chapter of our lives was about to begin. What would it bring?

CHAPTER ELEVEN

Morning dawned, bright and clear, with a cold wind blowing. The gong wakened us earlier than usual so we would have time for breakfast before the customs officials arrived. They would be aboard the launch that would take Southampton passengers ashore after customs processing. We were just going up to the dining room when the cry was heard, "Land! Land!" Everybody rushed out on deck. There, glimmering in the morning sun, were the famous white chalk cliffs of Dover. My mother had often told me about them. They were, in fact, her last glimpse of England, since she was never able to return.

I was excited to see them with my own eyes. We both gazed, entranced. England! We would do more than just view it from a ship's deck. We were actually going there. We would be among people with the same blood in their veins as ours. For the first time I truly understood what was meant by the old adage, "Blood is thicker than water." I could hardly wait to meet these relatives. We watched with the others until the chalk cliffs melted into the morning mist.

We had just enough time for a hurried breakfast before we reached Southampton and the long ordeal of going through customs began.

Breakfast over, we quickly made our way to the deck again to see all we could. The strange white cliffs fell behind as we steamed toward Southampton. We made good time, and soon caught our first glimpse of Southampton across the water.

We could see the launch skimming across the bay toward our ship. The sailors dropped anchor, the launch came alongside, the gangway was lowered, and a number of very important-looking men came aboard. They called for passengers to line up alphabetically, each deck or class separately by deck. We, being "W," were almost at the end of the line. We had been able to take care of some of the paperwork earlier, so the luggage inspection and a few other minor details didn't take long. We then followed the others to the waiting launch. Everyone was in a holiday mood. We waved gaily to the *Bremen* with only a trace of regret at our parting.

The little launch chugged merrily along until we reached the Southampton pier. Waiting for us was Cousin Muriel, Mother's cousin and my second cousin. She held out loving, welcoming arms to us. We had never seen her before, but I felt I knew her because of pictures I'd seen. She looked like Queen Victoria. Mother told us to look for someone who would have made a wonderful stand-in for that famous monarch. Cousin Muriel fitted the description exactly. She was a regal, stately, dignified lady with a loving heart. She was also a devout Christian, so we enjoyed much in common. She showed us a lovely time, from the train ride to her home in Bristol, to the many interesting places we visited together.

We saw old Roman baths in the ancient city of Bath. The Romans discovered these hot springs when they conquered Britain before the time of Christ. They made a lavish health spa out of the whole area of what is now Bath. Many of the fine old baths are still useable. We wandered through old cathedrals, damp and musty with age, but fascinating to our American eyes. We peeked at old, old houses with thatched roofs and mullioned windows, quaint and old-worldly. Funny little winding streets, rows of peaked houses exactly alike, pretty little stone churches – all intrigued us. We loved it.

Then it was time to take our leave of Muriel and go on to London for a few days visit with her younger sister, Marjorie. She was a trim, modern woman of the world, mingling with Lords and Ladies of London's high society. She was a breezy, natural person who liked horses, dogs, and people, in that order. I can still hear her asking us brusquely, "Well, well, so you are missionaries, eh? Then there must be gobs of things you choose not to do, aren't there? Would you be so good as to give me a list of things you might enjoy doing? She was so refreshingly honest and straightforward that Paul and I liked her from the start. We began to chuckle, and when she saw our reaction to her comical question she threw back her head and roared with laughter. Her laugh was so contagious we couldn't help joining in. After a good laugh, she hugged us, one on each side of her, and the ice was broken.

We had always wanted to ride someday on a doubledecker omnibus, so we told her that. We thought what fun it would be to see London from way up there on top of the bus. She thought it was a splendid idea, so we did that for a couple of days. We would jump out to see something interesting or historical, then hop back on. It was a wonderful way to get a good overview of that famous old city. We saw the changing of the guard at Buckingham Palace, wandered through St. Paul's Cathedral, looked at ancient tombs, found David Livingstone's tomb in Westminster Abbey, and shuddered in the gloomy Tower of London. We browsed through the fabulous British Museum and sat with Marjorie through a session of the House of Commons. We also took a close-up look at Big Ben.

One day we visited Madame Tussaud's Wax Works. Everybody who was anybody was beautifully and tastefully portrayed in wax. Many of our presidents were there as well as some of our villains. They looked so natural we excused ourselves if we got in front of one or accidentally bumped one. Marjorie loved it all with us. She probably had seen everything dozens of times before, but now she was seeing things through the eyes of her young American cousins and she fell in love with London all over again.

All good things do have an end, though, as we realized when we told Marjorie how we enjoyed ourselves with her and how much we loved London. We all cried a little at the train station and parted with hugs and kisses as Marjorie assured us she would see us on the continent some day. With a last wave, we boarded the train that would whisk us back to Southampton and our waiting ship.

English trains were clean, punctual, and fast. We enjoyed the ride to Southampton, even though the weather was chilly, dark, and windy, and it looked like a storm was brewing. We were picking up the *SS Europa* on this leg. It had just arrived from the States and berthed in Southampton instead of dropping anchor in the harbor, like the *Bremen* had done. As soon as passengers from England boarded she would depart for Bremerhaven, her German port. We would only be overnight passengers and had the good feeling of nearing our journey's end. We hadn't counted on the unpredictable channel, though.

We boarded in mid-afternoon, found our stateroom, and took a stroll around the ship. She was by no means as roomy and luxurious as the *Bremen*. Our stateroom was a little cubbyhole and the passageways were narrow and smelled musty. We could take it for one night, we decided, and thought no more about it.

The dinner hour, which was always so special on the *Bremen*, seemed tense and strained. We felt alone, too, not having made the Atlantic crossing with the others. They all knew each other and chatted a little in low tones. No one noticed us, but we were tired and didn't feel much like talking anyway. We missed our English cousins and the warm feeling of belonging. We missed the fun, laughter, and fellowship we had enjoyed during our two weeks in England. We decided the best thing was to retire early, get a good night's rest, and be ready for the long train trip the next day. We took a quick trip on deck, but it was snowing and terribly windy so we didn't stay long. We staggered below as the wind roared and the great ship tossed on the wild sea like a bobbing cork. We made it to our room without incident and were soon snug in our berths and sound asleep.

I don't know how long we slept till a shuddering jar awakened us. Rubbing sleepy eyes, we turned the light on to see our trunks pitching about the room like matchsticks. The ship lay dangerously to one side but, as a huge wave rolled against her, she righted herself and began lurching in the opposite direction. We put up our guardrails to keep from falling out of bed and prayed for our skipper, his crew, and all the passengers, that God would grant guidance and help in this time of trouble. I began to understand the old Anglican hymn that prays for those in peril on the sea.

Remarkably, we never felt afraid for ourselves. Amidst the tossing, rolling, and grinding of the ship and the roaring of wind and waves, we actually drifted off to sleep again, rocked in the cradle of the deep, a very rude and angry deep, rocking us unmercifully.

Then it was morning, but *what* a morning. Trunks and other luggage, left in the hallways for quick removal, were scattered pell-mell in every direction. The furniture in the lounge was a hopeless mess. The whole ship's interior was a disaster. I've always wondered if they ever got it back to normal again, because we debarked before anything was done about it.

The tables in the dining room had guardrails on them, too. We noticed a new group of people aboard we hadn't seen before. We asked about them and learned our ship received a distress signal in the night from a freighter. The *Europa* hurried to the rescue, reaching the sinking ship just in time to save captain and crew before the ship plunged to the bottom. Cargo and personal belongings all went down with the ship. These unhappy-looking guests were those rescued from that ship. We received another SOS, too, but when the *Europa* got there, nothing remained of ship or crew. The only remainder of the tragedy was an ugly oil slick on the turbulent sea. All these dreadful things happened while Paul and I slept. Most of the passengers said they hadn't slept a wink all night. They feared the ship would go down any minute. We all thanked God for His mercy and deliverance.

None of us wanted much breakfast. We were all too shocked over the happenings of the night to feel very hungry. Some of the passengers were seasick and spent much of the morning hanging over the rail, poor souls. Fortunately we had enough Dramamine left to stave off that miserable ailment, for which we were very thankful.

The sky was an ugly gray, some snowflakes were falling, and the sea was rough and choppy. Dishes on the table slid from side to side. We were glad for guard rails. Even the smell of coffee made our tummies feel a bit squeamish, but pots of hot tea with dry toast were a comfort.

We were behind schedule because of the storm and all that it involved, so we did not reach Bremerhaven until noon. Everyone's spirits lifted as we docked, and we all cheered. It was fun watching large containers being lifted and lowered to the deck by giant cranes. Land looked good to us, too, after the hazardous night. We didn't care about the weather so long as we were on land. It could be snowy, rainy, or foggy. The bottom line was that we were on good old *terra firma*.

Our future lay before us. We didn't know what it held, but we were content. Our Heavenly Father held us in His hands, and that was enough.

CHAPTER TWELVE

How good it felt to debark and stand on firm land again. Our legs were wobbly, but the long, dangerous night was over. We had survived it and were on the continent at last. We went through German customs, which didn't take long, and were soon off in a taxi with other passengers to see the town. Taxis were ridiculously cheap, especially when a group of people took one together.

Bremerhaven was a quaint, interesting, typical harbor city. We were aghast at the strong Nazi presence everywhere – swastikas waved from every public building as well as from all the homes and apartment complexes. In fact, every individual apartment had its own flag hung out. Pictures of Hitler were displayed in shop windows, often with candles burning before them. Large posters and many other signs and banners kept Nazi propaganda constantly before the people. They had nowhere to go to get away from that bombardment; they had to endure it. At that point, many of the people especially the young, supported Hitler.

People we met on the street seemed friendly, but somber and tense. They seldom smiled. We were so filled with joy we beamed at everybody, but, to our disappointment, very few responded to our happy mood. Actually, they regarded us with suspicion as though they were wondering, "What's your racket?" We felt sorry for them. Germany was a nation caught in a nationalistic trap.

We found the railway station and procured our tickets to Danzig with an overnight stop in Berlin. Berlin – that beautiful, glamorous, storybook city – we were going there! We would see it with our own eyes. These little tickets in our hands were the "Open Sesame" to all the wonders of Berlin.

The German train was clean and fast, but different from the English trains. Our third class seats were of golden oak and hard as iron. The first- and second-class cars were beautifully upholstered with a velvety plush, often in lovely colors. First-class anything was only a dream for us at this time, though, and we couldn't have cared less. We felt like kings, being privileged to travel and see all these wonderful things, and all because we had answered God's call.

The cars were divided into small compartments, each holding eight passengers. A narrow corridor ran the length of the car, with doors opening into each compartment. It wasn't a bad arrangement, but in such close quarters we all had to be pretty chummy. We must have provided some good and welcome fun for our fellow passengers as we tried to communicate with hands and feet and eyes. We had some good laughs. I guess our cubbyhole mates were glad for any break in the monotony.

The train rumbled on through the winter afternoon, passing villages, towns, and cities, dropping off and taking on passengers. That part of Germany is quite flat and uninteresting at any time. Now, with a light snow falling, it was bleak and uninviting. We were glad as the train came to a hilly area with fir woods. The trees were all standing in uniform rows like soldiers. It reminded us of Van Dyke's beautiful poem, "I love the German fir woods, in green battalions drilled." Not that we loved them all that much on that dull, monotonous winter day, but they helped.

We ate supper in the dining car, but it didn't compare with the elegance and gourmet touch of American dining cars. The food was nothing special, just something to eat. Maybe we were pampered too much aboard ship and by our adoring English cousins. In later years we found dining on German trains a pleasant experience.

We neared Berlin as darkness fell. We were glad to spend a night and part of a day there. Paul knew once we got involved in the work, there wouldn't be much time for the lighter things of life. He was really straining at the bit, but, as always, he wanted me to be happy. He knew how I loved people and new sights, sounds, and experiences. I loved him all the more for entering so whole-heartedly into all the things he knew I loved and enjoyed.

The city scenery was a pleasant change as the train rolled into brightly lit Berlin. We enjoyed its broad streets, beautiful department stores, palaces, and museums. Sophisticated little boutiques nestled between ancient cathedrals or fine old federal buildings. The train rolled past beautiful parks, the stately old university, and many other buildings that we couldn't identify. Finally we rolled to a stop at the impressive Berliner Hauptbahnhof. We hadn't much luggage to carry. Most of it had been sent on to Danzig, so we were free to wander about. We located our hotel, found our room, and could hardly wait to drop into bed.

Our modest little room was spotless, with huge, snowy, feather ticks on the beds. There were enormous square pillows to match. Actually, there were two or three pillows on each bed, the top one smaller than the rest. We didn't know whether we should sleep on top of those feather coverlets or under them. After studying the situation for a while, we decided we probably should sleep under those mountains of feathers. This proved to be correct. Later, after a hot bath and a prayer of thankfulness, we slid contentedly under those white mounds. To our joy, the cover and pillows were wonderful. They were soft and downy, warm and light. Perfectly delightful.

The next thing we heard was a knock on our door. A maid informed us it was the time we had requested to be awakened. We jumped out of the feathers and were soon down in the cozy breakfast room. We gorged on crusty rolls with fresh butter and strawberry jam, and a coffee-like beverage prepared from roast grain that reminded us of Postum.

After breakfast we were off to see Berlin by daylight. We wanted to see all we could before our train left in the early afternoon. First we went to the Kaiser's palace. What a place! The parquet floors were so shiny we could see our faces in them. All the sightseers had to put on felt slippers, called in German, *pantoffeln*. Everything in the palace was just as beautiful and charming as the floors. There were millions of dollars of gold leaf everywhere, and priceless paintings, lovely statuary, draperies, and furniture. It was truly a magnificent place.

There was so much to see and enjoy in Berlin. Some things seemed extra special. The famous Pergamon museum was one of the finest in the world. It fascinated us with the artifacts of long-ago times and places. There were priceless statues, drawings, paintings, and much, much more, salvaged from the mists of antiquity. This treasure, or at least much of it, was lost during World War II. What a pity that the Kaiser's palace, the museum, and centuries of noble architecture and invaluable treasures were obliterated in seconds.

We loved the *Tiergarten* (Animal Park). It became world famous as one of the first zoos in the world to display animals in their natural habitat.

We also enjoyed strolling hand in hand down that famous old street, *Unter den Linden*. We peeked into shop windows, dropped into quaint antique shops, browsed among lovely things of another place and time. It was romantic and fascinating.

It was a very special morning for us and ended all too soon. There was scarcely time to eat and return to the hotel for our luggage before catching our train. We decided to eat at the *Rathskeller* (Townhall Restaurant), just across the street. Paul had learned about them in his German class. They were supposed to be very good and typically German. It didn't take us long to scamper across the busiest street in Germany.

Paul had studied German for two years in high school and felt he had at least a nodding acquaintance with the language, traditions, and customs of the land. Here was a good chance for him to use his precious, hard-acquired German.

The tables were of natural oak, scrubbed almost white. Everything was sparkling clean. There were no tablecloths, but who needed them with tabletops like that? We studied the menu, which meant nothing to me. Paul appeared to be very interested in what they had to offer. I waited with baited breath to see how his German would go. Unfortunately, Paul had not learned food names, restaurant etiquette, and such things in school.

The austere waiter, who insisted on being called "Mr. Head Waiter" or "*Herr Ober*" when anyone wanted service, came bowing up to our table. He asked, or so we assumed, what we wanted to eat. Paul tried his best to ask the waiter what he would recommend. The waiter tried to tell us, but Paul just couldn't understand him. Then the waiter began to slap and rub his lower back in the most frenzied and undignified fashion. Whatever had gotten into him? He shouted in German over and over again, "*Nieren! Nieren!*" as he gestured.

We both tried to understand, but it just wasn't anything Paul knew. He would now and then give me an embarrassed look. He had wanted so badly to show off his German, poor guy.

At last the waiter hurried away to find someone who knew English. He soon returned, grinning happily. He began again slapping merrily at both sides of his lower back, shouting at the top of his voice, "kid-kanees, kid-kanees." He was trying to tell us about his good kidney pies, but it was so ludicrous, we all howled with laughter.

We eventually ended up with what we thought was roast beef with potato salad and green beans. It looked very appetizing. We tasted the meat. It was sour! Good old German *sauerbraten*. Well, there was still the potato salad and beans. We would enjoy those. Paul was very fond of green beans and one of my favorites was potato salad. We started blissfully on those, grimaced, and left the rest on our plates uneaten. We knew that German potato salad is usually on the sour side, but this was as sour as the vinegar that seasoned it. The beans were a German specialty, bean salad, and as sour as the meat and potato salad.

There was still a dessert, a lovely molded pudding. It looked so good we could hardly wait to eat it. At least something would be sweet. Paul started with a very large bite to help get the sour taste out of his mouth. I just couldn't believe the look on his face as he almost choked on that beautiful pudding. I quickly sampled a tiny bite. Sure enough, it, too, was even more sour than the other food. It had been made with sour wine as the liquid.

Sad and hungry, we paid our bill, leaving our meal practically untouched. Not to clean your plate, in the Germany of that time, was almost as bad as treason. Waiters and diners alike regarded us with distinct disapproval. We were sorry to have such well-developed American taste buds. We have had many a good laugh over it since, with both German and American friends.

As we walked along the street to our hotel we passed a candy store. How tempting those big gooey chocolates looked! We were so hungry for something sweet we felt we must have a few. We planned to enjoy them on our way to the hotel. I popped one greedily into my mouth, then one in Paul's. We both began to cough and gag. They were made of a strong, sour liquor, with a light coating of chocolate. We decided there was nothing sweet in Germany. For a minute we were outraged, then we began to laugh. It was one of the funniest things that ever happened to us. We could chuckle in later years when served cuisine that was strange or different. We were glad we had learned to take any kind of food or lodgings, customs or traditions, in stride and make the best of them.

We got to our hotel, picked up our luggage, and were soon flying along in the elite *Berliner Express*, one of Germany's finest trains. We raced over the winter countryside, through dark fir forests and lonely, leafless woods of birch and elm. We rushed passed charming, red-roofed villages, with tall church steeples dominating the village scene, stoping from time to time to take on or let off passengers.

Just as darkness fell at the close of the short winter day, we arrived at the border of the Free State of Danzig – *der Freistadt Danzig*. Richard Bronson, oldest son of Professor Bronson, a teacher at Northwest College, was there to meet us. We hadn't met before, but within five minutes we felt we had known him always.

He was a tall, handsome young man, with a refreshing frankness and a talent for putting people at ease. He was about our age. His fiancée had joined him about a year before and they had married in Danzig. Both Richard and his bride were a great asset to the mission. It was good to know we would be working with them. I looked forward to meeting his wife, Margie. I felt we would be friends if she was anything like her husband.

After boarding the train for Danzig, Richard told us about the mission program, which had many facets. There was the Bible School, the mission office where much of the overseas business was carried on, and other important projects. He told us about the customs and practices of the people in Danzig as well as in Poland. He told us at length about the Nazi takeover of Danzig and how the Danzigers wanted to join the German Reich. He shared his feelings about the German desire for expansion and possible imminent war. These were sobering and disturbing times in Europe. We tingled with excitement, realizing we could well be in the middle of whatever developed in the days ahead.

We were so wrapped up in the stimulating conversation we hardly noticed we were in Danzig until the train came to a grinding halt at the station. The missionaries greeted us warmly and ushered us in to a sumptuous meal. We spent a happy time of getting acquainted, then slipped away with Richard and Margie through many gates, walls, and doors, until we finally ended up at our own door.

We had a bundle of huge keys to get through all those doors and gates. Paul said he felt like a jailor. This room was only temporary until we found something better. We were tired after the sightseeing morning and the long train trip. Our tiny room was cozy and inviting. We tumbled thankfully into our clean white beds and were soon fast asleep.

Danzig was a wonderful old *Hansa Stadt*, one of several on the Baltic. The *Hansa Staedte*, or cities, were a medieval league of German merchants, known as the Hanseatic League. They had banded together for more security as they traded abroad. They were a power to be reckoned with in the commercial world of that day. Germans who lived in them, even as late as our time in Danzig, were proud to be citizens of a Hansa city.

Danzig was a charming, romantic old city, rich in medieval lore. We quite fell in love with it. The large, old, red-brick Church of Mary was said to be the largest Protestant church on the continent. From its squarish tower, one could look over all of Danzig and far out to the Baltic Sea. St. Catherine's Church was a little Gothic jewel located near an old millpond with an old water wheel. We loved it there, winter or summer. Paul took some beautiful pictures of it that we cherished over the years.

One of the most photographed places in Danzig was the old crane tower on the *Motlau*, a canal that ran through the city. The name in German is the *Krantor*, and it was used for loading and unloading ships that made their way up the *Motlau* from the Baltic. Many beautiful, historic buildings were destroyed in the war. Quite a few have been restored by the Polish people who fell heir to Danzig at war's end. They love this wonderful old Hansa city, too, and have tried to restore the most historic parts of the city just as they were. The Polish name for Danzig is *Gdansk*, and so it is known throughout the world today.

The *Motlau* cable ferry was especially charming. It looked like a raft, and passengers could stand or sit on a rounded bench for the few moment's crossing. It cost only a *pfennig* or two, less than a penny in American currency. It was one of the most exhilarating little outings one could imagine. Paul and I loved it and enjoyed a ride nearly every day, never tiring of the short little trip.

The political climate of Danzig at the time of our arrival was very tense. The Nazis had already taken over the city and the citizens were restless. They had one obsession: to become a part of the German *Reich*. How and when that would occur nobody knew, but that it would take place was a certainty in everyone's thinking.

Daily we saw the dreaded Blackshirts goose-stepping arrogantly down the street, looking proud and cruel. Something about them always struck terror in our hearts. We were informed to beware of them. They were known as the most cruel henchmen of Hitler. They would enter houses in the dead of night and drag away helpless victims who were brave enough, or stupid enough, to express opinions against the Third *Reich*.

The Brownshirts were also important to Hitler's plan. They goose-stepped their way into a place of prominence in the Nazi program. We hated to hear them marching down the streets, day or night, bellowing out Nazi propaganda songs in harsh, raucous voices. Even very young boys in knee pants, all dressed in brown, marched up and down the streets to militant songs led by an older boy.

Another thing that horrified us was that in every public place – parks, beaches, camping and picnic sites, soccer fields, restaurants, and anywhere else where people might like to go – there were signs conspicuously posted: *Juden unerwunscht* (Jews not wanted). We were grieved in spirit to witness man's hatred toward those different from themselves.

A beautiful, historic synagogue in Danzig was confiscated by the Nazis. It was earmarked for destruction in the coming May. They hung a large sign on it that stretched across the entire width of the building. It read, "Come lovely May and free us from the Jews."

Some Danzigers felt sorry for the Jews and risked imprisonment, or worse, by trying to help them. The majority, however, were fearful of getting involved in any way that might jeopardize their own safety. "Keep your nose clean at all costs" was evidently their uncourageous attitude.

One evening Paul came home late from the mission office, look-ing upset. He was carrying a load of magazines and papers under his arm. I had been worried, for he was usually very punctual. I waited for him with my heart in my throat. Deep inside I felt that all was not well. It was such a relief to see him at last, that I threw myself, sobbing, into his arms. He hugged me, then led me to a chair while he explained what had happened.

He had been summoned by the *Gestapo* to appear in their office immediately, without fail, or. . . . Paul went. There on a desk lay all our newspapers, magazines, and any other printed matter that might have the remotest hint of anti-Nazi propaganda. We had been missing our mail of this type and wondered what had happened to it. One of the officials seemed to be in command and did the questioning. What was our political stand in America? Were we spreading anti-Nazi propaganda? What was the general feeling in America toward the Nazis? What were we doing in Danzig? Had we been sent on some secret mission by the American government? On and on they went.

Paul lifted his heart in a silent prayer for wisdom to answer the questions wisely and carefully, in a way that would not upset the officials and yet give them the information they wanted. He told about his call, about helping in the Bible School, about how young people needed goals in life. He explained our American way of life. The official actually got quite chummy with Paul, which made him all the more wary. He knew he must weigh every word or he might have to eat them later.

The officer then stood, picked up our papers, and proceeded to show Paul why they had been confiscated. Paul couldn't help smiling as humorous and sarcastic little jokes, cartoons, or editorials were pointed out to him, with the comment, "We have nothing against you having and reading your papers, but we demand that you keep them for yourself and don't pass them on to anyone here." Paul thought that was fair enough and agreed to abide by this decision.

This disquieting episode, though it ended peaceably, was disturbing. From then on, if Paul was only a few minutes late I would get uneasy and nervous. If he got home a little early and I hadn't gotten home from the Bible School yet, he would start calling around, fearful I might have been taken into custody. It was an anxious period for us both. We couldn't go on like this. We prayed earnestly together and separately.

The secret police officer who had interviewed Paul came to the mission office one day. He had a friendly chat with Paul and invited us to go out to dinner with him that evening. Paul called to see if I wanted to go. We were both reluctant to accept, fearing some sort of trap. Paul had to speak very guardedly, with the police right there in his office, but in the end, we agreed. We had a perfect meal in the best hotel in Danzig.

The official was warm and friendly. He had brought us a few more of our papers that the post office had sent them. He informed us he had issued instructions to have all our mail sent directly to us in the future. He said he felt he could trust us to keep our part of the agreement. He wanted to assure us we could relax. There would be no more meddling with our mail or into our private lives. It was such a definite answer to prayer that, though we knew we must still be very careful, we praised and glorified the Lord in our hearts and settled down to enjoy the wonderful meal.

A week or two later Paul called to let me know he had invited our policeman friend for dinner the next evening. Could I arrange it on such short notice? Paul was jubilant. Herr so and so, the agent, had visited him again and they enjoyed a good talk. He told Paul an American in Nazi Danzig was pretty much suspect, no matter what he did or didn't do. He wanted to assure us that so long as he was in Danzig, we should bring any sort of political difficulty or problem to him and he would see we were protected. The same went for our whole mission.

Our new friend appeared to enjoy my crisp fried chicken, creamy mashed potatoes, a fresh vegetable, and apple pie. When we asked the blessing, he told us with tears in his eyes that he was brought up in a Christian family who believed like we did. We could see God's hand in all of this.

We had times of sharing and teaching him, our first convert in Danzig. We were saddened, though, that he feared for his position and even his life if he took a public stand for Christ. We were confident he privately loved and served the Lord, and we prayed for him over the years. He helped us out of several dangerous situations as well as sticky little matters with the Nazi government. He was a real godsend to the mission. We thank God for him to this day. He was our guardian angel in *Gestapo* uniform.

CHAPTER THIRTEEN

Paul wasn't happy about having to work in the office so much. He was trained for office work before he went to Bible School and was glad to help when it was a productive activity. He felt, though, that so much of what he had to do was just filling in time, busy work. He was frustrated and bored. He loved teaching in the Bible School where we both were on staff. He was a good teacher and the students loved and respected him. They called him Teacher, and he loved being known by that name. He delighted in studying, finding new and creative ways of presenting truth, digging out precious nuggets from the God's Word. He would have long, stimulating discussions with the students, which were a blessing to him and to them.

Paul always went back to the office, though. He did what was expected of him, giving his best. He seldom complained, but I knew what a trial this was for him. Still, in retrospect, we could see everything that happened then was part of God's school. It was training for bigger and more responsible assignments. In later years, Paul became one of the most patient and gentle of men. He was also a pioneer who dared to stick his neck out for what he believed God wanted him to do.

Paul was not sure how God wanted to use him when we went to Danzig. He knew, though, that God had planned some special type of ministry for him. Who did God use to reveal it? No one less than Adolf Hitler! Hitler had a way of inspiring young people to the point they would gladly die for him. His messages went by radio into schools, summer camps, playgrounds, anywhere and everywhere, where children were. They idolized him.

He made all his programs for children very personal, something like this: "You are very special to me, boys of Germany! You are mine, lovely flaxen-haired girls! Together we are going to conquer. You are Germany's greatest treasure. We'll show the world what German young people can do," and on and on and on. We saw and heard all this day after day.

Gladys in front of a chapel in Zappet, Poland, 1939

We watched the response of children and youth. They were eager and ready to be a part of Hitler's program. We watched the churches losing their children and youth. They entered Hitler's Nazi Youth by the thousands. Our hearts broke! These vital lives, the very future itself, the children, were excited, thrilled, enthusiastic. They were really turned on by the Nazis and their program.

The things of God, on the other hand, seemed dull, old-fashioned, uninteresting, and totally irrelevant to modern youth. No wonder our hearts broke! We prayed, "Oh, God, don't you have anyone who can inspire, thrill, and motivate children for you like Hitler does for his devilish purposes?"

Well, when you pray like that, you had better duck. God spoke to each of us when we were praying alone. Not in an audible voice, but in that still, small inner voice that people who love God learn to know. He simply told us, "You do it! You have seen what can be accomplished by a demon-inspired person. How much more by you, who are filled with my Spirit and have all my heavenly resources at your disposal. Go! Inspire youth for me! Bless them, lead them to the fullness of the Holy Spirit. Motivate them early to commit their lives to me. I commission you to this service. Do it!"

Paul told me of God's call to him. I shared how the Lord had revealed his will to me, too. He wanted me to work side by side with Paul. Together we would reach out to youth, from toddlers to teenagers and older. From then on our goal and reason for being was to introduce the young to the thrill, the excitement, the wonder and adventure of knowing Jesus and serving him with all their hearts.

Now, over fifty years later, there are missionaries, pastors, leaders, teachers, and writers everywhere in the world whose lives God has enabled us to touch and bless. Strange are the ways and workings of God when we take time to reflect upon them. He brought us over land and sea to remote Danzig to give us the vision and calling He planned for us.

We sometimes went out from Danzig to minister for a week or two in Poland. We loved these times of evangelism and rejoiced as people responded to the gospel message. We ministered mainly to simple farm folk, scattered far and wide over the countryside. They walked miles through all kinds of weather to get to the meetings. We seldom had seen such hunger for God before. We have never gotten a greater response to the message of life since. We loved these humble people, and they responded in like measure.

The political situation was very tense. The Poles feared and hated the Germans, and there was no love lost by the Germans for the Poles, either. The Poles were afraid Germany would invade their country, and they were not prepared for an invasion. Poland knew it would be suicide to resist. The Poles are a feisty people, though. They would rather die than surrender their freedom and be slaves to any other nation. It was a nerve-wracking, jittery time for the Polish people back then.

Chapel in Orlamo, Poland, where Paul and Gladys ministered, 1939

The Polish economy was also in bad shape. Poverty was a way of life for many. Jobs were scarce, and Poles often tried to sneak over the border to find jobs in Danzig. With the coming of the Nazis, the economy there had improved. It was almost impossible, though, for Poles to get jobs in Danzig after the political atmosphere became so tense.

We enjoyed our trip to Poland, but we were ready to return to Danzig. We were tired and hadn't had a bath for a long while. The food didn't always agree with us, either. We both suffered from dysentery. Still, the few unpleasant things were well worth it, compared with all the good times we had there.

When we were safely back in Danzig, even the little, everyday things like a good soap, toothpaste, or clean sheets seemed like great luxuries. We thought of the dear ones in Poland, so patient, so uncomplaining, so thankful for any tiny favor we could do for them. We felt like someone should whip us if we ever complained or found fault again.

A love and a burden for Poland was born in our hearts during the time we were there, and that love has remained with us all these years.

CHAPTER FOURTEEN

During the summer of 1939, dark shadows of war lengthened over Europe. Every day brought new incidents. We didn't know what to expect next. Anti-Semitic feelings were worsening in Germany, and they spread to Danzig. With horror we witnessed the atrocities of Kristall Nacht (Crystal Night). Store windows were smashed with bricks or anything else the wild mob could get their hands on. Then the looting began. If anyone tried to stop the rioters, they were beaten up. Jewish merchants, trying in vain to salvage merchandise, were harassed and humiliated. One of our missionaries agonized to see a band of Nazi youth gouge out the eyes of a helpless rabbi. Their buddies attacked anyone who tried to help him. This awful night will live forever in our memories as a blot on mankind.

All night long the crash of glass, the shouts of rioters, and the screams of the victims sounded in our ears, mingling with our dreams. We held each other close and prayed for God's chosen people. We slept fitfully, waking with each new din that reached our ears. That was the darkest night of our lives.

The following day dawned cold and grey. How could the sun bear to look upon man's inhumanity to man? We were very concerned about some dear Jewish friends. They owned a fine electric shop in the Jewish quarter. Should we try to visit them? It could be risky. Our longing to see how they were overcame our hesitancy, however, so we started out.

When we arrived at their street, we were just sick. Every shop had broken windows, smashed in doors, or other damage. Deathly silence reigned in the whole quarter. We heard no children at play, no women chatting comfortably together on the corner. It was like a ghost town.

As we stood before our friend's shop with its apartment in the back, we couldn't suppress the tears. It was a shambles! The expensive plate-glass show window was shattered, merchandise stolen or smashed, and our friends nowhere in sight. We went around to the back and pounded on the door. It opened a crack, and the frightened face of the shop owner peered out. He smiled weakly when he saw us and opened the door just wide enough to allow us to squeeze inside. Then he quickly slammed it shut again. We reached out to those suffering people, and they practically fell into our arms. We wept together for a few minutes. Words were so inadequate.

"Want to tell us about it?" Paul finally managed to ask.

With tears and gestures they painted a picture of terror, brutality, and destruction.

"We've had it!" one of the brothers bitterly announced. "We were compelled to flee Russia because of pogroms like this against our people. We lost everything and had to begin again from scratch here in Germany where we thought we would be safe. Now the terror has caught up with us. We're getting out while there is still time, if there is any time left. We'll show these butchers we are not licked yet, you'll see. We had already made arrangements to flee to the United States. Our funds are being transferred to a Swiss bank where the Nazi swine won't get their stinking hands on them. So it's farewell, friends. God bless you for all your kindness to us. We will never forget you!"

We grieved with and for them as we helped mark down merchandise for a quick closing-out sale. The brothers practically gave these fine appliances away. Their one thought was to get themselves and their families out of Danzig as quickly as possible.

One of the brothers told us, "Things are so bad that we often sigh as we turn in for the night, 'Oh, if it were only morning!' Then, when morning comes, we fear for life and limb and long for the night. That's not living, Paul and Gladys. We feel like a curse hangs over us no matter where we go. Will you both say a prayer for us before you leave?"

We stared at the family in astonishment, for just that morning in our devotions we read from Deuteronomy, chapter 28, verse 67. This is what it says regarding the Jewish people in exile because they had turned from God and were serving idols.

"In the morning thou shalt say, 'Would God it were even,' and at even thou shalt say, 'Would God it were morning,' for the fear of thine heart wherewith thou shalt fear, and for the sight of thine eyes which thou shalt see." We shared this verse with them, tears streaming down our cheeks as we talked.

"My God!" exclaimed the younger brother. "That is exactly what has happened to us in the past and is happening again now! I fled from Russia, where I was left for dead by a firing squad, with this terror in my heart, and now, again, we find ourselves fearing for our lives, hating the night and hating the day. Will this be our tragic fate forever?"

We tried to encourage the family to return to God if they felt they had failed Him. Paul reminded them of some of the beautiful Psalms of David that tell us of God's mercy and His grace. He doesn't keep His anger forever. He is slow to anger and plenteous in mercy. He is a loving, forgiving God.

They all listened attentively and bowed their heads as Paul drew us together with our arms around each other. He poured out his heart to the Lord for His suffering, sorrowing children. He prayed that God would keep and protect them in the days ahead and most of all to help them to return again to the God of their fathers.

It was time to take our leave. Any moment someone might come by. That could mean trouble for our friends and possibly for us. We all embraced once more, and they promised to let us know how things would go. They were still in Danzig with no assurance they would ever get out. We left them with heavy hearts as we heard the bolt slip into the lock behind us. Several days later we went by again. The shop was locked and deserted, the apartment cold and empty. Did they escape or had they been taken off to a Nazi death camp?

Some days later a very carefully coded note arrived with the cheering news that the whole Gruenspun family had reached England safely. Arrangements were being made for them to travel on to the land of their dreams, the United States. We rejoiced with them and praised the Lord for their deliverance. He still loves His chosen people. His loving hand had sheltered and protected this little family.

Years later we met the brothers again as we were going through New York. It had been very hard for them at first. Getting started and putting down roots in a new land isn't easy. They began with a few electric appliances. Many were the long, hard hours they put in, but it paid off. When we saw the family again, they were doing well and glorying in their new homeland.

The political climate in Danzig became more tense each day. Nightly, Hitler or Goebels made long, heated speeches on the radio, whipping the people into a furor of emotional agitation and war fever.

The Bronsons had a tiny baby daughter now. She was not well, so they felt it would be wise to take her to the States as soon as they could arrange it. The Nickoloffs had already gone to Bulgaria and left from there to return home. Several other missionaries were getting ready to leave, too. It looked like we and two other couples would soon be the only ones left.

We were young and healthy with no children. We weren't afraid for ourselves, probably because we were too naive and optimistic for our own good. Whatever the reason, we didn't want to leave. It was summer and we had some interesting plans in mind. There was to be an European Christian conference in Stockholm in June, and we wanted to attend. We hoped to spend the rest of the summer ministering in Poland.

The Stockholm conference was a wonderful time of blessing and fellowship. We booked passage on an Estonian coal boat. Another missionary lady accompanied us. We were the only passengers, so were allowed to dine at the captain's table in his cozy, private dining room. He was a friendly, pleasant person and spoke quite good German. We learned a lot about Estonia (which has recently regained its independence from what was the Soviet Union) as we chatted together at mealtimes or while lounging on deck. He loved showing us around on his tidy, ship-shape little boat. One would never have known it carried coal deep inside.

We enjoyed the couple of days on the boat, especially as we neared Stockholm. We wended our way in and out among many lovely little islands until, off in the distance, the skyline of Stockholm came into view. It was a beautiful picture, gleaming white in the afternoon sunshine.

We were met at the pier by friendly customs people. They offered us hot cups of excellent Swedish coffee to sip while they inspected our luggage. When they learned we were conference guests, they gave us a warm welcome. We were put on the trolley to the *Filadelfia Kirk* where the day services were to be held. Night rallies were conducted in the largest tent we had ever seen.

The Philadelphia Church is one of the largest in Sweden. It boasted six thousand active members then, almost fifty years ago. It must be twice that large today. This fine church was known all over Sweden, in much of Europe, and even in the United States and Canada.

As our trolley rolled to the church we were impressed with its attractive and practical style. Flags from all over Europe fluttered from poles put up for this occasion. The church was built in the round so that, no matter how large the crowd, no one was ever very far from the speaker. Three balconies jutted out over the congregation. Even those sitting in the top balcony had a good view of all that went on below. Many of our great church edifices today are built on similar lines, but it was a breath-taking spectacle then.

We would never forget that first night at the conference. Such well-known speakers and teachers as Donald Gee from England, Levi Pethros from Sweden, Watson Argue from Canada, and many others blessed our hearts with their anointed messages. We hadn't realized how starved we were for good spiritual food. It was a little taste of heaven on earth.

The few days in Sweden flew by too quickly. The conference with all its excitement and blessing was over, and it was time to return to Danzig. We both felt a strange reluctance about going back. We thought of the tension and uncertainty. We could hear, again, the thumping of Nazi boots on the cobblestones. Would we be in danger there? But we had made our decision to stay in Europe. Much as we would love to remain in this lovely land of peace and freedom, we knew our path led back to Danzig and Poland.

We traveled by train this time. The train took us south to Malmo. There we boarded the train ferry and were in Danzig by morning. Nothing had changed. The marching feet, the endless speeches, and the swastikas waving looked all too familiar. We hurried to our apartment and began to get ready for our Poland trip.

It was exciting to be going back to Poland. We rented a room with a friendly woman in the pretty city of Torin on the Wistula River. Our missionary friends, the Tobers, lived there. They went with us to outlying towns, villages, and farming communities. We taught and preached, prayed for the sick and hurting, and ministered in any way we could. Missionary Tober interpreted for us, as our German wasn't adequate yet. It was a precious time of blessing for all of us. Many of the dear farmer folk gave their hearts and lives to Jesus. Others were healed. Christians were encouraged in the Lord and built up in their faith.

Paul and Gladys in Olivia, a suburb of Danzig, Poland, 1939.

It was a tense time in Poland, too. People were restless and uneasy. There was much war preparation. Across the Wistula, the Poles could see the great German tank and troop build-up, ready to move at Hitler's command. The Germans had the finest, most modern weaponry known to man. The Poles knew they were no match for the Germans, but hoped for British help. When and where would the great German war machine strike? That it would strike was a forgone conclusion.

I wonder, now, that we were not more upset over all the war preparation going on. I guess we were too young, and too confident of being able to handle our own affairs, to realize the gravity of the situation. We could well have been caught right in the middle of the awful holocaust. We loved being in Poland. It was thrilling to see God use us among the people there, young and inexperienced as we were. The exhilaration of having a tiny part in the great move of God in prewar Eastern Europe probably helped close our eyes to the danger.

It was revival time. In eastern Poland, hundreds of White Russians were turning to the Lord. They prayed, then, for open doors to reach their fellow Russians just over the border. "Oh, God, make a way!" was their constant prayer. They had no premonition of how God would answer their prayer or how soon, and it was just as well they didn't know. It came soon enough and not in a way they could have dreamed of.

We sensed that this would be our last series of meetings in Poland. We tried to give the people something to live by, to grow on, and to take with them into the uncertain future.

Often in the meetings, people shared their fears and troubles with us. We encouraged them with the precious promises from God's word. Our favorite promise became theirs, too. It is found in Isaiah 41:10, "Fear thou not; for I am with thee: Be not dismayed; for I am thy God: I will strengthen thee; yea, I will help thee; yea, I will uphold thee with the right hand of my righteousness."

One night we held a prayer meeting in a country place. Many of the worshipers had never seen a train. Some hadn't even seen an auto close up. A plane flying overhead looked like a big bird to them. They asked us how anyone could ride in such a small thing. They traveled by foot or springless wagon. We did, too, when we were in that area.

As we were going from one to another praying with them about needs, we noticed one little women, a simple scarf covering her head and a shabby gray shawl over her thin shoulders. Her head was bowed, her hands folded on the rough, backless bench. Her shoulders shook as she wept softly into her hands. We slipped nearer and Paul handed her his handkerchief. She was so absorbed in her prayer, it lay on the bench unnoticed. We went nearer to pray with her. Suddenly she raised her head and, with closed eyes, began to speak in perfect American English. We were astonished! It was very startling to hear our native tongue in this out-of-the-way place. Most of the people here couldn't speak their own language well, and now this woman was speaking perfect English.

We listened intently to what she was saying. It was a message of hope and encouragement for us. "Don't be afraid. Trust me. I will be with you every step of the way. I will lead and guide you. I will bring you safely through every trial. Be of good cheer." The message was over. With face aglow she worshipped for a moment or two in English, then dropped her head again and continued her prayer in Polish.

When the meeting was over and the people were leaving, we hurried over to the woman and congratulated her on her good English, inquiring where she had learned it. She stared at us blankly for a moment, then informed us that she spoke no English or any other language except her mother tongue. Her friends confirmed this. They thought she was praying in her prayer language, "tongues," as it is often known. She thought so, too. It was awesome to realized God had come down into that humble cottage and used His obedient handmaiden to encourage and comfort His faithful young messengers.

We returned to Torin the next day. What a luxury to take a hot bath, wash our soiled clothes, and just rest an hour or two.

We hadn't heard the news since we left Torin, so Paul decided to turn on the radio and see what was happening. We dialed the British Broadcasting Company on short wave. Some music was playing, but suddenly it stopped. With a crisp British accent, a gentleman announced that a very important message was about to be aired. The German government and the Soviets had signed a mutual assistance pact. We could expect any moment to hear that the Soviets were entering Poland from the east and the Germans from the west. Any British citizens, or others from the free world, who didn't want to be caught in the middle should remain glued to the BBC for additional information.

Every few minutes further reports came through. Things were rapidly heating up. We could see that time was running out. Paul, in his quiet, unruffled manner, was a tower of strength for me. He decided that first we must call our American Consul friend in Danzig. He would know what was best for Americans caught in Europe. The guns hadn't gone into action yet, but this was the signal! No more meetings now.

"Oh, God! Protect your dear people who will be caught right in the middle of this pincer movement. Give them courage and strength. Grant them your peace!" we prayed.

Excitement was at fever pitch in the streets below us. People crying, the shouting of commands that no one listened to, the rumble of wagons and carts over the cobblestones. Church bells all over the city pealed out what sounded like a funeral dirge. It was a heart-wrenching moment. We often relived it in our dreams.

Paul called the American Consul. He was shocked and angry to learn that we had gone to Poland in spite of his warning. He didn't warn us this time. He gave a command as harsh as he could make it. Just three words: "GET OUT! NOW!" He didn't need to repeat it. We were getting out!

We said hasty but warm good-byes to people we could reach by phone. We told the Tobers of the Consul's command. They got in touch with Warsaw and found they had to get a special visa for Mrs. Tober, as she was still a Polish citizen. They assured us they would leave as soon as possible. They promised to see us off at the station the next day and then go on to Warsaw.

We packed our few things, being especially careful of our precious film. It had a story to tell of Nazi brutality and much, much more. We wanted the outside world to see it at all costs.

We were soon on our way to the station in an ancient taxi. Sure enough, the Tobers were there to wish us well. I can still see them standing on the platform waving their handkerchiefs and wiping away tears they couldn't control. They didn't get the needed visa. They had to flee to the forest to save their lives. Later they returned home for a few days. They got the check we sent from the Danzig border and lived from it until they were again forced from their home.

We never saw them alive again. He was murdered by the Russians while trying to protect the women in their group of refugees. His wife had to bury him with her own hands in a shallow grave. She was able to return to the States later. After the war, his sons moved his remains to the family plot in the homeland. What noble people!

I'm glad we couldn't foresee all of this tragedy as our train pulled out for Danzig. We were in life's springtime. Every cloud had a silver lining. Every problem was a challenge that would soon be solved. We were almost happy as our train rumbled over the rails. No premonition of the terror awaiting us at the Polish-Danzig border clouded our joy of being on the way home.

The details of our arrest at the border and how we narrowly escaped with our lives and possessions have already been related. After all these years, I can still vividly remember my terror as the Polish official rummaged through my things, handling and discarding our canisters of film. Our protecting Father was truly watching over us.

After our difficulties at the border it was exciting it to be actually on our way home. Our train turned out to be the last visa-free train to leave Danzig before the war broke out in all its fury. The first shots of the war were fired in Danzig. Dear friends of ours never got out. How we grieved for them and what a challenge it was for us. Did God have some special work for us to do, that He had spared us? Did He want us to pick up the torch the others had laid down and hold it high? We found out in God's time.

CHAPTER FIFTEEN

What a joy it was to pull into the Danzig station at last. We lost no time getting to our apartment. We were tired and drained from the ordeal of the past hours and looked forward to a hot bath and a good night's sleep. We hoped we could get our trunks down from the attic in the morning and get an early start on our long trip to Sweden and safety.

We rang the bell to our apartment. The door opened a crack and the nervous face of our landlady peered out at us. A look of shock and dismay crept over her features.

"You can't come in here," she whispered. "This place is full of Nazi troops. They just came in and took over and I'm utterly helpless to do anything about it. Please, please leave quickly and quietly. I'm not mistress of my own house anymore. Go away right now. Please do."

Nazi troops from Germany, disguised as tourists, had been slipping over the border all week. They took over Danzig and were quartered in every available house all over the city. There were even Nazis in our little apartment.

We turned helplessly away, wondering what to do next. Everything we owned in the world was packed in our trunks there, several stories up, in the attic. We had carefully packed before we left for Poland with the thought of just such an emergency. With a house full of Nazis, how would we ever get them down?

We prayed for help and guidance as we stood there in the dark outer hallway. All of a sudden Paul looked at me, eyes shining.

"I have an idea," he whispered. "Herr Kroll."

Herr Kroll was a railroad man and a member of the church we attended. We didn't have his number, but we ran to the nearest phone booth, looked up the number, and called him. Paul explained our plight and in his hearty, good-natured way, Herr Kroll promised to come right over. We hadn't long to wait. A terrible rumbling sounded down the street. There was Herr Kroll with a heavy farm wagon and a team of sturdy horses. He looked like an angel to us. The shabby old wagon was as beautiful as Cinderella's golden coach. What a hugging good time we had.

Herr Kroll was one of those special people who always seemed to know just what to do. Being German, he felt he could calm the landlady's fears and arrange to get our trunks down and onto his wagon without arousing undue suspicion in the house. He explained our situation to her. She relaxed and showed him a back stairway to the attic. We crept up like mice. The stairwell was dimly lit with a tiny, naked bulb dangling from the high ceiling. It cast weird shadows down the stairway, adding to our uneasiness. One by one, the men carried the four trunks down and out to the wagon while I stood guard. No one bothered us. How we praised God when everything was safely loaded. Herr Kroll thanked the landlady and we were on our way.

The old borrowed wagon creaked and groaned over the rough streets. We sat on the board seat with Herr Kroll. As he urged the horses forward, Paul and I were wondering where we would sleep and what the morrow held for us.

As though he read our thoughts, Herr Kroll turned toward us, and in his hearty way, announced warmly, "Of course you dear people will be our guests tonight. I will put the loaded wagon in an old carriage house back of our home and lock the door securely. It must be shielded from any unfriendly, prying eyes. In the morning we will go right to the train. I can arrange for your trunks to be bonded and sent direct to the United States without being inspected first."

No words of ours could express our gratitude to him for his kindness or to God for bringing such precious people to us. We were heartily welcomed in their home where a warm supper awaited us and a clean, white bed was turned down. We were tired after the hectic hours we had been through and retired as soon as possible.

We were up at the first streak of dawn. After a hasty breakfast, we gathered together for prayer. Herr Kroll committed us to the Lord. He also prayed for divine favor with his superiors, that all would work out well with getting our trunks off. After warm good-byes to Frau Kroll and the children, we were off with Herr Kroll in the grey morning light. The streets were almost deserted. The city was so quiet it was hard to believe it was filled with Nazi troops all geared for action.

We arrived at the station without incident. It was thrilling to see how smoothly and easily our luggage was handled and sent on its way. Herr Kroll told us it isn't usually so uncomplicated to bond trunks without inspection. God had taken charge again! The Krolls were truly God's answer to our need. They will forever remain locked in our hearts.

We were given our tickets for the visa-free train that would take us around through East Prussia and via Berlin to the train boat for Sweden. This was our plan of escape.

We still had about an hour until train time, so we called an American missionary, Herbert Schmidt, who was married to a German citizen. They lived in Danzig with their two little girls and were wondering what they should do. It was complicated for him to make the necessary arrangements, as his wife and children had to have visas for the States. That wasn't easy in those tense days. They came to the train to see us off, their two little daughters with them. The Kroll family was there, too. We prayed together, wondering when or if we would ever see them again. The Schmidts told us they would try to get things settled in Danzig and leave as soon as they could get away.

We waved from the train window until they were only a blur in the distance. The Schmidts never made it. For the second time, our train was the last to leave before the war broke out. Missionary Schmidt was arrested by the Nazis, his wife died, and the little girls and their grandmother disappeared into the seething caldron that was wartime Europe. They were only found again after the war through the intervention with the Soviets of President Harry S. Truman.

Our train hummed along through the warm sunshine. We felt both joy and sorrow. It was good to be on our way, but what about our friends who couldn't leave with us? Would they get out in time? Why were we the ones to get on the train? Did God have some special mission for us in the future? Paul stretched out his legs and looked at his feet, remarking with that quizzical smile of his, "I won't really feel safe until I set these two feet down on Swedish soil." I knew just what he meant!

The trip to Berlin was long and tiresome. The tension and political unrest unnerved us. We thought of the fun in Berlin in happier days and wondered why one nation wanted to fight another. Why couldn't people live in peace with each other? It was a relief to board the train that would take us to the boat. Evening shadows fell as the harbor lights came into view. It took only a few minutes for us to board the boat that would take us to Sweden and safety by morning.

The boat landed in Malmo, Sweden. A number of refugees were aboard her. Evidently the news had preceded us. Reporters and photographers swarmed all over the pier, buttonholing anyone they could. Camera lights flashed and anxious loved ones called out to relatives and friends who had been on the continent when the crisis started.

We seemed to be a special target. They called us Polish refugees. The questions they asked were pertinent and well chosen. Our answers gave them a rather clear picture of what was going on in Poland and Danzig. Some of them were Christian reporters from the *Filadelfia Kirk* daily paper. All news from Danzig, Poland, and the Soviet Union was censored, so the press was hungry for facts. It was quite an experience.

A lovely couple finally broke through the crowd and introduced themselves. They were from the *Filadelfia Kirk* and arranged to host us while we were in their city. They didn't speak much English, but we could understand them a little because of our knowledge of German. Swedish is also a Germanic language, so there is a similarity.

We had a wonderful time in their pretty home. They were perfect hosts, doing all they could to make us feel comfortable. It was fun trying to communicate with each other, using hands, feet, eyes, and other parts of our anatomy, such as nose, ears, or patting our tummies. Sometimes we laughed until we cried at the weird antics we went through to make ourselves understood. We felt comfortable with our Swedish friends, having lived and gone to school in the Pacific Northwest, which could well be termed "Little Sweden."

We spent about three weeks in the Scandinavian countries. We will never forget the kindly people, the open homes, and the royal treatment we received. We were fed the fat of the land as solicitous housewives tried to put some meat on our bones, as they expressed it. We really were thin after our summer in Poland, so they babied and pampered us. We lapped up all this attention like two hungry kittens that had just fallen heir to a bowl of cream.

We were invited to hold meetings in Sweden, Denmark, and Norway. People were eager to learn about all that was happening behind the Brown Curtain of Nazism. Only trivia or propaganda was allowed to filter out. We were cautioned in Denmark and Norway to be very careful what we said and how we said it, as both countries were full of spies and quislings. Sweden was neutral and didn't worry so much about it. She felt pretty safe but was making preparations just in case.

Our two big problems now were to find passage to the States and money to pay for it. Since we had sent our last mission check back to Poland at the Danzig-Poland border, we had no funds. From then on we were cast upon the kindness of others. We were, in very truth, refugees. Every steamship line we contacted was booked solid, mainly with Americans fleeing Europe. We tried everything in Sweden and then went to Denmark. We simply *had* to get a passage soon. Any day the axe could fall. War would rage in Europe. Shipping would be for goods and weapons to support the war machine. We could be trapped there.

Early one morning, hurrying excitedly through the quiet streets, a paper boy ran, shouting at the top of his voice, "*Krieg beginnt! Krieg beginnt!*" We couldn't read or understand Danish, but it was enough like German for us to grasp the blood-chilling message: "War begins! War begins!"

Paul hastily donned street clothes and dashed outside for a paper. Our hosts hadn't heard the clamor since their room was at the rear of the house away from the noise of the street. We ran into the cheerful breakfast room, Paul waving the paper wildly, begging for a translation. Our horrified host grabbed the paper. He began to read and to translate almost in the same breath.

Germany and Russia had declared war on Poland. England was siding with Poland, and France was about to. The German battle ship *Schleswig Holstein* was anchored off Danzig and had fired on Polish Gdynia. Danzig was in a turmoil. World War II had begun!

We knew that if we were to get out of Europe, it had to be very soon.

We placed the matter in God's hands. We were confident the God, who had brought us through all the dangers that lay behind us, could handle this one, too. Our hearts were heavy for our dear friends, the Tobers and the Schmidts. No word could go in or out of Poland or Danzig now. We could only pray for them and solicit prayer support from the churches we visited.

A vice admiral of the Danish navy, a devout Christian, invited us to spend a few days with him and his gracious wife in their palatial home while we tried to find passage to the States. This was a highlight of our time in Denmark. The vice admiral was very kind in trying to help us with our ship-passage problem, but even he couldn't get us on a ship that was already overloaded.

We sent a cable to REEM, the cable address of our mission, informing them of our safety and of our need for funds, but we couldn't count on our cable getting through, because all means of communication appeared to be at a standstill. We decided to go to Norway and see what possibilities for a passage we could find. We gave the *Filadelfia Kirk* in Oslo as our return address on the cable we sent. We loved Denmark and the dear people we met there, but time was running out. If we expected to get out of Europe, we had to find a way.

Norway is one of the most beautiful countries in Europe and her people some of the most friendly. We were invited to make our headquarters in the nice hotel connected with the church complex in Oslo. We visited shipping firms, travel bureaus, freight companies, and absolutely every other possibility during the day. In the evenings we were asked to conduct meetings in churches within the Oslo environs. Our experiences in Poland and Danzig were of interest to everyone. Our interpreter kept reminding us to be very careful of what we said, since Norway was full of spies. Some of their own people became informers through fear of the Nazis.

It seemed as hopeless to find passage from Norway as from the other Scandinavian lands. Our long-suffering interpreter went to the different companies with us. We couldn't have managed without him.

"Well," he sighed, "I only know of one more place. Let's pray before we go to it." So saying, the men removed their hats and we prayed for something to happen so that we could find a way to get home.

We had a couple of blocks to go and prayed the whole way. There stood a modest, two-story building, painted a dazzling white. It was the last shipping firm. We went in, hearts pounding. Our friend asked in Norwegian if they had a ship sailing within the week. They had. Could they take on two more passengers? They could. The smiling man at the desk let us know it was a tiny cabin with two very narrow bunks, but it was clean and the only accommodation left. He grinned engagingly as he added in perfect English, "Wow. You're sure the lucky ones. You came in at just the right moment." We couldn't have agreed more.

The ship was the sturdy little *Stavanger Fjord.* Before we knew it, we were booked up for the end of the week. We didn't have much to pay down, but the friendly gentleman listened to our story and was willing to wait. Now our faith would undergo some more testing, as we waited every day for our money to arrive at the church. We continued to trust God. He had proved Himself all the way. He still had everything under control.

It was the last day. The ship would sail the next morning. We were breakfasting with others in the hotel when our interpreter came into the breakfast room with a big smile on his face, carrying a yellow envelope. He handed it to us. It was our cable. It had arrived in the nick of time. God is never too late. The money was there, deposited in the church bank account. In short order it was in our hands and we were on our way to the ship company.

Our ticket was ready and waiting. It felt good to have it in our hands at last. Lighthearted as a couple of children, we hurried to the pier to see about our luggage. We had time to see the sights of Oslo, too, before dinner. That was a bonus after the hectic days of the past week.

The hotel arranged a little surprise dinner for us with the pastor, his wife, and some of the church elders. It was a wonderful evening. In the morning we were taken to the ship where friends from the church gathered to say farewell and wish us God's blessing. Everyone was so kind to us, it was hard to think of leaving them now. A few tears were shed as we wondered if we would ever see one another again.

We never did. Not long after, the Nazis marched into Norway. Many lives were lost. We never again made it to Norway during all the nearly forty years we lived and worked in Europe, but these precious people have lived on in our hearts. We will meet again some day where wars will be no more and tears are wiped away.

On that warm September day in 1939, we boarded the *Stavanger Fjord*. The gangway was hoisted, the anchor was weighed, and the hoarse, throaty blast of the whistle sounded. We slowly moved out of the safety of the Oslo harbor into the vast unknown. We all crowded on deck to get a last glimpse of old Europe that would never be the same again.

"Good-bye, good-bye, Europe. May God help you in the days, months, and years ahead. Don't forget that we are coming back some day to finish what we started."

Our trip was hazardous in many ways. We were overloaded as we transited the mined infested water. Passengers and crew alike kept a constant lookout for mines and lurking submarines. We had lifeboat drills daily and blackouts nightly. Despite of all this, we were a happy lot. All class distinctions were laid aside to accommodate the crowd. We were all in the same boat, figuratively as well as literally. We were caught in the maelstrom of war. All of us thanked God to be on this ship. We felt perfectly happy for any kind of quarters.

The captain of our ship chose to sail far north of the usual travel routes to avoid some of the dangers already mentioned.

Every evening a vesper service was held. Paul was asked to conduct it. People enjoyed singing the old hymns, especially the old Anglican chorale, "For Those in Peril on the Sea." They wanted to sing it every night and from their hearts, too. Another favorite was, "God Will Take Care of You." Paul brought short, relevant messages from God's word. One the people liked especially was about Jesus stilling the storm on the sea of Galilee. They loved his message on the Twenty-third Psalm and responded well to an excerpt from Ps.107:23-30 where those who go down to the sea in ships have trouble with storms and other dangers. Then they call upon the Lord and He delivers them from all their fears. It ends with the grand finale, "Oh, that men would praise the Lord for His goodness and for His wonderful works to the children of men." Ps.107:31

We never had a more attentive or responsive congregation than these nervous, jittery passengers on the good ship *Stavanger Fjord.* They wanted to be together. They were seeking comfort and encouragement. It was not to be found in the games, the swimming pool, or on the dance floor. These things provided momentary distraction from their fears and uncertainties, but they wanted more than that. They looked for this inner strength where it is sure to be found – in the Bible, God's word.

There were dangers all around us. Besides the mines and submarines, there were always the scouting planes from both sides of the conflict. First a German plane would buzz over us, studying our identity. Then, to our intense relief, it would fly off. Before long an English plane would follow, circle a few minutes, and disappear into the clouds. We all thanked God the two hadn't met over our ship. Paul, in his quiet, confident way, was God's man of the hour on that long, precarious voyage.

It wasn't all worry and fear, though. We met many wonderful people, among them several missionaries of various faiths. Little differences didn't matter in a time like that. We clung together, ministering hope and courage to other passengers. The meals were delicious, which did much to cheer sinking spirits. There were deck and lounge games that were fun for everyone, especially the children. A library of books to interest all types of readers was available. On what would otherwise have been the first-class deck was a pint-sized swimming pool, which everybody enjoyed. Best of all, the weather was lovely all the way, even off the coast of Iceland.

The beautiful morning finally arrived when the Statue of Liberty appeared, torch held high in the rosy dawn. Everybody crowded on deck. Men removed their hats. Men, women, and children fell to their knees on the rough deck, sobbing their gratitude to a loving heavenly Father who kept us and brought us to this moment.

The band suddenly started to play "The Star Spangled Banner." We stood straight, right hand over our hearts, and sang along. We hugged each other. We congratulated one another and the tears flowed as we gazed toward the shores of home. There she was at last! The unforgettable skyline of New York across the blue water. We pulled into the harbor singing, "Praise God from whom all blessings flow." We were home at last.

CHAPTER SIXTEEN

Excitement was at fever pitch as our staunch little ship moved in to take her place at the pier in New York. It was like a dream. Were we really home? Crowds on the pier clapped and cheered as the gangway was lowered and passengers began to descend. Those who were met by loved ones shouted greetings, blew kisses, jumped up and down, half beside themselves for joy. The rest of us shouted and clapped, laughed and waved, just because we were so happy.

As we trooped off the ship, those on shore showered us with fruit, flowers, candies, and confetti and screamed with excitement. Most of the goodies landed in the water, but we were able to catch some of them. It was a joyous celebration! We had almost forgotten how warm and wonderful Americans could be.

As soon as we were ashore, Paul checked to see if our luggage was there. It had come direct from Danzig and was waiting for us. As we went through customs, showing our passports and picking up mail, the agents greeted us warmly with a smiling, "Welcome home." To receive mail at last, after so long a time, was too tempting. We couldn't resist reading it immediately. The trunks made good seating so there amidst the bustle of the crowd we lost ourselves in our mail.

One of the first pieces we picked up was a yellow envelope. A telegram from my mother. In a few words she told us my father had developed a fatal heart disease and probably wouldn't live until we reached home unless we really hurried. I was devastated. We went through the rest of our mail in a daze, then took steps to get on our way. My heart was heavy as I thought of my healthy, vibrant father dying. It didn't seem real. We had to get there while he still lived. I needed to see him and tell him how much I loved and appreciated him. He needed to see me once more, too, and hear my voice. He loved Paul very much too, and Paul admired and respected him.

Paul found a good used car onto which we loaded our belongings, and we were on our way. We had arranged to meet with REEM in Chicago. They wanted a full account of all that happened from the time we went to Poland for the summer until we landed in New York. After a long but friendly conference with the leaders there, we picked up our mail. There was another telegram from mother, informing us that Dad was completely cured. He was a new man and we could continue our trip as formerly planned. We were overwhelmed with joy and thanksgiving.

Our friends at REEM rejoiced with us and immediately arranged meetings for us in the Chicago area. From then on, we held meetings all the way to Seattle. It was a good experience for us. We ministered in large churches with great congregations and in small, pioneer places. Sometimes we spoke to society's castaways in inner-city missions. We didn't preach. We just told our story as refugees from Poland. Everywhere, rich or poor, high or low, people wept with us for those who didn't get out and rejoiced with us for God's tender watch over us, just two of His kids.

We discovered in Poland and again in Scandinavia that we could depend on God's blessing and anointing in our meetings when we put ourselves and the ministry completely in His hands. Now, as we ministered in so many different kinds of places, we experienced anew how true this is. We were amazed at the response to an invitation to accept Christ as Lord and Master. We felt God was leading us to do more than just thrill congregations with an exciting adventure story. That was only an introduction to a loving, caring God who loves people personally and stands ready to help.

We enjoyed every minute of our long trip. Each state had its own beauty and interest for us. Driving through Montana was very special. The rolling plains, the shining mountains, the big sky, and the friendly, "Howdy, neighbor" people. We touched only a few places on Highway 10. Summer turned to fall and fall was fast becoming winter. We still enjoyed our trip in spite of cold weather.

We were thrilled to see whole herds of buffalo in the wild, and agile cowboys bringing herds of cattle hundreds of miles to new grazing grounds. It was startling when real American Indians, complete with moccasins, buckskins, and feathers, came prancing by on their pinto ponies. Of course it was only for show, even fifty years ago, but we loved it. We constantly marveled at the mind-boggling vastness and variety of America. We often found ourselves humming, "Oh, beautiful for spacious skies." As we reveled in the grandeur of Glacier Park, we rejoiced in our American heritage. We loved this land that was our land and prayed God would guard and protect it through this dark time in human history.

It was just a few days before Christmas when we finally drove into the Buck driveway in Everett. We planned to spend Christmas with the Bucks and the New Year with the Williscrofts in Yakima. My family was expecting us, so when they heard the car drive in, the door burst open and everybody came running with arms outstretched. It was wonderful to see them. A great moment of hugging, laughing, talking, and kissing followed. Mother and Dad looked happy and fit. Walter, the only child at home now, was a tall, handsome young man. His mischievous brown eyes danced as he looked me over, evidently deciding I would do, took me in his strong young arms, and gave one of his big bear hugs. My married sisters, with their husbands and children, were there to greet us, too. It was a glorious time of reunion.

Roland, still in college, beamed his pleasure that Paul and I were safe at home again. George, a graduate of Northwest College, had married and was living in California. We missed him with his puns and jokes. Al, the oldest, also lived in California, so he was absent, too. I missed the three older boys, but nothing could dim the joy of being with my family again.

Christmas days with the Bucks were all we could have wished. Paul had a good time, fitting right in with the family. He was anxious to see his family again, though, so we decided to drive over the Cascade Mountains a day or two earlier than planned.

The drive through the winter wonderland was breathtaking. Words are inadequate to describe the snow-capped peaks, the azure skies reflected in the rivers and lakes, the snowy landscape sparkling in the winter sunshine. It all combined to remind us once more how glorious our land is and how glad we were to be back in it.

As the familiar scenes around Yakima came into view, Paul got more and more excited. He loved pointing out all the dear old landmarks. He was like a small boy again, thrilled about coming home. I recognized, then, how homesick he was and how he had missed his loved ones. He never expressed his feelings much, but he had been longing to see them all the while we were on the long journey home.

We rolled to a stop before the nice apartment house where the family had lived since they came to Yakima so many years ago. Paul's hands were actually trembling as he stopped the car and ran around to open the car door for me. He was so eager to help me out, I almost fell on my nose. He managed to catch me in time and, laughing, we ran into the house and down to their apartment.

The Williscrofts hadn't heard us drive in, so the surprise element was doubly exciting as we bounced through the door. Everything was suddenly in an uproar. Children clamored for hugs and kisses. The parents beamed with love and thankfulness to have us back again. The brothers enjoyed a time of jolly backslapping, and everyone talked at once. Home! Is there any place like it?

Those were a great few days. It was fun listening to the brothers kid each other. The sisters-inlaw enjoyed comparing husbands, noting the likenesses and differences. The children had all grown so much and helped keep things lively. The parents hovered over us like a pair of robins with their brood. Mother Williscroft cooked all the goodies she knew her children liked. Dad went into long discussions with his boys over every controversial subject the sons touched on. It was family and it was fun.

Paul, especially, enjoyed visiting the Stone Church. He was invited to speak and thrilled the congregation with the saga of our escape from Poland. The young people asked us both to tell more about it in their youth group. They enjoyed planning little parties and socials for us, and we were delighted to attend.

In Yakima we heard the rumor that had I died in childbirth while still in Danzig and that poor Paul was trying to care for the baby and carry on alone. This rumor probably made the rounds because of the Bronsons having a baby. It was a hard delivery, and Margie did almost die. God was gracious and brought her through, but the mixed-up rumor got to Yakima and was devastating to our friends there. Fortunately Everett had not heard the rumor yet, so friends there were spared that shock. It was a strange feeling to see friends looking at me as at one risen from the dead. It left us quite shaken.

The holidays were over. We cherished every minute of every day, but now it was time to get down to business. We received many invitations to visit churches both in central and eastern Washington. Churches on the coast also wanted us. The itinerary was timely. Everybody was interested in war news. The churches were almost always packed. Not only members came, but many townspeople. Interest remained high from church to church. We were invited to schools, civic groups, women's clubs, businessmen's luncheons, and so on. We had long talks with pastors, principals, and leaders of all kinds. We learned a lot from our travel experiences, more than we ever learned in college. Talking with these knowledgeable people was a great learning experience for us, too.

Everywhere we went Paul showed his precious film from Danzig that I thought would be lost at the Polish border. People were fascinated by the scenes of Nazi flags flying everywhere. They could grasp the mood of the Nazis as they watched the Brownshirts and the Blackshirts marching to martial music. The crowds that flocked to the Nazi political rallies gave viewers a clearer understanding of Hitler's popularity. They shuddered over the "*Juden Unerwunscht*" posters in parks, on beaches, and in almost every public place. We even had pictures of *Kristall Nacht* showing the horrible destruction of Jewish property and, in some cases, physical abuse and disfiguration.

We bought war films, too, taken right after the start of the war, that people found very exciting. Paul made a commentary to go with the film. Recorded Nazi music accompanying it gave just the right mood. It was impressive. Sometimes we were asked to repeat our presentation three nights in a row so that everyone who wished to could have an opportunity to attend.

This was heady business for two relatively inexperienced young people. Looking back from this vantage point, I marvel at God's goodness and grace in keeping us unspoiled and usable. He allowed just enough troubles to keep us where He wanted us. Sometimes our projector bulb went out right in an exciting place. Another time the film would break once or twice during a showing and need to be repaired. The poor congregation would have to sit and wait. We caught colds or our voices gave out. We got tired and longed for a night off. There were times when it was hard to speak, moments when the right words just wouldn't come. These were all humiliating little experiences that kept us humble and made us aware once more how utterly dependent we were on God if we wanted to be used by Him.

God loved His kids and made sure pride wouldn't take root in our hearts and destroy us. In spite of these mishaps, the crowds kept coming and we kept traveling.

Winter blossomed into spring, spring became summer, and still we traveled. We looked constantly to our Father for guidance. It was no surprise, then, when we felt a nudge to attend the family camp in Montana near Yellowstone Park in a very lovely area. We drank in all the meetings like thirsty animals that suddenly found fresh water. It was a time of spiritual renewal. We met many old friends, among them college students we hadn't seen since we left for Europe. We enjoyed a mini-reunion, catching up on what was going on at school and delighting in being together again.

On Sunday afternoons we were asked to share our experiences in Danzig and Poland. There was special interest in our escape to Sweden and the voyage to America. Sometimes the listeners wept, sometimes they laughed. Always, though, we sensed the moving of the Holy

Spirit speaking to hearts. At the close of the service, Paul gave an altar call for a rededication of the whole person to the Lord for His service. Young people streamed to the front. It was a holy moment of consecration and committal as they waited before God. Some of these kids told us they felt God leading them into His service. They asked us if the next step should be Bible school. We encouraged them to wait before the Lord and ask Him to guide them step by step into the place He planned for them. Later some of these young people did come to Bible school and went out into the service of the Lord.

Through this visit to camp we were invited to many churches to show our pictures and tell our story. The Assembly of God was small in Montana in those days. Churches were far apart. We often drove all day to get to the next meeting. We got tired and hot, but people came from all around and God blessed and refreshed us together. We loved Montana and the people there.

We were scheduled for a service in Glasgow in Eastern Montana near the North Dakota border. We already knew some of the people there. They had come to a meeting in Wolf Point, the next town down the line, a few nights before. The church building was a simple wooden structure. It showed possibilities, though. There was a full basement that could be finished and made into Sunday school rooms and whatever else was needed. There was already a nice little apartment downstairs that could serve as a parsonage. Something about this little church intrigued us. We felt excited as the service began.

A pleasant, lively young pastor, Al Morrison, from Sidney, Montana, led the song service, strumming a tiny ukelele and getting the people into the spirit of the occasion. He later became one of our dearest friends, even visiting us in Germany. He held meetings in a number of churches there and blessed the people with his warm, lively style.

Glasgow was without a pastor at that time. They asked us to take the church. Again we felt a thrill of excitement. We arranged for the board and members to pray about this as well as for us. We would go ahead with our schedule for the summer, pray for God's direction, and let them know what we decided before we went back to the coast.

Glasgow is in the Fort Peck area. Fort Peck is site of a great earthen dam on the Missouri River. Many men had been employed on this vast project. Now the operation was finished and only a skeleton crew of skilled maintenance men remained, living in a neat little government-housing area near the dam. Most of the members of the Glasgow church worked on the dam. Possibly ten or twelve people, some of them with the maintenance force, remained in the church. A few more came from farms and hamlets in the area. The situation didn't look too promising, but we felt that if God wanted us to come, He would work it all out. We left it with Him.

The meeting in Glasgow that night was something special. Many people who came were Mennonites from one of their nearby settlements. They were happy to hear about their old homeland but, peace-loving as they traditionally are, they were saddened to hear how Germany had changed. The meeting was lively and the house full. Many came from other churches in town, interested to hear about conditions in Europe. There was a warm, loving atmosphere. We felt at home.

When the service was over, we greeted people at the door. Those from the church introduced themselves and hoped we would come back. The visiting townspeople thanked us for the presentation and also wished we would come to stay. Who could tell? Was it possible that little Glasgow, out on the plains of Montana, was God's destiny for us for years to come?

CHAPTER SEVENTEEN

We finished our itinerary in Montana. We were captivated by the freshness, open-heartedness, and warmth encountered from one end of the state to the other. Winter was fast approaching when we finally arrived back in Yakima. The big question now was whether or not we should take the pastorate in Glasgow.

We prayed, we talked to Paul's pastor, we asked advice of mature Christian friends and, above all, we searched our own hearts. It was good to have this input from others, but still we couldn't get Glasgow out of our system. We felt drawn there with irresistible cords. First was the need. They had no shepherd, no leadership, no direction. Second, the people in Glasgow had won our hearts during the short time we were there. Could we let them down? Last, we were unable to resist the urgent inner nudge. We finally wrote to tell them we accepted the pastorate in Glasgow, and peace came to our hearts.

We packed what we needed. Paul's parents helped us with pieces of furniture we lacked. His mother generously provided us with sufficient pots, pans, and dishes to start. We loaded a small trailer with our things and were on our way into a whole new experience.

The long trip over the snow-covered Rockies was hazardous in itself, but pulling a heavy trailer over those slippery roads was a nightmare. We enjoyed the beauty all around us more than we feared the dangers, so we had a good time anyway. We sang, quoted scripture, shared plans of what we hoped and dreamed for Glasgow, and counted the miles as we left them behind us. Eventually we left the mountains and traveled the rest of the way over flat tableland. Sometimes we couldn't see a tree as far as the eye could reach. We began to see signs – Glasgow 200 miles, Glasgow 150 miles, Glasgow 10 miles. It was a thrill for two bone-weary travelers. We were almost there.

Glasgow looked wonderful to us as we drove through the dark, quiet streets. We decided folks here retired early. When we rolled to a stop in front of the little white church we were suddenly wide awake. We were home. Here we would live for an undetermined number of years. Our children would probably be born here. If God blessed, we might see many people from miles around learn to know and serve Him. We would undoubtedly know good times and bad, joys and sorrows, ups and downs. One thing we knew, God had brought us there and He would supply every need. At the moment, we were glad just to be there.

The door to the parsonage was unlocked. Doors were seldom locked in Montana in those days. We went in to find the apartment cozy and warm, with hot food in the oven and a fresh cake on the table. A nice card lay beside the cake, welcoming us to Glasgow.

Our first gesture in our new home was to thank God for a safe journey over all those treacherous roads. The second was to commit ourselves to our heavenly Father. We needed His blessing and power in our lives. We promised to give Glasgow our best.

Before long we were pretty well in the saddle. We visited the homes of members and strangers alike. Every house was the dwelling place of people God loved. Most of the people welcomed us, but a few looked us two kids over with haughty ridicule and the curt remark, "We're not interested!" Dogs chased us. Doors were slammed in our faces. Sometimes we were scornfully reminded that, "This town already has too many churches for its own good."

Paul had never served a pastorate before, but he had kept his eyes open in all the many churches we visited in the past one-and-a-half years. His collection of dos and don'ts really piled up. Now he made good use of them, trying to avoid the don'ts and put the dos into practice. We made our own mistakes, too. We even turned a few dear saints against us.

One family stopped coming to church. We went to visit them, hoping to find out what the trouble was. They angrily informed Paul he hadn't shaken hands with them one Sunday. He apologized and tried lovingly to mollify them. It was a long time before they were happy with us, though. You can't win them all, but both of us learned from this mistake.

Our promise to God back in Danzig haunted us now. That longing and urge to reach boys and girls for Jesus still burned in our hearts. During visits in homes, we always invited the children to Sunday school. It was easy to get close to them. Just asking what a child's name was, or when his birthday was, brought a warm response from child and parents. If a family needed a ride, Paul offered to come and pick them up. Even when the parents weren't interested, they usually allowed their children to come. We trained some of the young people to teach, and some were already qualified teachers. People began to come to church. They brought their children to Sunday school. Paul enlisted men in a taxi service to pick up children whose parents didn't come. We discovered children really could be inspired for God. They loved to come and wouldn't miss Sunday school for anything. Many, now grown, are bringing children and grandchildren to Sunday school and church. It was an exciting adventure to watch God work in the lives of old and young.

Every Saturday some of the men came to work on the church. They put a floor in the basement and finished some of the Sunday-school rooms. A neighboring pastor came and plastered the sanctuary. The men finished a nice little office for Paul, just off the platform. The church began to look neat and inviting as the work went on, week after week. The women came and helped prepare hot meals for the fellows. Saturdays became social times of fellowship and blessing. People wouldn't miss them for anything. Things were beginning to look up.

People came from outlying areas to see what was going on. There were several Mennonite communities in the countryside around Glasgow. These frugal, God-fearing farmer folk, had churches in their own communities, but they loved to visit our church for anything special. They sent their high-school children to town during the school year. They lived with Christian families in town when they could. Some lived in cheap boarding houses. They liked to come to our church on Sundays.

The Lord laid these fine young people on our hearts, so we started a youth program for them and our own church kids. God moved among them in such beautiful ways. Many made a new commitment to the Lord. Some were filled with the Holy Spirit and all were blessed. There were not many youth in the church when we arrived. The ones who were there were not very stable. The Mennonite kids brought a breath of fresh air with them. Soon they and our own young people formed a fine, strong youth group.

Young pastors Paul and Gladys in Gasgow, Montana, 1941

Paul was always a serious, studious type. He was not a man to set the world on fire, but he was blessed with consistency and tenacity.

This helped him succeed where other, more gifted ministers often failed. He was tireless in his preparation for Sunday, spending most mornings in his study. Afternoons he made hospital or home visits to anyone who was sick or suffering. He went to minister's meetings and became acquainted with his clerical colleagues. The Baptist pastor took a fatherly interest in this young newcomer, acquainting him with some of the intricacies of pastoring. Paul appreciated his help, and they became good friends.

Paul was never an eloquent speaker, but his messages always carried food for thought. People came to see what was going on and very often stayed to seek God. The congregation began to grow. The church was filled with young life and vigor. It was meeting a need in the town. The young pastor was appreciated and respected. God was working.

Everything was not all sweetness and light however. The loose ends at the Fort Peck Dam project were finally tied together. Most of the remaining workers were laid off. They left town to find jobs elsewhere. Our growing congregation began to disintegrate as one family after another moved away. Before long we were almost back to where we had started. A man of lesser character and less inner strength would have given up and gone off to seek greener pastures. Not Paul. He was faced with a challenge, and he accepted it.

"There are many people left in Glasgow who need God. We're staying, honey. Let's believe God for another miracle in this little church," was Paul's response to my suggestion that maybe it was time for us to move on, too. That was his attitude all through this bleak period.

Trust God we did. Church growth was our main thrust in prayer for days and weeks. But we didn't only pray. As the Lord guided and different possibilities came into our minds, we tried them out. We visited homes. Paul sent out literature. He posted placards on lamp posts and telephone poles, in store windows, and anywhere else he could find an appropriate spot. We passed out cute little Sunday school invitations to school children going by and spoke to individuals, old and young, about the church program. That wasn't all, though. Paul delighted in telling anyone who would listen about his wonderful Friend and Saviour.

We invited good speakers now and then. Sometimes Paul enlisted a good singing group from the area. He left no stone unturned to reach his goal. The church people helped, too, by inviting neighbors, friends, and relatives. Best of all, we were united in our prayers and in our action, with one goal in view: to reach our town with the gospel. We banded together in a covenant of prayer – -at home, at church, in odd moments during working hours, wherever an opportunity presented itself. Our slogan was "Pray for Glasgow." Pray people into the church.

What was the result of all this? People began to come to church. New people moved to town and found their way to our church. Sunday-school children excitedly invited parents and brought them along. Turned-on high schoolers brought their friends from school. It was exhilarating to see how everybody cooperated. The church began to grow again. People gave their lives to Christ. Once more our little church was a source of blessing in the community. Paul had accepted a challenge, and God honored it.

War fever was mounting across the United States. Great defense projects were booming. People in smaller towns were being lured away because of the urgent need for workers in these factories, with the promise of high wages. There was an exodus of small-town workers to the large industrial areas. Glasgow was no exception. We watched helplessly as our healthy, growing congregation began to dwindle a second time to a mere shadow of what it was.

Glasgow was long thought of as a town of transients. Now it was living up to its name. There were, of course, families who owned their homes and were quite firmly established. Most of these were business and professional people with stable incomes from their business or practice. They remained. Some were in our church, which was a comfort. The majority, however, were more transient. They packed up and followed the crowd to wherever jobs were to be found.

Pastor Williscroft didn't give up. He didn't leave. He didn't despair. He did some strong knee work, however. Once again he organized the church into a prayer patrol. The tiny remnant that was left prayed and believed for a miracle.

To everybody's surprise, the federal government decided to put an airport in Glasgow to support the military. That brought construction workers to town. They brought their families with them. Some of them were already church members and sought our church as their place of worship. Paul wasn't sleeping, either. He visited the building site, talked with people, witnessed to them, and invited them to church. Some came. They liked it and invited others. Once more we saw God at work, melting the hearts of these tough men on the construction crews. Men, their wives, and their children gave their lives to Christ. Paul knew these people wouldn't be permanent. They would leave as soon as the airport was finished. With this in mind, he preached teaching sermons to build them up in their newfound faith. They were wonderful people, a blessing to have in the church.

Eventually the airport was built. The workers went off to other jobs, the new converts and their families among them. Our church seemed empty and lonely for a few weeks. Then the airmen and maintenance people came, and the church began to build up again.

Our district superintendent laughingly complimented Paul on his talent for winning people for other churches, since our congregation changed so often. They found the Lord in Glasgow and soon moved away to be active members of another pastor's church. That was good, though. Were we only building up churches, or were we building the Kingdom of God?

The children of the church in Glasgow, Montana,
where Paul and Gladya were pastors, 1941

The years in Glasgow were happy and fruitful. We made many friends and were accepted in the town. The church, even with its changing congregations, was known and respected. It was exciting to watch God work among us. Children were now, as always, a very important part of our ministry. Our church was full of them. Young people were also a strong element in the church. We were thankful for all God did among us and gave Him the glory.

Something was missing, though. The years came and went, but we were still childless. We longed and prayed for a baby. We had been married about four and a half years, and the church was more stable, the congregation reasonably permanent. When I awakened one morning feeling nauseated and miserable, we thought it was only a touch of stomach flu that was making the rounds in our area. It persisted, though, so I visited our family doctor. After a thorough examination, he grinned as he said, with a twinkle in his eye, "Mrs. Williscroft, you have the oldest malady known to women."

I stared at him a moment, then shrieked, "You mean, ah…you're telling me, ah…that I'm pregnant? You're telling me I'm going to have a baby?"

He nodded, smiling warmly. "You are in about the sixth week, I'd say."

Then he went on to give me instructions on prenatal care. I was so excited I hardly heard a word. I wanted to hurry home and give Paul the earthshaking news. I hugged the good doctor, slipped out of his office, and danced on cloud nine all the way back to the parsonage.

When I got there Paul was out. Wouldn't you know? I simply must share my joy with someone right away. Who should I call? Mother, of course!

She was almost as excited as I, even though she already had a number of grandchildren. Like most mothers, she gave me lots of good advice. Then I called Paul's mother. She was delighted and immediately sent baby a gift. Dear Mom Williscroft was a generous, giving soul.

After Paul returned and I told him the news, we celebrated the rest of the afternoon and all through the evening with embraces, kisses, smiles, and my tummy soother, Coca Cola. From that day on,

Paul handled me like a piece of Dresden china. One would think this was the first baby ever to come into the world, and I loved every minute of it.

It was early in October when we first knew we were having a baby. We reckoned he would arrive near the tenth of June the following year. The months of waiting and preparation were precious for us. Almost daily we laid the little new life that was developing in my body into the hands of the Friend of children. We gave ourselves anew to the Lord, praying for wisdom and guidance to bring up our child to know and love Him, too. We fixed a little corner of our one bedroom into a nursery with pictures of babies on one wall and one of Jesus above the little crib. I painted the crib a soft ivory and put cuddly pastel decals of lambs on it. I happily hemmed diapers and crocheted pretty baby things. It was a time of perfect contentment and joy for us both.

The church went wild when they heard our secret. They gave us a big shower with enough pretty things for two or three babies. Some were pink and feminine. We surmised some of our people were hoping for a little girl to grace the parsonage. Well, that would have been nice, too, but somehow, we felt we were getting a boy. We wanted and prayed for a son. He would be like his father. Perhaps he would even go into the ministry some day, if that was God's plan.

The days and weeks flew by. Christmas was only three weeks away. It was Sunday evening, December 7, 1941. We came home from the evening service and flipped on the radio just in time to hear the awful report of the bombing of Pearl Harbor. We couldn't believe our ears. We listened to terrible reports of our ships being bombed, our boys dying, the unpreparedness of our navy there, and the deception of Japan. I was in such a state of shock for awhile, we feared we would lose our baby. I was young and healthy, though, so, with God's help, baby and I came through it without any real damage.

We planned to spend the holidays with both sets of parents. A girl from the church went with us to visit friends on the coast and to help with the driving.

We were driving along early one morning just out of Ellensburg, Washington. We hadn't quite reached the dangerous canyon yet. Our young friend was at the wheel while Paul and I were sleeping. We woke up with a start when we felt the car slipping and sliding. We had hit black ice, and the car was out of control. A huge ammunition truck was behind us. Another vehicle was coming toward us on the two-lane highway. It looked hopeless. There was nothing we could do.

Paul was in the front passenger seat. He reached for the wheel and tried to bring the car out of the slide. No use. It continued to careen crazily right into the path of the ammunition truck.

My concern was for the little life I was carrying. *Oh, God, please don't let anything happen to my baby,* was my heart's cry as we went into the spin. I held my two hands tightly over my abdomen as I prayed. We held our breath as we all committed ourselves into God's care. Suddenly it was as though unseen hands took hold of our car and glided it gently backwards down an embankment on the opposite side of the highway, with its front wheels barely visible over the edge of the road. We felt the small trailer we were hauling touch a barbed-wire fence behind us, then we came to an easy stop. The car coming toward us whizzed safely by, and the truck, with its deadly cargo, drove on without incident. We knew our heavenly Father had taken charge of the situation that morning.

To us it was a miracle. There wasn't a scratch on the car and only a minor dent or two on the trailer. Cars stopped to help, and soon our car and trailer were back on the road. We drove on, rejoicing. What a mighty God we serve.

The holidays were wonderful. Both sets of parents pampered us to our heart's content, and I got special attention because I was sick every morning. I rather think both mothers enjoyed bringing in that steaming cup of tea to the bedside. Paul couldn't do enough for me, either. I think we both cherished each other and the new life we were bringing into the world, even more since the near tragedy.

It is a mystery why vacation days go by so fast and ordinary days can sometimes pass so slowly. In no time we had to get back to our flock and the duties of a pastor and his wife. The return trip was uneventful. It was actually good to be back in our little parsonage again.

The church knew we needed another room with a new addition on the way. The men got together and added one to the two rooms we had. It was so nice to have it, especially when we had overnight guests.

It was a sunny June morning, June the 9th. I woke with awful pains in my back. They got worse so we decided to call the doctor. He ordered me to the hospital immediately. Little Robert Grover first saw the light of day at exactly two o'clock that afternoon. We all came through with flying colors, although at times the doctor and I wondered if Paul would make it. He survived, however, and was the proudest, happiest daddy in town.

I could hardly wait to bring the baby home and lay him in the pretty little bassinet the church ladies had given us at the shower. I had often looked longingly at it, dreaming of the day when our baby would be sleeping there. That happy day came at last. We brought our little Bobby home and tenderly tucked him into his cozy nest. He was a happy, contented baby, and we were happy, contented parents. Our joy was complete.

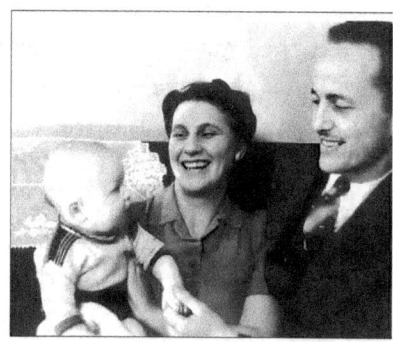

Bobby Williscroft is born, 1942

We gave him the middle name of Grover after Paul's father. He was a proud grandfather and quite devoted to little Bobby whenever he got a chance to see him. We gave Robert to the Lord as soon as we knew he was on the way and again after he was born. When he was two months old we brought him to church where we officially dedicated him to the Lord. District superintendent Leonard Palmer officiated. As he held our little son in his arms, the baby suddenly smiled up at him and reached for his moustache. That brought a ripple of amusement into the otherwise solemn service. It was a very special moment for us as Pastor Palmer held our baby in his arms and repeated the beautiful, sacred words of the dedication ceremony.

✳

World War II was raging all over the world. Boys from our church were being drafted and going off for training amid waving banners, songs, and tears. Daily the papers printed names of those killed or missing. It was a solemn, patriotic time. Women were knitting socks, rolling bandages, or helping in USO centers. We were all buying Liberty Bonds. Even children saved pennies to help in some way. In churches, pastors preached patriotic sermons and their congregations sang patriotic songs. Everyone prayed for loved ones on the front and for the dreadful war to be over.

To our joy, the church held its own. In this time of national crisis people came to church who hadn't made a practice of it before. People felt they needed God and one another for comfort and support. Even the prayer meeting was well attended. Prayer became important. It was during this time that prayer breakfasts and days of prayer in the community became popular. It was a hard time, but it was also a good time. It seemed to bring out the best in people.

Our little Bobby was fast growing into a loving, mischievous little boy. He was truly a child of the church, everybody's baby. He loved it and seemed to thrive on it.

We were happy in Glasgow. The people loved us, the church was healthy, and we were getting along well. Little by little, however, a strange restlessness crept over Paul. He was conscious of that familiar nudge he knew so well when it was time for a change. He felt God had other plans for him now, but what and where? We made it a matter of concentrated prayer.

Then a call came from a church in central Montana. Was God leading us to Conrad? Yes, indeed He was, and we knew it. It would be hard to leave Glasgow. We loved the people and they loved us.

It was an emotional farewell, but we were learning that life is made up of meetings and partings. Through our tears we could see the shining rainbow of promise. Glasgow will live forever in our hearts.

CHAPTER EIGHTEEN

Conrad was a pretty little town about fifty miles north of Great Falls. It was typical small-town USA, with broad, tree-lined streets, attractive, well-kept homes, and a church on nearly every corner. The little church we would pastor was a simple, white frame building with a large lawn in front and a high green hedge on three sides. It wasn't elaborate inside, but it had a good "churchy" feel about it. The parsonage was in the back part of the church building. One room opened into the next like a string of railway cars. The furnishings were simple, but adequate, and it had a homey, lived-in feeling.

The Sunday school accommodations were not as good as in Glasgow, but we felt we could fix that by having some of the classes in our apartment. We had a vision in our hearts of what God could do in this little church. Paul dedicated our ministry there to the Lord before we ever held a service in the church. He believed and trusted God for His moving and blessing upon our ministry as well as upon the dear people to whom we would minister.

The congregation in Conrad was larger than in Glasgow. It was a pleasant, welcoming group. We noticed the people were quite "church conscious" and seemed satisfied with the status quo. It was an above-average congregation in intelligence, education, and ability, consisting of business and professional people, several good musicians, teachers, and farmers. This was a settled community. People owned their homes, for the most part, and seemed satisfied to be where they were. It was quite different from the shifting population of Glasgow.

We often missed Glasgow but found Conrad a challenge. There were areas where we felt we could render the church a positive service. One was visitation. Some of the church people enlisted in this ministry as well and became quite adept at it. New people were reached through this systematic visitation program. Some of the experiences in homes visited were hilarious, others sad. We met people at the grass-roots level. The youth and children's work was especially near to our hearts, and the Lord helped us see some exciting results.

The youth work was a real joy. These kids could be motivated to attempt difficult, but exhilarating, projects. Paul asked them to determine the most promising young person in town and, as a group, pray for him or her until that person accepted Jesus as personal Savior.

They found that person, a fine young man in his senior year of high school. He worked after school and Saturdays as bag boy in a local grocery store. Since the town was small, everyone knew and liked him. When the Junior Chamber of Commerce selected him as the young man of the year most likely to succeed, that was the clue the kids needed. The poor guy didn't stand a chance with our ardent young people zeroing in on him. They met at the church several noontimes a week to pray for him. They prayed at home in their devotions. They requested prayer for him in the regular church services, times without number. They prayed after church in one of the smaller rooms. These were a bunch of turned-on kids! Summer vacation came. Popular and studious Frary Buell, their prayer target, won a scholarship to a good college in the East.

Summer melted into autumn. School started, and Frary left for college. Our young people started back to school, and they kept on praying. The weeks and months flew by. It was Christmas time, and vacation had begun. The Christmas young-people's service was already in progress when the door softly opened. Everybody turned to see who was coming late, as people so often do in smaller churches.

There stood Frary Buell with a friend. The kids went wild. They clapped and welcomed him royally. Then Frary gave a beautiful testimony. He had given his life to the Lord at college, in Campus Crusade. When he got home, he inquired where a lively Bible church could be found and was referred to ours. His high-school friend, Don Patten, was home from Missoula, Montana. They got together and discovered that both of them had given their lives to the Lord while away at college. Our young people felt God gave them double measure for all their praying.

Frary finished college, went on to seminary, and then to a Third-World country as a missionary, where he labored for many years. Later he and his wife went to Scotland, where he pastors a fine church. We were in touch with him while we were in Germany and planned to visit him in Scotland, but Paul was called to higher service before we could go.

Frary's friend, Don Patten, finished his studies in Missoula, served the Lord faithfully, and has recently retired from a prosperous business in Seattle, in partnership with God and honoring Him in all he does. He has a lovely Christian wife, and they have raised a fine family. Don is also a serious, talented writer, author of *The Biblical Flood and the Ice Epoch*, of *The Long Day of Joshua*, and of *Catastrophism and the Old Testament*.

One of the Conrad girls, Beulah Bokma, was a registered nurse and a radiant Christian. She dreamed of having her own car and saved toward that end. One day the Holy Spirit whispered to her heart. "Why don't you buy a car for a missionary first? You can get one for yourself later, you know." Beulah was obedient. The national youth organization had a project of raising funds for equipment to help missionaries do a faster and better job. They purchased cars, Jeeps, boats, planes, bicycles, motorcycles – even printing presses and much more. This was one of the greatest mission endeavors by young people ever promoted at that time.

Beulah gave the money. A struggling missionary was blessed and encouraged and Beulah tasted the joy of giving. It didn't end there. Our youth group received an impressive document from the missions headquarters one day to find they ranked first in per-capita missions giving of all the youth groups in our denomination. They were awed when they received a banner and a large, beautiful, golden loving cup. They displayed it proudly in the church and sometimes in their young peoples' room. Beulah was a beautiful example and inspiration to all of them on the joy of giving.

Our young people were so excited over Frary and Don they wanted to take on another challenging goal. We discussed different ideas with them until we all came up with a thought we felt they could actually believe in. Sometimes young people are turned off if they are encouraged to take on more than they can trust God for. Their new project was to pray that a person a month would come to the Lord in our church. That would be twelve a year. The kids were comfortable with that number. So the praying began again. Not that they hadn't prayed since their prayer campaign for Frary. But this was praying very definite prayers. In many cases, they were for definite people: friends, relatives, and schoolmates.

Those kids prayed all year long. They loved to pray. It became an important part of their lives. They would often greet each other with, "Hey, did you get your praying in today?" or, "Who'd you pray for today?" It was one of those things that a youth pastor dreams about, but hardly dares hope for.

At the end of the year as the kids tallied up the score, there were exactly twelve new people who had taken a definite stand for the Lord. This was heady business for those kids. They could have kicked themselves, then, that they hadn't trusted God for more people. They had learned the life-changing truth of the power of prayer.

I was pregnant when we moved to Conrad. It was one of those miserable pregnancies where I was sick the whole nine months. Our doctor in Glasgow informed us, after Bobby's birth, that we probably wouldn't have any more children. We were terribly disappointed but reconciled ourselves to being a one-child family. Little Bobby refused to accept that. He wanted a sister, so we told him to pray to God to give her to him.

When we knew a baby was on the way we encouraged him just to pray for a baby and not specify either a boy or a girl. Maybe God might know a brother would be better for him than a sister. The poor little guy was incensed to think God might give him something he didn't want. He glared at us accusingly and grumbled, "God wouldn't give me a brother when I asked Him for a sister!"

His little-boy faith never wavered all during the long, trying pregnancy. In fact, he tried to share some of the misery with me. Often during the day I would drop wearily on the bed murmuring, "Oh, I'm so miserable!" Bobby would come then, climb up beside me, and in the same plaintive voice, repeat, "Oh, I so missable!"

The days, weeks, and months slipped by. My nausea lasted the entire time. Both Paul and Bobby were sweet and sympathetic. They did all they could to help and cheer me. Our joy over having another child outweighed any discomfort, but still I found myself counting the days until it would all be over and I would be myself again.

Late in February Paul had to leave for Springfield, Missouri, to attend a national Sunday school convention. That was back in the golden days of the Sunday school, when it was considered one of the most important outreaches of the church. Paul was the district Sunday school representative for Montana and needed to be at the convention. The only problem was that I was nearing the time when the baby was expected. Paul hated to leave, but our doctor assured him the baby wouldn't arrive for at least two more weeks. Our fears allayed, Paul left, cheerfully expecting to be back in plenty of time for the big event.

I waved as long as the car was in sight, then turned to go in, when an awful pain struck me. Mother Williscroft was with us again. She took one look at my stricken face and dashed off to call the doctor and inform the hospital. One of our kind deacons took me to the hospital.

At high noon our little daughter made her appearance. When the nurse laid her in my arms, I could only thank and praise the Lord for this beautiful child I was cradling. First I examined her carefully to make sure that Bobby had his sister. Then I looked over each tiny toe, kissed every wee finger, touched those miniature ears, and ran my hand gently over those masses of dark hair on her little head. She was perfect and, to this mother's eyes, the loveliest thing in the world. I ached for Paul to be there to adore her with me. I was almost angry at the poor old doctor for not knowing better when our baby should arrive. My calculated date was much more accurate than his. If we had only gone by my calendar he would have been with us.

These negative thoughts ran through my mind for awhile. Then I felt ashamed of myself. Paul needed to go. We promised each other God would always have first place in our lives. Now He had given us a precious little daughter who was healthy and perfect in every way, and I lay there feeling sorry for myself. I felt so unworthy of all God's goodness. Holding my baby to my heart, while tears rolled down my cheeks onto her soft, dark hair, I gave this little one into God's great Father hands, begging Him to never let me put her or anything else before Him. His peace stole softly into my heart again. I was content even though Paul was hundreds of miles away.

A telegram was sent off to him with our good news. Paul's answer came the following day expressing as much joy and regret as a telegram can convey. He promised to cut his time in Springfield short in order to be home with us as soon as possible. My world was in order again. It all happened on February 24, 1945. Just forty-three years later on that same day, Paul went to be with the Lord.

When Grandma went home and told Bobby he had a darling little sister, he wasn't even surprised. He gave her that clear-eyed look only young children can give and remarked, "Grandma, I knew God wouldn't give me a brother when I asked for a sister." He could hardly wait until we brought her home. Every day when Grandma came to see me, he sent little drawings, small toys he loved, and other tokens of his affection for the wee sister God had given him.

Paul got home while I was still in the hospital. He lost his heart completely to his pretty little daughter. He never quite got over the fact that he wasn't there to witness her arrival, but he was very relieved that both of us were fine after the hard pregnancy.

We always felt that our Beverly Ruth was a special gift of God to us because, humanly speaking, she shouldn't have joined our family. She was a happy, contented baby and grew into a sweet, sunny little girl. Bobby adored her, showing her off to visitors as his baby. Now our little family was complete. We enjoyed our children and were very thankful for both a boy and a girl, knowing there would probably never be another child.

Bobby and Beverly Williscroft in Conrad, Montana, 1949

We noticed, however, that as Beverly grew out of babyhood, all was not well with her. She fainted often in her carriage. Sometimes, for seemingly no reason, her face turned blue and she gasped for breath. Every childhood illness was life-threatening for her. Our family doctor couldn't find any cause for these symptoms. He thought it must be some childhood weakness she would undoubtedly outgrow. She did appear to be getting better as she grew older. That laid our fears to rest for the present, but we were still troubled with unspoken questions.

The war ended at last. We were away at youth camp and didn't even know the bomb was dropped and that Japan had surrendered. On the way home we stopped to get gas, showing our ration coupons. The attendant looked at us as though we were from the dark side of the moon.

"Wouldn't you like me to fill her up?" he asked uncertainly.

"Can we?" Paul asked with astonishment. The amused attendant delighted in telling these weird people all that had taken place while we were hidden away at camp. It seemed like a dream that peace was here at last. On September 2, 1945, Japan surrendered. Germany had surrendered on May 8, 1945. The world was at peace for the moment, but how can there be any real and lasting peace when our world has rejected the Prince of Peace?

The years passed, and we were still cozily ensconced in our little Conrad nest. We had promised the Lord we would go back to Germany after the war. We began to feel gentle nudges in our hearts. They were very disquieting, but we were busy and happy.

Then Paul's health began to fail. He had been troubled with ulcers, and now they flared up again, growing steadily worse. He became gradually weaker until, one Sunday morning, he collapsed at the pulpit and had to be carried out. Some of the deacons rushed him to the hospital. There it was discovered his ulcers had been bleeding for some time, causing his weakness. After several blood transfusions he felt stronger. Dear Beulah gave him all the tender, loving care of which she was capable. He improved rapidly and was soon at home again, though still too weak to carry on his normal pastoral duties.

This was a severe testing time for us both. I tried to take on some of his ministerial activities, while still handling the Sunday school, youth work, Women's Ministries, and our home and children. I was also, at the time, representative for the women's work in Montana. It was too much, with Paul's health so precarious. God was speaking to both of our hearts about returning to Europe, but Paul was too ill and I too busy to pay much attention. About this time God began to speak to Paul in no uncertain terms. Sick as he was, Paul was compelled to listen. The still, small voice he knew so well left no room for speculation.

"It's time to go back, Paul. The war is over. Remember your promise!"

Paul was always eager to obey the Lord. He longed to do whatever he felt God wanted of him. Now, in his weakness and need, he cried out, "Oh, Lord, I'm willing to go, I want to go, but I can't in this condition. The mission would never send me. Lord, if you will heal me, I will start getting ready right away. I will know it isn't just myself attempting something."

God heard him and honored his request. Almost from that minute his ulcers began to heal. Each day brought added strength. He was like one reborn, his eyes sparkling, his step springy. Paul was eager and excited about getting back to Europe now. Just one problem still remained. Me.

I didn't hear God's voice as distinctly as Paul did, probably because I wasn't ready to. I was afraid, terribly afraid, to return to Europe, especially to Germany. I suffered from a dreadful nightmare that began soon after we returned to the States. It returned time and time again to haunt me whenever I thought of Germany. I dreamed I was pushing a baby carriage on a rutty mountain road. It was night and raining. The dark forest all around was dripping wet. Behind me I could hear the *thump, thump, thump* of Nazi boots coming nearer and nearer. I froze in my tracks, knees like soft soap. I couldn't move. The thumping boots sounded so near I began to scream! At that point I always awakened in a cold sweat, screaming helplessly. After the children came, the very thought of taking them to Europe threw me into a panic.

Paul felt powerless in the face of my terror. He knew it was time to go back to Germany and he was ready and willing to go. Yet he knew that he couldn't force me, feeling as I did. He was always gentle and comforting. I was ashamed of my fears and longed for victory over this hang-up. I begged him to pray for me, after we'd talked about it. Prayer was his lifeline and pray he did. It was only a matter of a week or so when God performed the miracle.

It was a dream that frightened me out of keeping my promise to God about going back to Germany. God, in his infinite love and wisdom, gave me another dream. Normally I'm not a dreaming kind of person at all. I dreamed just like everybody else, but I never paid any attention to my dreams. My new dream was clear and precise, unmistakably from God.

I dreamed we were standing on a hilltop overlooking a large city. It was evening and the setting sun cast a golden light over the buildings. The windows reflected the sunset and shone like pure gold. Suddenly, from the center of the metropolis, there was a dreadful explosion. A huge mushroom cloud rose into the sky. A ghastly wind blew around us, flinging twigs, pebbles, and other debris crazily in every direction. Strangely, though, not a hair of our heads was ruffled. Nothing touched us. We felt strong arms around us, shielding us from every harm. We looked up to see who it was. There was Jesus holding us to Him and smiling lovingly down upon us. We were literally, "Safe in the arms of Jesus." Then I woke up.

Peace flowed into my heart. Floods of joy filled my whole being. I was at peace with God, myself, and the thought of going back to

Germany. Sliding over to Paul's side of the bed, I woke him up and crawled into his loving arms. Snuggling down, I shared my dream with him.

"Oh, honey, I'm ready to go with you now to the very ends of the earth!" I sighed happily. We had waited for God. He had answered. It was time to move.

There was much to do before we could finally leave for Europe. We applied to the Assembly of God missions headquarters for missionary appointment to Germany. When that came through, we resigned from the church in Conrad with mixed emotions on our part and on that of the church, as well. It took awhile to arrange for a successor, so we stayed on in Conrad for a while. When we finally left, it was to take the kids and me to Grandma's, together with a trailer loaded with our belongings.

Paul needed a hernia operation before he could get a clean bill of health to go to Germany. We decided it would be best to have it done in Conrad where he could be looked after by our family doctor. It would be nice to have Beulah there to nurse him, too. He would stay only a day or two in Yakima and then hurry back to Conrad for his surgery.

We planned to spend a year in Yakima, making that our headquarters while we did our deputation in the churches. Paul's mother had generously invited us to stay in her home during this time. She even offered to baby-sit our two lively children while we traveled. She was one of the most generous people I've ever known.

The trip to Yakima was delightful. We chose to take Highway 10 so we could visit Yellowstone Park. The children loved it. To see the bears on their hind paws begging for food was such fun. They never tired of watching Old Faithful Geyser spouting off every hour or the bubbling pools that looked like water boiling in a teakettle. There was so much for little eyes to see and delight in. Then we drove to Boise, Idaho, to visit the Roland Bucks for a few days. The cousins had a wonderful time together as did we oldsters. We saw each other so seldom and there was so much to share, we talked and laughed and rejoiced with one another for hours on end.

The delightful days in Boise went by too fast for all of us. It was hard to say good-bye, for we knew we wouldn't see each other again for years. We promised to keep in touch and departed for Spokane to visit my sister Margaret and family. We were invited to speak in the First Assembly of God there. Our children sang and we shared our hopes and dreams for Germany.

We left Spokane and drove on to the Tri-Cities. My brother, Walter Buck, and his wife, Phyllis, were pastoring in Richland. That was another happy time for all of us. In Walt's fine, growing church, the children sang and we shared again the needs of a crushed Germany. The children enjoyed Uncle Walt's fun and humor and adored Aunty Phyllis for her gentle, loving ways. The cousins loved every minute together. Our children thought we should stay there and live with the Bucks. Why not? They had never enjoyed themselves more anywhere.

Once more our farewells were emotional, since we knew it would be a long, long time before we met again. Our children would be denied the joys that cousins share even more than siblings. Children's sorrows are, fortunately, short-lived. Before long our two were excitedly looking forward to Yakima and seeing dear Grandma again.

Grandma, with her cookies and pies, her loving and spoiling, was very special to Bobby and Bevy. They never quite loved anybody in the same way they did this kindhearted little lady. Now they were going to spend a whole year with her. They could hardly wait.

It isn't a long drive from Richland to Yakima. Almost before we knew it, we were driving down a shady street to stop in front of Grandma's comfortable home. The children almost fell out of the car in their eagerness to see their grandmother. She came running to greet us with arms outstretched. She was a widow now. Dad Williscroft had passed away a few years earlier. They had only lived a couple of years in their new home before his death.

Life was different for her after his passing, but she was a plucky woman and soon put the pieces of her life back together again. Lloyd and John, with their families, had moved to the coast, but whenever they or we could arrange a visit with Mother, she welcomed us with open arms. Mother Williscroft had given her life to the Lord a few years before Paul's father passed away. She loved Him and His church, never missing a meeting if she could help it. She made many friends at church who were a great comfort after she was alone.

My parents had died within a year of each other. Paul's mother was now our only parent, and we cherished her. Where else would we rather stay for a year than with Mother in sunny Yakima? As she led us into her home and closed the door, I thought, We are also closing the door on another chapter of our lives. Soon a new door will open. What will it hold for us?

CHAPTER NINETEEN

The year at Grandma's was a busy, happy time. We studied German several hours a day. It is a complicated language, but quite logical, in that words are usually pronounced as spelled. We had most of our difficulty with word endings and articles. Every noun has a gender and one must know the gender to speak the noun correctly in every context in which one wishes to use it. German friends were often highly amused to hear us talking unconcernedly in their cherished language, making a table into a lady and a fly into a man. It was small comfort to notice that most Americans learning German had the same problem. We felt German, thought German, dreamed German, but when we spoke it, it was never a hundred percent right. For example, *der Baum,* a tree, is masculine; *die Kastanie,* a chestnut tree, is feminine; while *das Mädchen,* a girl, is neuter. It's easy to get mixed up.

While we were with Paul's mother, we both found jobs to help out with expenses. Paul was a trained accountant, and found a good job with a firm in Yakima. It was fall when we arrived and the wonderful

Yakima fruit was ripe, so I found it easy to get a job in the cannery. There didn't seem to be any other kind of temporary work. I enjoyed the cannery, though. It was a good experience. I needed to get down to grass roots, to feel and identify with people in all areas of life. I felt I learned a great deal that would help me understand and relate to people.

Christmas came and went with all its joy and excitement. The new year, 1950, a census year, would soon be upon us. We were asked to help with census taking and gladly accepted, since our jobs were finished after the holidays. This would be another good learning experience. We were each given a special section of town to work and a map of all the streets, houses, apartments, and any other sort of dwelling in that section. We met about every type, color, race, and religion one could imagine. Sometimes we had to beg, persuade, coax, sway, entreat, or even demand that people let us in, or cooperate after we were in. Talk about a training course for working with people! It was fun, too, for we met many wonderful and interesting people. We both were glad when it was over, however. It was time to get on with our plans and preparations for Europe.

We needed to purchase clothing for ourselves and the children to last over a period of at least four years. Conditions were such in Germany that we probably wouldn't be able to buy things we might need for a long time to come. The idea of being prepared is all well and good, but how does one know how much a child will grow in a year, two years, or even in six months? We tried to guess and also talked with mothers of children the ages ours would be over the years we were planning to be away.

People were helpful, but in the end we used our own common sense mixed with a good dose of imagination. Our mission, as well as missionary friends, encouraged us to take along books, games, records, and toys suited to the ages our children would be while we were away. This proved to be wonderful advice. We were thankful over and over again for the entertainment, knowledge, and pure fun the two enjoyed for hours on end with these things we had taken with us.

Another big adventure we launched into was to buy our first home. It was a pretty little English-type cottage with three bedrooms, a large living room, handy kitchen, bath, and utility room, located in Union Gap, a suburb of Yakima, Washington. We were able to put a small down payment on it, install good renters, and let it pay for itself while we were in Germany. We planned ahead so that when we retired it would be paid for and we could just move in and live rent free in our own home. This, however, was not to be. True, it was paid for and totally free of debt, not long before Paul's death, but he was called to higher service before he was ready to retire. When I retired due to poor health, it was too much house for me alone. I was able to sell it for a good price, so we never did know the joy of living in it as its loving owners.

The children enjoyed attending school in Yakima. Bobby was in the second grade, Bevy in kindergarten. They brought home good report cards and glowing remarks about having the nicest teachers in the world. "Bet the teachers in Germany won't be as nice as the teachers here!" they usually added when talking about teachers.

We spent as much time as possible preparing them for living abroad. The language, customs, homes, schools, and churches would all be very different. There would be many adjustments for two little people, but being so young was also much to their advantage. Children adapt quite easily to changes, and childhood is the best time to master a new language. We didn't attempt to teach them any German, since ours was so imperfect at that point. They would learn it quickly at school and in play with German children.

We visited many churches during that year. We took the children with us during summer vacation. They won the hearts of our congregations with their loving, innocent ways and happy little songs. Sometimes one or the other would give a little testimony. They had both given their hearts to Jesus when they were very young. They had heard about Him every day of their lives and loved Him from earliest babyhood. Bobby often waxed quite eloquent in his testimony. He still possesses this ability in his relationships with people. Bevy was more shy, but her gentle manner and sweet smile won her many friends. If people were especially warm and friendly, she could get carried away. Then she would prattle happily about whatever was in her heart, even if it might have been better left unsaid.

For example, she and Bobby wanted a baby very much, only Bobby wanted a brother and Bevy a sister. They could argue for hours over who would get what. One day, just to keep the peace, I asked how it would be to have twins, a boy and a girl. Why, they could even name them. How about Bruce and Bonnie? We often played pretend games like that, and Bobby knew this was just for fun. Not Bevy. For her it was the perfect solution to a knotty problem. Mama said it, so it must be so. Evidently, a thrilled little girl began a rumor that didn't stop for awhile.

One night after service, a lady approached me, stood awhile looking me over from head to foot, and finally remarked, "Gladys, do be careful. In your condition it isn't wise to be on the go as much as you are. Remember, you hold two little lives under your heart." I stared at her in utter amazement. Maybe my mouth hung open, I don't know.

She could see my puzzled look and laughed as she continued. "Now, now, don't look so surprised. Your precious little girl told me all about the twice-blessed event."

At last I managed to stammer, still bewildered, "I'm sorry, but I can't imagine what in the world you are talking about. You surely have the wrong person."

First she gave me an icy stare, than relaxed a bit and chuckled as she continued. "Your daughter told me you are going to have twins, a boy and a girl. The children will name them Bonnie and Bruce. Bevy was very excited and happy as she told me all about it. It's a cute idea to share it with the children, but don't you think it's a bit early to name the babies? Why, you might have two boys or two girls. That would destroy the children's confidence in you."

I confess, for a second, I could have turned my precious little girl over my knee and spanked her soundly. As for this dear lady, studying me with eagle eyes, I itched to tell her, in no uncertain terms, what I thought of women who prodded little children, trying to get some juicy morsel out of them. Suddenly, though, the humor and ludicrousness of the whole thing hit me and I started laughing.

Then it was the woman's turn to look mystified. I explained our game to her, assuring her I never dreamed Bevy would take it all as gospel truth. That was typical of our Bevy at age five. I should have known better. I had a lot of explaining to do before my little girl understood we really were just playing a game. There would be no baby brother or sister. This funny little happening has become a legend in our family. We've had many good laughs over it.

During the school months, Grandma Williscroft was the adored baby-sitter. She enjoyed the children and dreaded the time when we would leave. She told us she cherished every moment she spent with them, although they weren't perfect, by any means. Grandmothers are very special people where children are concerned, though, and our two were no exception. In fact, they grew rather adept at playing grandma and mother against each other. That could have created problems, but we were glad for someone to care for our children when we were away. Grandma really had their welfare at heart, so it wasn't hard to overlook little difficulties that arose now and then.

While the two of them were with their grandmother, they both came down with whooping cough. Bobby was a sturdy little guy. All through his childhood he was able to throw off diseases children are prone to with very little effort. When it was all over he seemed none the worse for it. Not so with poor little Bevy. She almost died with every sickness she contracted. It was so with whooping cough, too. Bobby never went to bed with it and was well in a few days. We thought we would lose Bevy. With every cough she began to choke and pass out.

Paul was traveling, so all the responsibility and burden rested on his mother and me. The doctor came often, keeping a watchful eye on her. Grandma and I prayed night and day. It broke our hearts to watch our little golden-haired girl fight for her life, gasping, choking, and finally coming out of it limp and almost lifeless.

God was good to us in those trying days. The church was praying and friends everywhere joined in the prayer battle for our daughter's life. A day came when I saw the crisis was near. God would take her or heal her. She was too weak to fight any longer. A spasm of coughing started, but it faded away. She smiled weakly at us, tucked her thin little hand under her cheek the way she usually did to go to sleep, and immediately fell into a deep, healing slumber with the tiny smile still on her lips.

"Thank God," Grandma and I murmured softly so as not to awaken our darling.

For days I had been up day and night with Bevy. I was utterly exhausted. Grandma made us a hot cup of tea, then led me gently to my bed and tucked me in.

I don't even remember how long I slept, but I woke to Bevy's little voice asking Grandma for a piece of bread and peanut butter. It was the loveliest music I ever heard. From that day on she kept improving until she was again our pretty, funny, elfin little daughter. I'll never forget Mother Williscroft's love and selfsacrifice during Bevy's illness. It's one of those lovely warm memories in the album of my soul.

Gray November was upon us, the time we planned to leave for Germany. After her long convalescence, Bevy was eager to help, anxious to please, and getting in everybody's way. Bobby felt quite grown-up and pleased when we gave him permission to get all his things together, letting us know what he wished to keep. The rest would be thrown away or given away. He really did quite a nice job of it, so we let him decide to whom he would give what he didn't take with him. We even let him help a little with the packing.

At last everything was packed and ready to be sent off, and our train tickets were in our pockets. Arrangements were made for ministry stopovers along the way to New York and our ship. We thought this would be good for the children and give us opportunity to see old friends and make contact with new churches. It was with mingled anticipation and sorrow that we drove to the station. It was just after lunch. Most of our friends were at work, so not many were able to see us off. Mother Williscroft tried hard to smile, but Paul and I, as well as Mother, felt we would never see her again. Sadly, this proved to be true.

The whistle sounded. We ran out. Passengers had detrained and were greeting loved ones on the platform. A burly trainsman shouted over the megaphone in clipped tones, "All aboard!"

A last kiss, another hug, one more handshake, and we clambered aboard, still waving as the train pulled out. We were traveling on a deluxe Empire Builder, a Great Northern train with a panoramic, sight-seeing deck. The children were quite impressed and wanted to spend most of their time up there. We shared their enthusiasm. As the hours sped by, we enjoyed the changing scenery of majestic mountains, rushing rivers, and all the rest of the glory that is America. Paul instructed the children in the geography and history of the places we passed, so the time on the train was pleasant and profitable.

It was a wonderful trip! The stopovers were fun and rewarding for all of us. Usually there were children where we stayed, and that made our children happy. New York was mind-boggling for them. They looked up at those tall buildings and wanted to go to the top of every one. Bobby kept shouting excitedly, "Daddy! Daddy! How tall is *that* building? Can't we go up in it, Daddy? Daddy, Bevy wants to go up, don't you, Bevy? Can't we, Daddy? Can't we, please?" Well, you know what happened. Daddy took them up to the top of two or three of the tallest buildings. They thought that was heaven and enjoyed it immensely. The Empire State Building was their favorite, of course. We thought we would never get them down.

A highlight of our stay in New York was when Paul found the name of one of our Jewish friends from Danzig in the phone book and called him. He arranged to meet us where we were staying. We had a wonderful visit with him. There was a lot of catching up to do on all that had happened since we last saw each other. He and his brother were prospering business men, he in New York, his brother in Boston. Their English was improved and both had acquired American citizenship. How proud and happy they were over that. Our friend insisted on taking the children to Coney Island while we took care of some business. It was a wonderful afternoon for them. When he brought them to our quarters later, he exclaimed over and over how much he enjoyed the hours with them.

The few days in New York were over too soon. It was time to board the little Dutch ship *SS Veendam*. Mr. Gruenspun, our Jewish friend, came to the pier to see us off. He was our only well-wisher as we left the shores of America that time. We will long remember the love and kindness shown us by this dear man and his lovely family.

The fall voyage to Europe was all one could wish. The weather was remarkably mild and pleasant. The rolling Atlantic was blue and sparkling in the sunshine, with gentle, white-tipped waves lapping at the sides of the ship. We met many interesting people and enjoyed some stimulating conversation. Traveling with us was a fine couple high in the Ethiopian government. He shared with us a humiliating experience in one of our southern states. They were sightseeing by bus. When they were boarding one morning, the driver ordered them to the back door. No blacks could enter by the front door. They related their experience without malice or bitterness. It just came out as they described their trip to America. We felt embarrassed and heartsick. Thank God it is different now!

Another interesting acquaintance was an engineer on his way to Turkey to oversee the building of a large dam. We enjoyed talking together. He was a warm, caring person, motivated to help when he observed the problems and needs of that poverty-stricken land. We shared our burden, the spiritual as well as physical needs of crushed and broken Germany. To our surprise, he pointed out our goals were even more important than his. He won our admiration and esteem just because he cared about people.

Among the many captivating passengers aboard was a young Dutch woman who had seen her whole family butchered by the Nazis during the German invasion of Holland. She was very bitter, and when she heard we were on our way to Germany to bring hope and salvation to this shattered people she became almost hostile.

"Let them all go to Hell. They don't deserve anything better," she screamed. "They made Hell for millions of people. Now they can taste it themselves."

She was so vindictive – poor, heartbroken little soul. She had suffered more horror and tragedy than one small human could endure. She had been visiting friends in the States who fled Holland just hours before the Germans marched in. Now she was on her way back to Holland, and every turn of the ship's propeller brought her nearer to the scene of her anguish.

As she saw we were ready to close this conversation, she made one parting shot. "You Americans are so good and *so dumb*." I've often recalled that remark.

Another passenger was a young man on his way to Paris to study French cuisine. His name was Jim, and a more affable, delightful young person would be hard to find. Our children loved him, and he attached himself to our little party. We invited him to spend the holidays with us in Switzerland. Sure enough, there he was on our doorstep one frosty day just before Christmas. Our kids just whooped for joy. More about him later.

Paul wasn't the only clergyman aboard, but he was asked to hold a Sunday morning service in the first-class salon. We always felt this was a direct move of God. Many of the passengers needed what we could share.

Paul brought the only message he knew: John 3:16. "For God so loved the world that He gave His only begotten Son, that whoso-ever believeth on Him, should not perish, but have everlasting life." He then issued an invitation to accept this Son of God as their own Savior. Several responded, among them our precious Dutch lady. Paul counseled and prayed with the others but motioned for me to minister to her.

She knelt, weeping, as she poured out all her hurt, her anger, her unforgiveness, at Jesus' feet. He forgave her, too, and made a brand-new woman of her. She even looked different. Her stern, unsmiling eyes were warm and kind. Her hard mouth was tender and smiling. Her harsh voice became soft and sweet. She rose from her knees and threw herself into my arms, crying, "I can't believe it! I don't hate anymore! I love everybody! Can't I come to Germany with you? They need to learn to love just like I did, and I want to be one to tell them." In a moment of time, Jesus had changed a bitter, revengeful woman into a loving child of God.

The children loved the deck games, the swimming pool, and running around the ship to explore everything. Everyone was their friend. Bobby, especially, was buddy-buddy with the officers, passengers, and crew. He was their little shipmate and enjoyed many privileges, such as sitting at the wheel with the helmsman's hand on his as he steered the ship along. Bevy, on the other hand, loved to curl up on somebody's lap and listen to stories or the sailors chanties. She was a really beautiful little girl with her long golden curls, delicate features, and fairylike movements. Our engineer friend took a special fancy to her and hardly let her out of his sight. He called her his little princess and was her devoted slave.

We were all very proud when Paul was champion of the Ping-Pong tournament. All our friends were rooting for him – the children and Mama, too. Bobby was the braggiest boy on the ship after that. Nobody's daddy was as good as his daddy. I'd often sigh and cry inside myself, *Bobby, Bobby, whatever will become of you, my darling? Will you use all that joy of life, that bubbling enthusiasm, that power of persuasion, for God or for yourself?*

The last night at sea was a gala evening featuring a fantastic buffet, games, skits, music, and all the trivia of paper hats, noisemakers, tin horns, balloons, and prizes. The jolly, plump Dutch captain was right in the center of everything. We allowed the children to stay up and enjoy the fun for awhile. When the more adult fun began, we slipped quietly away to our favorite corner of the family lounge.

We were reading *Black Beauty* at bedtime every evening. There were only a few pages more to read, so there in our cozy corner, Mommie, Daddy, and two sleepy but attentive children reveled in the happy ending of a beautiful, intelligent horse's misfortunes. With a kiss and a prayer, we tucked them into their bunks for their last night's sleep on the trusty little *Veendam* that bore us safely for ten days and nights across the wide Atlantic.

The next morning, shortly before noon, we docked at the pier in Rotterdam, Holland. All the color and excitement of the waterfront was ours to enjoy as the ship began unloading. We watched until lunch was announced. After lunch we went through customs on the ship. Then we watched excitedly as the gangway was lowered and the long-awaited cry sounded over the megaphone, "All ashore! All ashore!"

We took a last quick look around the ship that had served us so well. We shook hands with the pleasant stewardesses, stewards, and crew who did so much to make our voyage unforgettable. Paul caught Bobby's restless, active hand in his. Bevy slipped her little hand trustingly in mine, and we led our children down the gangway into a brand-new world.

The children, as well as their parents, were all eyes as we stood on the pier and looked around us. The buildings were so different, tall and narrow, with peaked roofs. The canals with their little boat taxis were fascinating. The rosy-cheeked men, women, and children all around us looked friendly and kind. Our children stared as they listened to the strange sounds of the Dutch language the people were speaking. The land was flat as a pancake. The whole city was cut through by innumerable canals. Tulip time was long since gone, but beautiful fall asters and chrysanthemums bloomed profusely wherever there was a little soil. We liked what we saw of this old Dutch city on the mouth of the River Rhine.

Somebody was calling our name. "Williscroft! Williscroft!"

We looked around, and there were the dear Waldvogels, whom we knew only through correspondence. They were waving and smiling as they beckoned us to follow them. They looked as loving and sweet as they sounded. They were both on the plump side. He was tall and dark. She was short and blonde. They came by car from Basel, Switzerland, where the mission headquarters were temporarily located and where we would be living. We had only hand luggage with us. Trunks and other heavy luggage had been sent right through to Basel.

The car was large and roomy, so all six of us fitted in very comfortably. The drive through Holland and Belgium was very interesting. We drove through many World War II battle sites, including the Battle of the Bulge area in Belgium. Walter Waldvogel and Paul entertained the children with exciting tales of fierce battles and brave men for miles on end as we drove through those places that we heard and read about only a few years before.

Scars of war were everywhere: a house with the roof blown off; a barn partly burned. The earth all over was pock-marked by combat. Pretty stone walls were broken down. Pastures had great craters in them from hand grenades or artillery. I felt such a horror of, and hate for, war as we drove through all this devastation.

We found a little hotel, where we spent the night. Early the next day we started out again. This time we drove through France. This was exciting, too. We stopped at an interesting old graveyard. Its tombstones were all broken and tumbled down from the fierce fighting of French and American troops against the Germans. Again I felt the terror and senselessness of war. The tears fell for all the precious young men who bled and died there, friend and foe alike.

As we stopped here and there to take pictures or look at historical war sites, the children scampered happy and carefree through the remains of bombed-out houses, schools, shops, and churches. What did they know of the tears, the blood, the agony that had happened here where they were playing?

We were tired and spent from the long drive and the emotional strain of what we saw and felt. Our mood seemed to affect the children, too. They sat quietly, with sober little faces. Now and then one of them would ask a question that the scenes of the day had evoked.

"Daddy, why do people go to war? Will I have to go when I'm big? Do you think I would die?" Poor little tykes, trying to figure out a grown-up's topsyturvy world.

We were thrilled to see the lights of Basel come into view. The border crossing didn't take long. As we drove into Basel, no words of mine can adequately describe the feeling of security, freedom, peace, and hope that tingled in the very air. There were no scars or remainders of war anywhere. Instead we saw happy faces, well-fed, well-clothed people. Flowers were still blooming, birds were singing, children were shouting and laughing at play. There were cars in the streets, shops chock-full of good things to eat, to wear, to enjoy. I don't think we ever realized before how we had taken these things for granted all our lives. Now we woke up to the hard reality that material things can vanish in a moment. Nothing is enduring but the Rock, Christ Jesus.

The Waldvogels had rented a room for us until we could find an apartment. They had one in mind that we would see tomorrow. Now they took us to the room to unload and rest awhile. We all took catnaps and then went out to eat. We were hungry and the Swiss cuisine is very good. It is a sort of combination of French and German cooking. After dinner Walter and Bertha brought us to our room and urged us to get a good night's sleep before meeting with the Kindermans and the office staff the next morning.

It was good to be alone as a family again. Our room was small, but clean and fresh. There was a couch that opened into a bed for the children, so we would make out fine.

CHAPTER TWENTY

The next morning we went to Waldvogel's for breakfast. Bertha made a real American meal of it. We feasted on ham and eggs, toast and juice, finishing with a lovely bowl of fresh fruit. It was a wonderful treat and we enjoyed every bite. Bertha was one of those choice children of God whom everybody loves.

After breakfast we accompanied the Waldvogels to the headquarter's office. It was nice to see the Kindermans after so many years. They loved our children. Theirs were all in the States now, and how they missed them! We chatted for awhile and Mr. Kinderman briefed Paul on some of the areas where he would be active. Then we were off to see the apartment.

It was pleasant strolling along the quiet street, peeking through high, iron-grillwork fences to look at tall old houses, manicured lawns, and formal gardens. The weather was sunny and mild for mid-November. It was interesting to see a little of the city where we would probably be spending at least a year.

We arrived at the address of our apartment. It was on the ground floor of a rather prestigious older house. The landlady, who lived on the second floor, greeted us coolly, we thought, when she saw the children. She took us to the apartment, which wasn't too bad, but old and musty. The furniture looked ancient, but attractive. It was too old to be modern, but not old enough to be antique. The two bedrooms were quite large and pleasant. The living room was about the same size, but longer and not as wide. The kitchen in the back was dark and opened onto a sort of terrace where creeping vines kept most of the sunlight out.

We looked at each other. We didn't know anything about Swiss houses. Maybe they were all more or less like this, so we finally decided to take it. We moved in that afternoon.

The landlady was no longer young and had a nervous, high-strung temperament. She looked the children over suspiciously as they carried in their toys and books. The look on her face told us she was about to prepare for the worst. She gave us a contract to fill out and sign. No visitors after ten in the evening. No baths or radio after ten p.m. No loud talking in the halls at any time. She noticed Bobby casting wistful glances at the pretty garden in the back with its neat flower beds, shaped shrubs, and trim gravel paths. She quickly pointed out to us some small print we had overlooked in the contract: "Garden not available to tenants." We sighed sadly. She hadn't shown us the contract until we were safely moved in. There was nothing to do at this point but try and make the best of it. Maybe we could move later.

After being in the apartment a week or two, I was almost a nervous wreck trying to keep the children quiet. One afternoon there was a tap at the door. There stood the friendly landlady. She actually was smiling a little.

"Your children are so nice and quiet, I've decided to let them walk in the garden," she informed me. "But they must never step off the paths onto the grass or get near my plants or shrubs. Is that clear?"

It was. All too clear. They wanted so badly to play in the garden I finally let them go out there, watching awhile, just to be sure they didn't get into trouble. Bobby held Bevy fast on the hand as they demurely trotted along the gravelly paths. Then I began to chuckle. Along behind them came the landlady, rake in hand, carefully raking away every trace of little footprints. I'm sure she was a good woman at heart, but she never had children of her own. Anything that altered her routine was very distressing for the poor lady.

Much as we loved Switzerland, we often wished we were any other place than there, and all because of the lady upstairs. We couldn't please her. Nothing we did was right. I was near despair. The children were getting cross and unhappy. Paul spent long hours at the office or days and, often, weeks ministering in Germany. I sometimes wished we were back in the States where we were comfortable and at home.

Eventually, though, we got the children settled in their respective schools – Bevy in kindergarten, Bobby in the third grade. School lasted from eight in the morning until one in the afternoon. Then they had lunch, a little rest, a short recess, and it was time for English schooling for Bobby.

I taught him his third grade all the way through. We both loved it and became real friends in the process. All of these school hours kept Bobby busy and out of the landlady's hair. He was the restless one. He just *had* to keep busy. Bevy would quietly play with her toys for hours on end. She never needed to be entertained or played with. Oh, she liked it well enough when she was with a playmate, but she was just as content alone. Anyway, we enjoyed peace and quiet with our landlady now, and I was very thankful.

Christmas in Basel was lovely. It snowed, much to the children's delight. Dear missionary friends joined us and did much to make it a merry time – the Ted Bards, Aunties Emma Decker and Jean Waltz, Bertha and Walter Waldvogel, and our young friend Jim, from Paris, who was learning to be a good French cook. We managed to find places for everybody to sleep and were one big happy family.

One evening we trimmed the tree. Everybody helped, even the children. We listened to carols on the record player and laughed and talked between drinking mugs of steaming chocolate and munching on my homemade Christmas cookies. We invited our landlady to join us and experience a real American Christmas, but she wasn't quite ready to go that far with a houseful of foreigners. Too bad. She'd have loved it.

We all helped prepare the big Christmas dinner. I can still see Ruth Bard making the turkey stuffing. She prayed over every move. "Oh, God, let this stuffing taste good. Don't let it be too salty. Make the rosemary taste like sage, please. You know Gladys doesn't have any sage on hand. Please don't let it be too moist or too dry, Lord. You see it's all for Jesus' birthday and it has to be the best." On and on she went. She was such a darling. God was as close and real to her as anyone in her family, maybe even closer. We laughed and teased her, but loved listening to her.

Jim told us he thought we missionaries were the funniest, dearest people he ever knew. He said it was the richest, fullest Christmas he ever enjoyed anywhere or any time. He wouldn't have missed it for the world.

We walked through snowy streets to church on Christmas morning. All over the city church bells were ringing out the glad tidings of Jesus' birth. A pale winter sun was shining on the snow, making it sparkle like a million diamonds. Winter birds were huddled on the branches of leafless trees, twittering and chirping their own Christmas carols. Frolicking children with new Christmas sleds were merrily trying them out on the snowy streets. Family groups wended their way to church, Bibles and prayer books tucked under their arms. We rejoiced in the old Christmas story, old but ever new. We sang the lovely carols, and coming out of church we greeted each other with the hearty German greeting, *"Frohe Weihnachten!"* We walked home again, the snow crisp and crunchy under our feet. We arrived at our apartment with rosy cheeks, pink noses, and voracious appetites.

We women bustled about basting the turkey, mashing potatoes, thickening the gravy, dishing up the food, and finally calling everybody to the loaded table. The tree sparkled with its twinkling lights, the candles on the table glowed warmly, and the holiday food, piled on the snowy cloth, looked and smelled delicious! We gathered around the table and Ted Bard, the senior among us, prayed. It was a thanks to God, a commitment of all of us to Him and a benediction for God's grace and glory to hover over us and over that Christmas day.

It was a real American Christmas. We felt it was the way God intended His children to remember and celebrate His Son's birth. We didn't feel lonely or strange. We were family. Everyone felt literally surrounded with love, warmth, caring, and joy. Later, as we compared notes, we found that all of us felt the same way. It was one of our most memorable Christmases.

※

The holidays were over. Everyone returned to pick up the threads of daily living, but for us, the loveliness of Christmas still permeated our home. The tree remained until it was almost bare, because the children loved it. Christmas music still softly sounded from our record player, filling our hearts with the peace of Christmas.

After a week or two of activity in the Basel office, Paul took a trip to Germany for a time of ministry in the churches, feeling for the pulse of God's plan for the new year that we had entered. In the meantime, the Montana youth presented us with a neat little car through the *Speed-the-Light* program. Speed-the-Light was a very fine project arranged by leaders in our denomination. Young people would take jobs in their free time, and the money they earned would go for cars, planes, bicycles, and every other kind of transportation vehicle one could imagine. It was good for the youth, as well as a real blessing for the missionaries. The Fiat station wagon was a great help; now Paul did not always have to depend on busses or trains. We appreciated the Speed-the-Light program more than ever and were grateful to our dear young people in Montana. Over the years we have received many cars from them and could never have carried out our heavy program without this sacrificial giving.

We were able to move to a beautiful apartment in a very lovely part of town in early spring. It was nicely furnished, and the kids had their own rooms. At last they could have the room the way they wanted it. Both of them enjoyed that to the fullest.

The apartment was on the ground floor and the landlady, with her twelve-year-old son, lived above us. She was a friendly, warm-hearted lady and a model neighbor. Her pretty grounds were for everyone in the house to enjoy. What a pleasant change from our former situation. The children, too, often talked about that as they played in the grassy yard to their hearts' content.

We all loved Switzerland. One lovely memory of our stay there is walking along a shady street on a spring morning. The sweet, dewy fragrance of the blossoming linden trees filled the mild spring air. The spreading branches of the linden trees sheltered countless birds, their lovely song enhancing the beauty of the morning. A lump fills my throat as I remember it now, so many years later.

The zoo was within walking distance and boasted a lovely pool as well as the *Tiergarten* (animal garden or zoo). We got the children season tickets, a gift from the Sidney, Montana women's group who adopted them. The ladies couldn't have done a nicer or more practical thing.

The children spent part of almost every day at the zoo. They could walk there. It was only two or three blocks from our apartment. Sometimes they took a lunch, but usually they came home to eat. Then they took a little rest, as the custom in most of Europe is, and spent the rest of the warm, lazy afternoon at the pool.

One late afternoon when they were at the zoo, Bobby called me. He had met two English girls who were vacationing in Switzerland. He thought they might be lonesome to hear some English and invited them to have supper with us. Could they come?

What could I say? We always kept an open house so the children learned to be friendly and hospitable, too. Bobby was just practicing what he observed at home. Yes, of course he could bring them, in about an hour.

I flew around baking and frosting a cake and quickly preparing a light, cool summer meal. They arrived right on the dot. I was glad the table was prettily set and everything ready. The girls were lovely, and we spent a pleasant evening with them. Bobby was very proud of his guests, and both children gave them the red-carpet treatment. The young ladies were quite impressed with them.

One girl remarked she always heard American children were rude and illmannered. She smiled, took Bobby and Bevy's hands in hers, and graciously told them that they proved her wrong. Bobby looked lovingly up at her and said, "Do you know why we are nice? It's because Jesus lives in our hearts, isn't it, Bevy?" Bevy nodded, smiling her sweet, shy little smile. I took the beautiful opportunity then of pointing those two precious young ladies to their Savior. Bobby opened the door to heaven for those girls in his innocent, boyish way.

One weekend the children and I accompanied Paul to Germany. We were moved, distressed, and depressed by all we saw. Paul often told us about it, but no words can describe the utter destruction we witnessed. It was five years after the Armistice, but great cities like Hamburg and Frankfurt, Munich and Stuttgart still showed the awful ravages of war. Many people were trying to make the semblance of a dwelling in basements under the rubble of their destroyed homes. There in the damp and the dark they bravely lived and worked, ate and slept. Women and even children could be seen on the rubble heaps, scraping off bricks to use again, hopeful of rebuilding their homes. We thought the people very industrious as well as courageous, doing everything possible to put their lives together again.

We listened to many wonderful stories Christians shared with us. A pastor in Bremerhaven lived in a house that stood all alone. Surrounding houses had all been destroyed as the bombs fell. When the warning siren sounded, he and his family didn't run for the shelter. They sat in their own home and prayed and sang, encouraging each other in the Lord. If the air raid lasted longer than usual, they fell to their knees and interceded for their neighbors and friends. When the war ended, their house stood alone, practically unscathed. It was a refuge for the sick, wounded, and homeless. It became a symbol of help, encouragement, and loving Christian service. The pastor tended the suffering, comforted the sorrowing, buried the dead. The whole family spent themselves in serving others.

During vacation time, our ministry as a family was always in Germany. Christians met in schools that were still standing, rented halls, homes, or sometimes in refugee camps. Some gospel tents were provided by Sweden and other lands. A year or two later, Missionary Olga Olsson brought a tent from the States, and God used it in her ministry to the German people.

There was a great hunger for God in those postwar years in Germany. The last shred of faith was shattered for many. Thousands lived in a total vacuum. They believed in Hitler. He betrayed them. Could they ever believe in anyone, God or man, again?

It may sound paradoxical, but this was definitely harvest time in Germany. It didn't matter who preached or where. People flocked to the meetings, and many found new life and hope. They were mainly young people. The gospel message was a ray of light in their darkness and despair. They responded to it wholeheartedly. Our first Bible students were among these eager, open youth.

German pastors held conferences in the spring and fall. We missionaries were invited and tried to help and fit in as much as possible. They were times of teaching, sharing, encouraging, and waiting upon God. These German leaders were, for the most part, fine, solid, faithful Christian gentlemen. We felt honored to work side by side with them.

We were often in Germany for weeks at a time during school vacation. It was always a thrill to return to Basel and breathe again the good Swiss air and be in a whole and healthy land once more. It was depressing in Germany to see so much ruin, sadness, and despair. We needed to come back to Switzerland to recuperate before returning to the pain of Germany.

School began again in Switzerland. Paul now traveled alone on his trips to Germany. This was difficult for him. He loved and needed his family. God was always first in his life, though, so off he went with a smile and a hug for each of us. It was hard for me, too. I knew how he felt, but I also appreciated his dedication and inner strength. We all missed him, and the children prayed daily for Daddy in Germany.

One early fall day Paul arrived from Germany, announcing he and our missionary colleagues had found an appropriate building for a Bible School in Stuttgart. It was formerly a palace and in fairly good condition. A few alterations were needed to fit it for a school, but much of that could be done after the students arrived. The price was right and the mission had endorsed the purchase. Classes would begin as soon as possible, and we should be there.

We talked it over and arranged to go to Stuttgart the coming weekend. We would try to find something before Bible School started.

The children and I were excited. We didn't like the thought of leaving Basel but had always known that our permanent home would have to be in Germany. Basel was just a pleasant interlude.

The time had come for a change. There was much to be done. We couldn't have any regrets now. Our place was in Germany. We were ready for whatever awaited us across the Rhine.

CHAPTER TWENTY-ONE

It was mid-September of 1951. We had lived in Basel for ten happy months. Bible School classes were to begin October 1. Taking the children with us, we drove to Stuttgart the following weekend as planned and visited several real estate agencies. Most of the places we saw were in damaged houses on streets still ugly with rubble heaps. Only this weekend was at our disposal and the agencies were closed on Sunday. We were beginning to feel a bit desperate, when finally an interesting listing at another agency was shown us.

The agent said the apartment was small and on the third floor of a new house. It was located in Frauenkopf (which is German for Woman's Head), a woodsy section of Stuttgart quite far out in the suburbs. A streetcar line ran almost to the place, and it was considered one of the best residential areas of the city. We began to get excited. It sounded like what we wanted. The agent drove ahead, and we followed, getting more interested every minute as we drove away from the city, debris, damaged homes, and sad-looking people.

Finally we turned off the main road and drove through lovely woods with houses tucked away here and there among the trees. We loved it. At last the agent parked before a three story white house just across the road from a forest, red and gold in its autumn finery. The children were ecstatic. They could hardly wait to explore the woods and check out the neighborhood.

We followed the man up two flights of stairs to a little attic apartment at the top. It *was* small. There were two tiny bedrooms, a wee bit larger living room, and a very small kitchen. The living room boasted a wonderful view of hills and valleys far off in the distance and a pretty red-roofed village in the valley below us. We took it. It looked and felt like ours. It was home. Who cared if it was small? We loved it and would manage somehow.

On our way back to the city, we drove down a steep hill. Here and there between the trees were glimpses of Stuttgart, bathed in sunset light. At one place was a glorious view of the city. It shone golden in the setting sun. We felt compelled to stop. Piling out of the car we stood on the bluff, gazing out over the city. The windows reflected the glowing sky. I had a strange feeling of having been in this very spot before. The bluff, the trees, the sun reflected in the windows, the calm evening light. When had I seen it? Paul and the children were with me. That much I could remember.

Then it dawned on me. This was the place I had seen in my dream that long ago night in Yakima. This was the spot where God had made it plain to me that He was in charge. It was here He had made me willing to go back to Germany. This time, of course, there was no atomic explosion. The peace of God was the same, though. Jesus' presence was as real as before, even though He wasn't visible. It was awesome. I shared my experience with the family. They, too, were awed.

Even little Bevy smiled up at us and in her sweet, little-girl way, said, "Isn't it nice to have Jesus here with us." We all knew this was the right place for us and that the Lord would be with us there.

We drove back to Basel, packed our things, and got ready to say our good-byes. We had lived less than a year there, so we were surprised when neighbors and friends came to say adieu. They brought little gifts for us along with their well-wishes. Some even wept as they hugged us, promising to keep in touch. We were deeply touched and felt even sadder about leaving. But a new phase of our lives was beginning, and mixed with the tears was a thrill of anticipation and expectancy as we started on our way.

It was fun getting settled in Frauenkopf. The children loved the forests and gently rolling hills. They soon got acquainted with the neighborhood children and were quite a sensation with their American ways. The dialect in Stuttgart was different than in Basel, but being children, they soon picked it up. Alas, their parents weren't so fortunate. We knew only high German, and that far from perfectly.

The European Headquarters office moved to Stuttgart along with the missionaries. Now everyone was busy getting the school ready for classes. The building was, at one time, a palace of the House of Liechtenstein. There was still gold paint on doors and window frames. It was a nice, roomy place, but definitely not intended for a school. It was simply a dwelling. Most of the rooms were large and airy, and made adequate classrooms or dorms. There were others that could, in a pinch, be used as small apartments for teachers or staff. Some of the teachers did live in the building, so it was well filled. We took only boys in the school at that time, so there wasn't much of a problem about sleeping arrangements.

In the beginning the teachers were Gustave Kinderman, Ted Bard, Walter Waldvogel, and Paul Williscroft. Now and then guest teachers came for seminars of a few days or a week. A fine young German man, Gerhard Wessler, helped in the teaching program, too.

The student body was mainly from North Germany the first year. A finer, more promising group of young men would be hard to find anywhere. They loved God. They felt His call on their lives and were willing and ready to undertake anything for the Lord. A number of them had fought in World War II. Some were wounded and would be partially handicapped the rest of their lives. Some of the boys came early and helped paint and repair.

Paul's main thrust was Christian Education. This was a brand-new concept for the students, especially children's work. I don't know for sure if they considered such activity beneath their dignity. As future pastors, missionaries, and other servants of the church, to work with children seemed unthinkable. It took a long, long time before they were ready to accept such an unusual idea in Germany.

This was a great challenge for Paul. Anything difficult was always a motivation for him to give it all he had.

The German language was always a problem for him, too. That was strange, considering his German background. He never did really master it. One day he needed a fresh stencil for the mimeograph. He sent a student to bring one. He came back with a big mattress on his shoulders and a perplexed look on his face. In German a stencil is called a *matrize,* but dear Paul had asked him to bring a *matrasse*, a mattress, confusing the two words. When he saw the mattress, it was his turn to look puzzled. Some of our mistakes in German are still good conversation starters all over Germany.

In the midst of those early, getting-started years, John Kolenda joined our missionary team. Ted Bard was sent to start a Bible School in Egypt. He was an experienced Bible School man, having served in prewar China for many years. After Egypt, he went to Hong Kong to help out in the Bible School there and later came back to help us again in Germany. He was a great man, loved by students and teachers alike. Gustave Kinderman returned to the States, too, about the time Ted Bard left. We felt a little shorthanded for awhile, but John Kolenda was a godsend and a blessing. It wasn't long before he won all our hearts and was one of the best missionaries ever to work in Germany.

It was soon time for the first graduation of *Berea Bible School*. Excitement was at fever pitch. Who will be valedictorian? Who salutatorian? What should the graduates wear? What should we do about a banquet, reception, or something to honor these dear young people? They had given up everything to come to Bible School and deserved a special send-off. One by one the problems resolved themselves.

It was still a time of rebuilding and finding their way for the Germans. Most were poor. The economy of West Germany was not yet strong as it later became. The students couldn't earn money while attending school, so they were pretty much dependent on what we missionaries could do to help them. New suits for graduation were out of the question. A nice pair of trousers might have been possible for some, but not an entire suit.

Then a package came from the States. In fact, it was a large carton. We tore it open. Jackets. A whole carton full. They were a lovely soft cream color, and there were exactly enough for every graduate. The boys were all sizes from quite tall to very short. The miracle was, there was a size to fit every one of them.

They looked stunning at graduation time in their snappy jackets with dark pants and ties. How we thanked our heavenly Father for planning it so perfectly. This was only one of the beautiful lessons of faith the students and their teachers learned during Bible School days. The fellows left school ready to believe God for anything, and God never let them down.

John Kolenda brought direction and leadership to the school. He sized up our problem of trying to interest German churches in a strong Sunday school program. We had absolutely no tools to put in their hands to help them get started. John encouraged us to stick out our necks and try to start a Sunday school paper.

Paul got hold of an old mimeograph, set it up in a little back room, and we were in business. It was primitive, but we put together a paper for boys and girls. Later he sent one of the graduates, who had a flair for this sort of thing, to a good printer. There he learned color work and many other little tricks of the trade. They found a used Rotoprint and set it up to replace the poor old worn-out mimeograph. The children's paper looked lovely now. Churches went for it. Children devoured it. It was soon a valued tool for work with children in Germany.

Little by little the student picked up new techniques and was really on his way. Paul believed in him and stood by him, helping in any way he could. We were all glad for the *Treasure Chest*, as the paper was named, but churches need more than Sunday school papers to build up strong schools. They needed lesson quarterlies, visual aids, how-to materials, and much, much more. Finances were limited; possibilities of getting hold of more funds appeared nonexistent.

Then we heard about Boys and Girls Missionary Crusade, a children's project to collect funds for children's work on mission fields. We got in touch with our missions leader in Springfield, Missouri, who helped us get English quarterlies to translate into German. He sent us the negatives for printing color visuals, as well. I don't think we would have a Sunday school program in Germany today if it hadn't been for Phil Hogan. BGMC (Boys and Girls Missionary Crusade) paid for translating the quarterlies. The program was getting off the ground at last.

Our warmest thanks goes to so many who shared in this effort. I think of the Speed-the-Light youth project, which provided us with funds for a better printing press. I remember women's groups who provided good stories to translate, print, package, and get out to the churches, and the assorted award trophies they spent hours making. It was a cooperative effort, this Sunday school endeavor. I am thankful for all the German Christians who helped translate, print, bind, and otherwise prepare the quarterlies. Now there are quarterlies for every age, including adults. May God continue to add His blessing to this great work, carried on now by the Germans themselves.

Paul's vision for reaching, teaching, and training the young was like a fire in his soul. Nothing was too much or too hard.

He would sit in his office phoning until the wee small hours, talking with pastors, planning seminars, working out details of conferences or forums, arranging teen camps, prayer weekends, and other youth or children's activities. He would often work at his desk after it was too late to phone anymore, until he could no longer keep his eyes open. Then he would stumble upstairs and literally fall into bed. He did this night after night. His days never seemed long enough for all he wanted to accomplish.

Paul was a man of habit and routine, but he was always looking ahead for new avenues to explore, fresh viewpoints to introduce, exciting possibilities to look into. In some ways he may have gone too fast at first. All these things were too new and different to be readily accepted.

In other ways some of our young German friends felt he was behind the times by not developing such novelties as TV games and other technical possibilities. Paul was a stable, steady sort of person, cautious of activities that could intrigue the child and be more meaningful to him than the lesson they were meant to convey.

We hadn't been in Frauenkopf long before we started a children's meeting in our apartment. We soon had a living room full of kids.

They loved it, and it was sweet to see them tiptoe up the uncarpeted stairs, trying not to disturb the other tenants. They removed their shoes outside the door, setting them in neat rows along the wall. In spite of all our efforts not to disturb anyone, there were complaints. The landlord finally prohibited us from holding the story hour in our apartment, so we moved to our garage under the house. The group kept growing. Children came from all over Frauenkopf. The landlord decided too many children were coming into his yard every week. He took back his garage, with the pretense that he needed it.

The children were inconsolable. We encouraged them to pray, and we all prayed together. We could keep the garage until the middle of the month. That gave us a little time to look around.

A wealthy factory owner and father of children who came to the group invited us to use their rumpus room for our group. It was a change for the better. We had more room and were in a nicer place.

More kids kept coming. Some were young teenagers. Even the large party room was soon too small. We felt we must do something else. Then we had a bright idea. Why not divide the group by ages? Well, why not? This change was the turning point in our endeavor to reach children and teens for Christ.

We had the six-, seven-, and eight-year-olds at two o'clock on Saturday afternoon; the nines, tens, and elevens at three thirty; the twelve through fifteens at four forty-five. We were exhausted when the last group went home, but what a triumphant afternoon. They were such super kids.

Every group had a lesson appropriate for that age. We could really communicate. The teens would ask questions that troubled them. They asked about all sorts of things that this group needs answers for. Their questions were sharp and pertinent. One after the other, they gave their lives to Christ. The younger ones loved the songs, stories, and handwork.

We had finally found a place where we were welcome. Each Saturday was a rich learning experience for us as well as for the young people we ministered to. As they learned to know and love Jesus, they took the good news home and shared it with parents, grandparents, and others who might make up the household. One girl with an older sister shared Jesus with her. She also gave her life to Christ. Later she met and married a young minister and has been helping at his side for many years. There was quite a revival atmosphere in Frauenkopf. Anywhere in the whole area, one heard our story-hour songs and choruses sung by women hanging out the wash, by men mowing a lawn or tending a flower bed. We were invited to homes where we shared Jesus with open-hearted parents and other family members. God was working in Frauenkopf and lives were being changed. The gospel is indeed the power of God unto salvation (Romans 1:16).

As the work in Frauenkopf grew, even our graded groups became overcrowded. I shared this problem with the deaconess of the state church, who was also a dear friend of mine. She thought she might be able to arrange for us to use the children's facilities in her church for our groups. They were used only on Sundays anyway. Most of the children who came to us went to that church on Sunday. Frau Deaconess felt it would be a good thing if their lovely accommodations could be used more often. She was able to work it all out, so for the rest of the time we were in Frauenkopf, our groups met in that lovely church. We were very thankful to the pastor and elders of that state church for opening their doors to us. I'm quite sure many of those children are today pillars in that church. Anything done for Christ is lasting.

Paul was sitting in an American snack bar in Germany one day when a young GI came and sat at his table. They began chatting and the young man shared with him some of the problems that servicemen and women have. He told of many who were Christians at home but went off the deep end in Germany. They were lonely, frustrated, homesick. They drank too much, spending hours in beer halls or other drinking places. They got involved with the wrong type of women. They did just about everything they shouldn't do.

Paul caught a glimpse of the spiritual and moral bankruptcy of our troops in Europe. He often filled in for chaplains who were on leave or on duty elsewhere. Now he felt it was time to get busy and do something tangible and concrete for our troops in Germany.

Cooperating with Chaplain A.C. Summers of Robinson Barracks, in Stuttgart, a Sunday night interdenominational rally was started in the Crossroads Chapel in downtown Stuttgart. It was called, "The Words of Truth Revival Hour." It soon became one of the most popular events in the area. GIs, married and single, officers and their families, and even young Germans attended. Everyone enjoyed this happy, more or less unstructured rally. It was beautiful to see a shouting Nazarene or Pentecostal praising the Lord with heart and hands and voice, as the old song goes. Kneeling beside him, a conservative Presbyterian or Episcopalian quietly and reverently worshipped the way he was accustomed to doing in his own church. Nobody criticized anyone else for the way he worshipped. We have never seen a more tolerant, respectful group of Christians serving God together than in this wonderful rally at Crossroads Chapel in Stuttgart.

The chapel was always full. People found God. Our tiny apartment was bursting at the seams with GIs, hungry for a little family life. Some came for prayer and counseling. There was hardly a spot in our home that was not stained with the tears of lonely, seeking GIs who wept their way to God there.

Three young men from that rally stand out distinctly in my memory: Jack Hetch, a Quaker; Paul Case, a Lutheran, as I recall; and Paul Shields, a Nazarene. All three were devout Christians. They loved us and came to our home often. All the servicemen and women were free to come any time of the day or night, but these three spent almost every free minute there, especially Jack.

Jack was dark, short, stocky, and a bit on the aggressive, argumentative side but warmhearted and loveable. He took our Bobby under his wing, and they became great pals.

Paul Case was of medium height, slender, with brown hair and blue-gray eyes. He was a gentle, sensitive person whom we learned to love and appreciate very much. A long time later, when he was out of the army and in college, he was part of a prayer group who helped with our support in the field. This type of quiet action was characteristic of Paul Case.

Paul Shields was well over six feet, with dark hair, blue eyes, a rosy complexion, and as big-hearted and friendly as he was tall. He was musical, played in the army band, and was, generally speaking, an all-around guy and everybody's friend. Interestingly, these three types represented all the boys who came in and out of the rally, our home, and our lives.

We sometimes took a few of the teenagers from Frauenkopf with us to the rally. They liked it and told the others how good it was. Then they wanted to come, too. We didn't have room in our little Fiat for so many, so the GIs got permission to bring a big army truck to Frauenkopf to pick them up. Soon they had a whole truck full every Sunday evening. Many of those teenagers gave their lives to Christ at the rally. It was an enormous incentive to them when they saw big, husky, good-looking young servicemen get out of their seats, march to the front, kneel at an altar, and surrender their lives to Christ. From that little Frauenkopf group, there is today a missionary to Africa, a Christian doctor, a youth leader of several thousand Catholic young people, and several others in leadership positions. Most of the others are dedicated Christian laymen and women.

Besides the Frauenkopf groups, I felt led to start a story hour for American children at Robinson Barracks housing area. I was already teaching a large primary class in the army chapel Sunday school. There I noticed the needs of the children and knew I must try and help as many as possible, not just the primaries. I planned it for after school one afternoon a week. The large, well-lit attic of one of the army housing units was made available to me. It was furnished with chairs and a few other needed pieces of furniture and we were in business. Children came in droves. It was beautiful how God moved in the hearts and lives of boys and girls. Many are serving the Lord today because of that story hour.

I have an open letter from Chaplain Summers about this work and also about our family. Paul kept it among his things all these years. I found it after his death:

To Whom It May Concern,

1. The undersigned chaplain has been the Protestant chaplain for Stuttgart Sub-Area (Formerly Post and District) since 4 July, 1952. When I arrived, I found that Chaplain (Lt Col) Hudson B. Phillips, was using Rev. Paul Williscroft as a regular supply at the Robinson Barracks Chapel, while he

conducted the service at the Crossroads Chapel in downtown Stuttgart. This arrangement continued until the new chapel was constructed at Robinson Barracks. Since that time, Rev. Williscroft has been an acceptable supply at various chapels in the area.

2. For over three years Mrs. Williscroft has been the very competent and efficient teacher of the primary department of our chapel Sunday School. This class has consistently been the largest and the children have been thoroughly instructed in the Holy Scripture.

3. For a long time, the Williscrofts lived in Frauenkopf, a suburb of Stuttgart. They worked with an attractive group of German youth. About eighteen months ago, Mr. Williscroft and I sponsored a German-American Evangelistic Service at the Crossroads Chapel Sunday nights. The Frauenkopf young people along with other Germans and our American soldiers, have been faithful attendants. It is the only service of its kind in the Area and is filling the chapel each Sunday evening. There were 149 present last Sunday.

4. Bobby and Beverly Williscroft, their children, have been faithful and helpful in our services.

5. Many U.S. soldiers have enjoyed the hospitality of the Williscrofts' home. My family and I have been there on numerous enjoyable occasions.

6. In conclusion, I have found the Williscrofts to be friendly, capable, efficient, prayerful, and thoroughly Christian in my relations with them. There is no family that I will miss more as I return to the United States. I commend them to you without reservation.

Signed
Augustus C. Summers
Chaplain (Major) USA

We felt very unworthy of such high recommendations, as we only did our Christian duty. This fine introduction, however, did open doors to military chapels for us all over Europe, so we were thankful for it. Chaplain Summers and his dear family were an inspiration to us as well as a lovely example of what a military chaplain can do and be. He was Presbyterian by denomination, but he belonged to us all as a true man of God.

CHAPTER TWENTY-TWO

We lived in the Stuttgart area for four happy years. Bobby attended the American military dependents school. Bevy was such a frail, wee thing we decided to keep her at home. I taught her the Calvert Course, a very good home-schooling program. I had taught Bobby his third grade in Basel, and he did very well in it. Bevy started first grade. As it turned out later, she really received her first and second grade in one year. When we sent her to the American school after that, they just didn't know what to do with her. She was ready for third grade, but she was so tiny and delicate they hesitated to put her there. She was a good pupil, and we knew she would be bored in second grade, so the principal finally decided to let her go into the third grade. She did very well and loved being in school at last.

The last two years in Stuttgart, we sent both children to a very fine private school, the Mertz Schule. This school specialized in many new and interesting teaching methods, as well as unusual and practical subjects. The children enjoyed it, and their German improved immeasurably. They rattled it off like natives. How we envied them.

For some time now, we had all been wishing for more room in the school building. Another missionary lady had joined our ranks, dear Olga Olsson. She was originally from Sweden but more recently from the States, where she had attended Bible School and college. The school was really crowded. It would be good to locate it more centrally, too. At that time the majority of students were from North Germany. Stuttgart was a long way for them to go. At the very beginning of the Bible School, one of the students, Reinhold Ulonska, pedaled all the way from Hamburg to Stuttgart on his bicycle. He eventually became the leader of the main German organization.

It wasn't easy to find just the right place to relocate the school. Where should it be? When should we do it? What sort of building would suit our needs? Should we build or look for something we could move right in to? The German leaders, with John Kolenda, started looking around. Wiesbaden, the capital of the state of Hessen, is a beautiful health resort city and not far from Frankfurt. The men looked around there, as it would be an ideal city for a Bible School. The large metropolis of Frankfurt, on the River Main, was nearby. The city on the River Rhine, Mainz, is also close. In fact, the men looked over all three of these cities, thoroughly, but just couldn't settle for anything. There were possibilities, but the buildings were either too big or too small or needed too much renovating. The most insurmountable obstacle was the cost. They were all too expensive for us.

We prayed until our knees felt calloused. We asked our American friends in Germany to pray with us. We had our supporting churches praying, too. Probably the only ones who weren't praying for a new location were our dear German youngsters in Frauenkopf. They felt it would be the end of everything if we left, poor kids. I wonder if they prayed we wouldn't find a place. At least we were beginning to think so. Finally, in a village located about thirty kilometers south of Frankfurt, nine kilometers north of Darmstadt, and not far from Wiesbaden, we found the right spot.

It was a partially finished factory building on a two-acre site. Actually, it looked pretty awful. The grounds were full of weeds almost as tall as the unfinished walls. The whole setup looked so abandoned and forlorn, Olga and I wept when we saw it. I think Paul felt nearly as dejected as we ladies, but he wasn't quite ready to commit himself. Half hidden in the weeds stood two small cottages. Old tires and other junk littered the few places where the weeds hadn't taken over. A more desolate, hopeless, utterly impossible site was beyond one's imagination. What did our brethren see in it?

I'll tell you what they saw. They had a vision. Especially John Kolenda. They saw green lawns, bright flower beds, a neat, three-story building, glistening white in the sunshine. They saw tall poplars casting long shadows across the lawn. They visualized the tiny cottages transformed into cozy bungalows where instructors could live comfortably with their families. Clearest of all, they saw hosts of happy, laughing, young people pouring in and out of the building where they were preparing themselves for Christian service at home and abroad. Where there is no vision the people perish. John Kolenda had a vision.

The building in Stuttgart was sold and the new property in the village of Erzhausen was purchased. Then the work began. Students came early to help. John Kolenda was motivator, inspirer, persuader, and sometimes the pusher of the whole project. First the weeds, bushes, and debris had to be cleared away. At last the building began. The students, led by John Kolenda, worked almost day and night. They planned to finish the ground floor first and continue with the further building program as time and finances allowed.

When the day arrived for school to begin, the building was far from finished. The roof over the first floor, at least, was in place. Despite the unfinished state, school started on time. The walls felt damp inside. Even the floors were still in the raw, but that fine group of young men felt that a dream had come true. They were actually in Bible School preparing themselves for the Lord's work.

They were in school all morning and worked on the building before school mornings and every afternoon. They studied all evening. I don't know how they did it. They were probably tired all the time.

The work went forward. The walls were painted, the floors were finished with a type of shiny dark material, the class and dorm rooms began to look livable, and everybody's spirits lifted. The kitchen and dining room were still unfinished, but at least food could be prepared and served.

We didn't move to Erzhausen the first year the school was there. Earlier we moved from Frauenkopf to a larger, more commodious apartment in another area of Stuttgart. We were still close enough to Frauenkopf to carry on our work there. It wasn't as easy for us and the young people, and the community missed the fellowship we'd enjoyed living among them. Since our landlord gave notice he needed his apartment, we had to move. Our new place was a condo. The owner had been transferred to another part of Germany and was happy to have us take over his nice apartment. We enjoyed the roomier accommodations, and the children didn't even have to change schools.

Paul spent the school week in Erzhausen teaching and helping where he could. He was also busy getting the publishing work set up there. One of the new students was very interested in this work and was a great help as long as he was in school. He later went as a missionary to Kenya where he was able to use the printing skills he learned with us.

Paul came home every Friday night. He was active in army chapels and busy with the rally at Crossroads Chapel weekends. The children and I missed him but were glad for the weekends.

That year in the new school flew quickly by. It would be our last year in Stuttgart. We had put down roots in this fine old *Swabian* city. Many of the scars of war were disappearing as the industrious Germans, with the help of the Marshall Plan, cleared away rubbish, put up modern new buildings, beautified streets and homes with flower beds, trees, and fresh, grassy areas here and there. Our work among the American service people was blossoming and so was the German work. We were happy and content. The Bible School year ended. Paul came home for the summer, only returning now and then to take care of the publishing work.

We spent a busy, happy summer, including a wonderful trip to the Holy Land. Summer was drawing to a close. The children would be returning to school. Bible School would soon begin.

We were thinking all summer about moving to Erzhausen for the next school year if we could find an apartment. The children and I were not too happy about that. They loved the Mertz school in Stuttgart and hated to change. Paul and I were not very enthusiastic about it either. We wondered what educational possibilities existed in a village like Erzhausen. Probably none, as far as Paul could find out. Well, I could tutor them at home if the worst came to worst. That didn't leave much time for missionary work, but it was something to think about.

We took a family trip to Erzhausen one weekend to see what possibilities existed. We spent a day in Frankfurt looking around for apartments as well as schools. There were some good schools, but we couldn't find housing. Wiesbaden was the same. Darmstadt is a smaller city, and the kind of place we wanted seemed nonexistent. As we came back to the Bible School, tired and discouraged, dear Grandpa Kolenda, as our children and the students lovingly called him, made the suggestion that we move into one of the little cottages on the property. They were living in the other one. He thought we might be able to sort of camp there for a few months until it could be enlarged. This was a good idea, and we decided to do it. We drove back to Stuttgart with exciting plans in mind.

There was a lot to do before we moved. We had to arrange with our landlord to sublet his apartment again. An army family decided to take it. We couldn't use all of our furniture until the cottage was enlarged. The army family could use it, so we left everything but the most necessary articles. These included our personal things, our books, office equipment, and the children's belongings.

Bobby and his sister wanted to pack their own beloved possessions and had a dreadful time deciding what to take and what to give or throw away. Poor Mama had to nearly break their hearts by constantly reminding them how small our house would be. Where would they put all that stuff? No, they couldn't take all those rocks they gathered in Frauenkopf; a few samples maybe. That was all. Finally we were all packed and started off in the Bible School Speed-the-Light van.

We were heavily loaded even though so much was left behind. The VW van rolled merrily along in spite of the load. We were laughing, talking, and singing favorite choruses when suddenly the van slumped down to the right in the front end and began swaying crazily all over the busy autobahn. We braced ourselves and began praying up a storm. Then we saw the right front wheel rolling groggily down the autobahn in front of us. Paul tried desperately to bring the wild van under control, praying as he worked. Little Bevy, who adored her daddy, kept praying, a bit hysterically, I must confess, "Jesus! Jesus! You are helping Daddy, aren't you? Aren't you?"

To our amazement and joy, the van abruptly eased over to the right shoulder and Paul brought it to a gentle stop without further incident. I can still hear Bevy's excited little voice as she called out to Paul, "See, Daddy! Jesus was helping you, wasn't He?" We all joined in answering a hearty, "He sure was!"

The German automobile club was soon there to help us. The axel had broken under the strain of our load. They found another and soon had us fixed up. We were on our way again and arrived in Erzhausen a few hours late, but so thankful for God's love and watchful care over His children. We were in Erzhausen at last, the little village that would play such a prominent part in all our future ministry until the Lord called Paul to higher service.

CHAPTER TWENTY-THREE

Erzhausen. Our new home. In retrospect, I always think of our cottage there as "The Little House on the Campus." It consisted of two rather large rooms, plus a pantry and bathroom. The children slept on narrow army-surplus bunk beds in the pantry. They didn't mind that in the least. Besides the Bible School grounds, there were fields and woods to explore, lots of village children to play with, and friendly Bible School students to spoil them. They felt like calves in clover.

Besides all those good things, Grandma and Grandpa Kolenda lived just over the driveway in the other cottage. There the children were always treated to fresh cookies, cupcakes, shiny red apples, or whatever treat dear Grandma Kolenda happened to have on hand. This was almost as good as living at Grandma Williscroft's. We received a telegram just before we left Stuttgart informing us of Paul's mother's death. This was a blow to all of us, but utterly devastating to the children. The Kolendas were a comfort and blessing in this time of sorrow.

The first thing on our agenda after we moved to Erzhausen was to see about the children's schooling. We thought the village schools might not be good for their German. We wanted them to speak a good high German without any of the dialects around us. The Erzhausen dialect was used almost exclusively among the villagers. Our kids picked up a lot of it just playing with the children in the neighborhood. We finally decided to send Bobby to a good boy's *Gymnasium* or middle and high school in Darmstadt.

We were often shocked to listen to Bevy talk about German history, literature, music, and culture. They are all well and good to know and appreciate, but our daughter had truly become a little German girl. Everything German was right and the very best, in her book. She often came home from school singing, *"Deutschland, Deutschland, Ueber Alles!"* at the top of her lungs, while she knew nothing of the grand old American patriotic songs and hymns. She did it once too often. We knew it was time for our little German girl to attend an American school.

There was one not far from us at the Rhine/Main air base. She could catch a German train to a small nearby town. From there she could ride on the American school bus to her school. It proved to be a good decision. The adjustment was not easy at first, but little by little Bevy learned to accept and enjoy the best of two worlds. She was glad and proud to be an American again. At the German school, peer pressure tempted her to try to disguise her nationality. German art, music, and culture still appealed to her, but she also cherished her own heritage. That was as it should be.

One of the first things we attempted after getting the children located in their respective schools was to start a Sunday school before the morning service in the Bible School chapel. Our children brought friends and those playmates brought other children, until there was a wonderful group of youngsters coming every Sunday. Students and staff workers gave time and effort to help with the teaching. We even formed an Adult Bible Class, unheard of in Germany at that time. Students took turns teaching it, thereby improving their own knowledge of the Bible, as well as developing their teaching skills.

A graduate student was leader and promoter of the fine children's program. He planned outings, picnics, programs for Christmas and other holidays, and was a good all-around children's worker. We couldn't have accomplished the wonderful work there without the help of Richard Breite. He is now the Royal Ranger leader for Germany, as well as helping develop this great program in Switzerland and Austria. He is small in stature, but one of the biggest men we know.

We had a few weeks before Bible School started to get as settled as possible in our cramped quarters. It was fun trying to see how livable we could make it under the circumstances. Our living room served as bedroom, office, and family room. It looked cozy and inviting, though, in spite of such general use. The kitchen was quite large and had a warm, comfortable atmosphere, with its green linoleum, cream and green cupboards, and cream-colored electric range. At first we had only cold water in the house, but no one complained. There was a little wood or coal heater under the water tank in the bathroom, so if anybody had the will or energy to build a fire, we could have a warm bath now and then. It really wasn't too bad. In fact, it was much better than the old washtubs Paul's family and mine used when we were small.

To help us better use the limited space, Bobby pitched a tent in the front yard, and camped out for most of the summer. When it rained, and it did a lot during that summer, I felt so bad for the youngster, but he insisted in staying in his tent. It was an adventure for him, and set the tone for the rest of his life, which was eventually filled with incredible adventures and daring-do.

The opening day for the Bible School seemed to sneak up on us. There was much still to do. I can see the dismayed looks on the faces of the new students who hadn't seen the school before. It really did present a most inhospitable appearance. They took it all in stride, however, changed into *grubbies*, and pitched right in with a will.

A welcome dinner was served in the dining room. Some of the students gathered lovely colored leaves and made the room look like an autumn woodland. It was really beautiful. Germans are some of the most artistic people in the world. Often they made out with very little. Setting a pretty table is one of their talents, and that evening was no exception. We had a lovely time together as the students introduced themselves and we teachers and staff welcomed them to the school. Those eager young faces, glowing with anticipation, were an inspiration. We and the other teachers were deeply moved. We pledged ourselves to give our utmost to so instruct, guide, and motivate these precious young people, that they, in turn, would give of their best to the Master.

The next day classes began in earnest. Paul was again deeply involved in his Christian Education classes, even grading the students on what they did and how they did it when their turn came to teach the adult Bible class. That was a real incentive to study and thoroughly prepare themselves, as well as the lesson. There were a number of very promising students in the freshman class. We were glad to see the delight some of them evidenced in the study of the Word and the excitement they felt over some newly revealed truth. It was especially exciting for them to dig out a gold nugget of scripture for themselves.

Between classes, housework assignments, and study, the building program went forward. One outstanding student, Gottfried Weichert, was a bricklayer by trade. He said once he had the feeling he never got through with his work. We surely could never have finished even the ground floor without Gottfried. In spite of his heavy schedule, he was selected as valedictorian of his class when he graduated. Everybody was proud of him. He came illegally out of East Germany to Bible School, so it meant a great deal to him to have this opportunity to study.

About a month after school had begun, John Kolenda wanted to get started with enlarging our cottage. He enlisted Gottfried and several other fellows who had building experience to work with him on this project.

It was amazing how quickly it went. On Christmas Eve they were finished enough so I could arrange the furniture, hang curtains, and put up the Christmas tree. It was wonderful to have three bedrooms and to use the living room for just that purpose. Bobby took down his tent and came indoors, although he insisted that he really didn't mind the snow.

We had so much room we hardly knew what to do with it at first. We had discovered that people can get along with much less than they ever imagined.

That was a very happy Christmas. We were all together in one place, the Kolendas, the Williscrofts, Aunties Olga and Emma. Others joined us, too. First we celebrated with the students. They planned and put on a nice program for us. After they left to spend Christmas with their families, we missionaries and a few students celebrated together.

It was good to have our own grounds, which were now white with snow and very Christmasy. Our children felt more at home here than anywhere we had lived except Frauenkopf. We were just one big extended family. According to missionaries from other fields, this is not always the case. How thankful we were for the dear Kolendas, who had the sweet ability to spread peace and harmony wherever they went.

The New Year dawned. The students came back and classes started again. Winter months sped by. The children enjoyed school. Bobby, whom we were beginning to call Bob now, was learning to speak German like a native. Beverly, on the other hand, wasn't as good in the language as she had been, but she was more American. Building activity went on, but not as strenuously as before. There was always some building work to be done. The students called it "building school" sometimes. John Kolenda continued to be the good spirit that hovered over everything.

Paul was a person who quietly went ahead and did what he could without any fanfare. He was developing the publishing work further by printing the official magazine of the German organization and other materials. He was also getting more involved in the servicemen's work. On American holidays he organized rallies at the Bible School for servicemen, their families, and, of course, for the single fellows. Military wives brought their specialties, and we enjoyed delicious potlucks together. These events were always special, and many were saved and filled with the Holy Spirit in that little Bible School chapel.

Paul usually arranged one or two servicemen's retreats a year in the Bible School, too. They lasted a few days and were wonderful times of spiritual refreshing for all who attended, missionaries as well as service people. Facilities were primitive and inadequate. Everything was more or less make-do, but who cared? These were days of heaven on earth. Those who could make it always said afterwards that they wouldn't have missed it for anything.

Paul often traveled long distances to visit Christian servicemen's groups on the different military bases. These were a blessing for the service people as well as for us. We really learned to know people by mingling with them in their own setting. It was always a satisfying and fulfilling experience.

A monthly newsletter was sent out to individual service people as well as to groups. Paul encouraged the service people to write in and let us know what was going on in their area. These reports were printed in the newsletter, besides announcements of coming events, births, weddings, and, sadly, sometimes deaths. Some of the responses from individuals were very heartwarming. This type of spiritual help and encouragement was badly needed among our troops overseas. The Lord had so beautifully worked it all out.

CHAPTER TWENTY-FOUR

It was furlough time. For six long years we had been away from our homeland. The children had almost forgotten America. They had both been small when we left the States. Now Bob was a teenager. Bev was a preteen. They were sweet, well-adjusted youngsters, completely at home in Germany, or anywhere in Europe for that matter. Their friends were in Germany. Their schooling was almost all German. The German language was like their mother tongue.

They didn't know it, but there were major changes ahead. They would be faced with a whole new culture: people, schools, foods, life-styles, church customs, and much, much more. Many missionaries' kids cop out at this point. We tried to prepare them for some of the differences, but weren't very good instructors, I'm afraid. We had been gone too long ourselves and probably suffered as much culture shock as they did when we got back to the States. Furloughs were due every four years, but Paul was involved with so many projects it was difficult finding time to break away. Finally, after six years, both of us realized that we needed to wind things down and take a leave for the children's sake as well as for ourselves.

It wasn't easy. Who would carry on? How would we divide the responsibilities? Difficult as it was, we found that we were expendable. That was good. Richard Breite, took over the Christian Education classes in the school. The young German printer took on the task of printing the materials the translators gave him. Olga Olsson took on the servicemen's work, even writing and getting out the newsletter each month. Olga is one of those people who does anything she undertakes well.

For the six years we had been in Germany, Paul had given himself wholeheartedly to the work at hand. He was tireless in getting materials out, while planning and preparing for the future. Now there were two children's take-home papers, quarterlies for all ages, new stories in English with a German translation placed inside, besides many other stories and new materials of all kinds. He planned and worked out interesting Sunday school conventions in three major cities: Hamburg, Bremen, and Frankfurt. They were well attended and an inspiration to everybody. Bible School students helped us put the conventions over. They were wonderful. We couldn't have handled the huge task without them.

German churches were beginning to take a close look at what was going on. One leading pastor wrote in his paper that went out to many churches, large and small, "The Amerika Mann is doing something for our churches that will bless tomorrow. He is teaching our people, through his ministry, how to reach, teach, and guide our children into an experience with the Lord, so they can be leaders of the future."

Paul left a rich heritage for Germany in the field of Christian Education. He became a symbol, a legend, from east to west, from north to south, creating a strong teaching program in German churches. Sometimes he was loved and honored. Other times his work would would be taken lightly or even looked down upon. People couldn't understand why an intelligent man who could be spending his life doing great things should stoop to reach children.

Paul's philosophy was that children, too, are a real and important part of the Great Commission to go into all the world and preach the Gospel to every creature. As we made plans to be away for a year, he faced a difficult time reconciling the need to go with the need to stay. His teacher heart feared for the still fragile structure of the Christian Education program he was developing. Would it survive the change? Without strong leadership, could the dedicated team of young people carry on under the pressures of skeptical church leaders? Only God knew.

Paul possessed faith that moves mountains. He knew how to lay all his anxious fears into the strong hands of the mighty God he served. With a peaceful heart he committed his faithful helpers to the Lord and was ready to turn his face homeward. Van Dyke's famous poem became very personal to all of us:

> Oh, it's home again, and home again,
>   America for me!
> I want a ship that's westward bound
>   to plough the rolling sea,
> To the blessed Land of Room Enough
>   Beyond the ocean bars,
> Where the air is full of sunlight
>   and the flag is full of stars.

Westward Ho! We were on our way in a VW van, with two thrilled Bible School students and two excited kids. We headed for Paris, the City of Light. The children chatted happily about all they would see: the Arch of Triumph, the Eiffel Tower, and lots more. They loved to show off their knowledge. We took the students along to help with the driving and to bring the van back to the school. It would be their first trip to Paris as well as their first sight of the ocean. Our children felt like old pros, since they crossed that ocean once and would do it again in just a day or two. They loved sharing their knowledge with the boys. All of them were having a grand time together, their last for many months.

I remember Paul quietly enjoying all the chatter. He loved his lively children and his happy, optimistic wife. They brought color and movement into his busy life. He was the perfect picture of the quiet, confident husband and father, content with his family and his God.

We had a wonderful time in Paris. We had been there before, and it was great fun showing the boys around. We had army friends stationed in Paris and nothing would do but that we all stay with them in their comfortable, roomy home. They did all they could to make our stay something long to be remembered. They had a homelike name, Captain and Mrs. Green, just like my grandfather on Mother's side of the family. He, too, was Captain Green, but a sea captain. Our army Captain Green took a few days' leave and showed us everything worth seeing by day. Since she worked during the day, Mrs. Green joined us in the evening. Then we saw Paris by night, while the daughter of the family baby-sat the children. We enjoyed the lights, the elegant shop windows, sampling a good restaurant or two, and seeing Paris at night from the Eiffel tower. It was a real fun time for all of us.

The last morning the Greens went with us to Le Havre to see us off. We were sailing on the French ship, *SS Liberté*. We wondered why it looked so strangely familiar until someone informed us it was the old *Bremen*, given to France after World War II.

We dined together aboard ship, as we had ample time before sailing. What a merry gathering around a large oval table. We laughed and talked, sharing the good things of the Lord until a shout rang out, "All ashore that's goin' ashore!" in a loud, nasal twang. We walked our friends to the gangway, hugged the students, expressed our warm appreciation to the Greens, and our friends hurried down with the other guests. We watched and waved until they faded into the gentle afternoon haze.

The deep, throaty whistle sounded. We stood on deck and watched as the great ship turned around and headed for the open sea.

It was a lovely voyage. The children were older, and we could do more things together as a family. We enjoyed shuffleboard and played it on deck every day. It was summer and the weather was beautiful the whole trip. We spent long hours on deck reading, promenading, swimming, or just getting acquainted with the many interesting passengers.

There is something about an ocean voyage that brings people together. Cultural, ethnic, or any other differences are forgotten. We are just people, shut in together for five days or a week. One does pretty much the same things together every day: eating, playing, talking, walking, exchanging experiences, and exploring each other's minds. No matter how often you travel by ship, there are always differences – a different ship, different passengers, different situations – but still, it is much the same. It is romantic, exciting, and fun. We missed these wonderful voyages after air travel eliminated most of the great passenger ships.

Paul loved playing with us in the afternoons. He spent his mornings in the stateroom or in a deck chair above, studying, planning, and dreaming, too, of possibilities, ideas, promotional activities, or anything that would further the Christian Education program in Germany. Whenever a new thought or a bright idea struck him, he would call me. He simply had to share it. Then we would talk together about how it could be worked out to fit into the German situation. I always appreciated his sharing of dreams, plans, and inspirations with me. Often I could help him put them into operation when the time was ripe.

The days melted into each other, and before we were ready to leave our floating island, we pulled into New York harbor.

On our first voyage this had been a thrill. Now it was a bit routine. We really were happy to be back in the States again. Paul called our Jewish friends, but didn't have time to look them up. He had ordered a VW station wagon in Germany, to be delivered in New York. He needed to pick it up and settle all the paperwork involved in getting it out of customs. The missionary home was still in use at that time, so it was a friendly, pleasant place to stay until all our business was taken care of.

The children enjoyed the great city. We took time to let them see some of the sights from their more mature perspective. That was fun for us all.

School would soon be starting and a whole continent had to be crossed to reach Yakima, Washington. We made many pleasant stops along the way, speaking in churches, and enjoyed seeing old friends again. Finally we drove into Yakima, but it wasn't the same. There was no loving grandma to welcome us. There was no cozy house, fragrant with homemade goodies, to make ourselves at home in. It was all different. Our precious Grandma was in heaven. We missed her dearly.

Loving friends invited us to stay in their home until our own little home in Union Gap would be ready for us. The tenants had moved out, but there were repairs to make before we could move in. These things kept us busy for a week or two. Oh, the joy when everything was ready to move into our very own home, the first we ever had. No words can express the thrill we experienced when we walked over the threshold and were home at last.

It was fun picking out a piece of furniture here, another there, until our home was furnished. Some of the things were from yard sales or were otherwise used stuff, but our home looked pretty and homelike. I chose a pink and gray color scheme. We were delighted over how nice the house looked when everything was completed. People said it looked professional, as though an interior decorator planned it. That was an encouragement, because I actually did not have much to work with. We enjoyed our little home and wished we could take it with us when it was time to go back.

That year in the States was good for us. The children went to different schools. Bob went to high school in Yakima every morning. Beverly attended a fine junior high just down the block from us. It was a time of transition and adjustment for the whole family. Paul did most of the deputational work alone as I couldn't leave the children during the school year.

Bob liked high school. One of his teachers had taught Paul many years earlier. Bob experienced trouble fitting in, however. He was very European in his thinking, much more so than we realized. He was ahead of his peers in most subjects and sometimes acted arrogant and superior. I conferred several times with his teachers, explaining the European school system and why Bob was having a hard time. They were lovely and promised to help all they could. About the time we were ready to go back to Germany, he began fitting into the American system.

Beverly had no trouble adjusting as she had been enrolled in an American school for the past year. Her trouble was different. Boys and girls her age never dated or even mildly flirted in Germany. She was a pretty little thing, and all the junior-high boys liked her. She wasn't prepared to handle this sort of thing and didn't know what to do. When she first started junior high, a boy asked her to go to the fair with him. She was dumbfounded and told him in no uncertain terms that she was just a little girl and didn't go places with boys. What kind of upbringing did he have, anyway? Who did he think he was, asking her to go someplace with him alone?

Well, word soon made the rounds that Bev Williscroft was a naive kid who wasn't weaned from the cradle yet. Poor Beverly. It took her a few months to live that down. She didn't budge an inch from her strong stand, though. Eventually the kids learned to know her and liked her for herself. I was relieved and happy when our home was full of boys and girls again, having wholesome fun together.

Summer vacation came at last. Paul promised the kids a long trip when school was out. He scheduled meetings in California, New Mexico, Texas, Louisiana, Oklahoma, Arkansas, Nevada, and Idaho. We had bought Bob a pair of *Lederhosen* (leather pants) in Germany and Beverly a pretty *Dirndl*, (Tyrolean dress) to wear in our missionary meetings. The kids looked like Heidi and Peter in the story of Heidi. They sang together and were a popular part of the Williscroft team. They tired sometimes of always singing the same songs, wearing the same clothes, watching the same slides, and hearing the same missionary appeal. We understood. We tired of it, too, and needed constantly to pray for a new touch from the Lord, a fresh anointing of the Holy Spirit on our lives and ministry.

Even so, it was a fun trip. Everybody loved Disneyland, the White Sands National Park, Yosemite, and all the other natural and man-made wonders. We had almost forgotten how vast and glorious America is. The children acquired a brand-new appreciation for their wonderful homeland.

Along the way the kids were able to meet relatives they had never met or hardly knew. There was Uncle Al of Buck Knife fame. How exciting it was to go with him through the factory. Their joy knew no bounds when Uncle Al gave each of them a nice little Buck Knife. That was their dearest treasure for a long time. They were deeply impressed as they observed their uncle's deep Christian faith. They had never met a businessman before who let God be his senior partner. There are many godly businessmen who have done this, but, living abroad for so many years, our children didn't know any.

Uncle Roland, author of the best seller, *Angels on Assignment*, pastored a large church in Boise, Idaho, and was a great favorite, as was Uncle Walt, also a pastor and a real fun person. There were the aunts and cousins. Bob promptly fell in love with those cute girl cousins. Beverly had fun doing "girl things" with her younger girl cousins. This was a never-to-be-forgotten trip for all of us. Seeing loved ones we hadn't seen for years, doing some of the most interesting sight-seeing we ever dreamed of, and then, the good meetings. We made friends for the work in Europe who remain true and faithful to this day. They caught the vision of Europe as a mission field, and that was one of our main goals.

God blessed and cared for us over all those thousands of miles until we drove into our yard in Union Gap. I look back on that time with warm memories and a grateful heart.

CHAPTER TWENTY-FIVE

The beautiful year in our own home, and the family trips for our deputation, were over. It was time to return to Germany. We loved being in the States, but a part of us had remained where our work was. The people in the Bible School were precious to us. During our travels, we visited many bookstores, gathering materials we thought would be helpful in the Christian Education program in Germany. We visited the Gospel Publishing House in Springfield on our way to New York. They were wonderful, giving us barrels of large Bible picture rolls, smaller lesson pictures for beginners, and quantities of other useful children's materials.

Permission was given to translate and print in German any of their materials we wanted. We felt like millionaires and could hardly wait to get to Germany and start translating. Paul planned to turn the materials over to qualified Germans for translation. This way the German would be correct and all the natural, idiomatic expressions, so important for translations, would be used.

The trip to New York was old hat by this time. We decided it would be fun, and educational for the kids, to visit our nation's capital. We had time for a short trip before sailing time, so we headed for Washington, D.C. It was cold, frosty December weather, but that didn't bother us. We bundled up and saw the sights. It was a good experience for everybody. Paul and I had never been there either. We all knew and enjoyed the great capitals of Europe but hadn't seen Washington. We spent a wonderful day absorbing history, glorying in our government, admiring buildings and monuments, and feeling terribly patriotic.

We drove back to New York in the early evening, chattering all the way about the things we had seen. Paul explained, or tried to, the intricacies of our government's operation to the children. He told them about our freedoms, our Bill of Rights, and our Constitution. He wanted to instill into them a wholesome pride in their country and a humble gratitude that they were born Americans.

The next day we sailed on the great and beautiful ship, the *SS United States*. For a winter crossing, we had unusually fine weather and calm seas. It took just five days, the best time we ever made from New York to Germany.

We arrived in Bremen, where we were met by a couple of our students. What a happy reunion that was. As we drove into the school grounds, we were met by a joyful welcoming committee and led to the dining room, where a feast was prepared. We felt at home again.

Other people were living in our little house on the campus, so Grandpa Kolenda rented a large old house for us in the small town of Griesheim, just a streetcar ride from the pretty city of Darmstadt. The house was a hundred or more years old and was in the process of being renovated. It looked clean and inviting when we went to inspect it. The workers were just finishing up last-minute details. There was a second building behind the house that we hoped, in time, to use as a servicemen's hospitality center. Behind that building was a large garden plot. That made Paul's eyes sparkle. He enjoyed puttering in a garden.

Griesheim is between seven and eight hundred years old. Deep under the old Lutheran church, workmen were digging to find and repair a water pipe. They struck something larger than a water pipe and discovered part of an ancient Roman ruin. It was the most exciting thing that had happened in or around that old church for years.

Our house was on a quiet street, nestled among other old houses of about the same vintage. A small group of Hungarian and Yugoslavian refugees lived in Griesheim. They were Christians and thrilled to know that missionaries were going to settle in their town.

The Kolendas opened their home to us for a week after our arrival in Germany, since the house in Griesheim wasn't ready yet. A nice group of refugee Christians visited us one evening at the service in the Bible School. They shyly approached us, with outstretched arms and smiling faces, warmly welcoming us to Griesheim. They needed a place to worship and hoped we would hold services in our home. It was encouraging to know they were there.

We were able to move into our house before Christmas, much to the joy of Bob and Bev. It was a different kind of Christmas than usual, with hardly time to buy presents or bake holiday goodies. We did manage a little tree, which the kids enjoyed helping decorate. The festivities at the school were lovely, though, and helped make up for our quiet Christmas at home. I don't think any of us minded not celebrating in our traditional style; it was enough to be back with our dear missionaries, students, and helpers.

The building behind our house had one medium-sized room on the ground floor and two upstairs rooms. We talked the possibilities over with John Kolenda and finally settled for using the ground floor as a little prayer chapel for GIs who came to visit us. The upstairs rooms could be sleeping quarters for men who needed lodgings for a night or two.

From that time on, as men learned about our hospitality home, hardly a weekend passed without a house full of GIs. Bev and I prepared meals, made up beds, and racked our brains to figure out how to feed ten hungry men when we had planned for only the five who had announced their coming. It was always fun, and a real challenge. How could we stretch the potatoes, the salad, or the dessert? I often prayed, "Lord, please multiply this meal, like you did the little boy's loaves and fishes so long ago!" We would watch with bated breath, as a full table of boys would eat and eat, but the bowls of food didn't seem to diminish much. I have carried away what was left with a grateful heart, thanking God for my own special miracle.

As time passed and lonely, homesick GIs sought refuge and comfort in our home, there was hardly a chair or couch without a few tear stains. Those were the places where men had prayed the sinner's prayer or struggled through some deep spiritual battle to a glorious victory. Sometimes those tears were shed by a heartsick boy who had just gotten a Dear John. The old hymn, "Love That Will Not Let Me Go," was balm to many a broken heart as we sought to minister to such needs.

We loved working with servicemen. Paul often said he'd like to have a whole church full of them. They were disciplined, dependable, great guys. We hear from some of those fellows still, who are now grandfathers. There are pastors, missionaries, and Christian workers in various areas of need, who once left their tears on our couch or chairs in Germany. Were the results worth all the effort: the shabby furniture, the wrestling in prayer, the countless meals, the hours of listening, of counseling? Yes, a thousand times, yes. It was a highlight of our ministry in Germany.

As the servicemen's work grew, Paul, with the help of our Assembly chaplains in Europe, was able to organize retreats for service people in beautiful Berchtesgaden in the Bavarian Alps. This was one of Hitler's favorite haunts. Under the jurisdiction of the American military presence in Germany, it had become one of the most popular retreat centers in Europe for military personnel. The retreats became so popular there were often five hundred or more present. These have been times of spiritual refreshing and inner renewal for thousands over the years. They are still a highlight of the servicemen's ministry in Europe, although they no longer are held in Berchtesgaden.

The big holiday rallies held at *Berea* were a great time for the students as well as the military people. Thanksgiving was always extra special. Americans brought turkeys, pumpkin pies, delicious salads, and all kinds of goodies. This was a real treat for us missionaries, too. We looked forward to this event from year to year as much as the GIs did. For us it was a touch of home; for the students, a rare and wonderful dining experience from a faraway land.

As the servicemen seemed to enjoy being in our home more than in the little chapel, we felt God leading us to invite the refugee Christians to join with us in services there. They were happy for that. There were several young people among them. Some had already given their lives to the Lord. Others were open and ready.

John Kolenda held a good evangelistic service in a rented hall in Griesheim soon after we started services in our chapel. Townspeople came as well as our small group. Several gave their lives to Christ, among them a young man and woman from the refugees. There was a wonderful atmosphere among us of victory and looking forward to God's continued working.

After the special meetings, more and more people came to the chapel. We held a training course in children's work for the young people. They drank it in and could hardly wait to get a Sunday school started. We began in a nearby school building. Paul put articles, ads, and announcements in the local paper, a weekly, and in several of the Darmstadt dailies. That brought the kids. They came in droves, alone, with older brothers and sisters, and often with a mother or grandmother. We used the school all summer. The children kept coming and were excited about it. The young people learned their lessons well and did a wonderful job of teaching and otherwise working in the Sunday school.

Before school began in the fall, Paul began to plan, pray, and work toward keeping up the good work in our limited quarters. He motivated the young people to pray, visit, and encourage the children to continue coming. We held planning sessions where the youth sat with us and helped us think through just how and where we could have the various classes. We decided to use our large garage as the assembly room. Then classes were to be held in our living room, all three bedrooms, and even in my kitchen. We were beginning to warm up to the idea of having the Sunday school on our own premises. We could feel freer and not be so bound to certain rules and regulations that schools always seem to find necessary. We could hardly wait for school to start.

The first Sunday after school started we held Sunday school, as planned, in our home. Some of the town children didn't come, but many of our neighborhood youngsters did attend. They hadn't come to the school. The attendance remained about the same for awhile. Then new children were invited by friends and they, in turn, brought their friends. We worked together, prayed together, and believed God together. We sent cards, visited homes, and made phone calls. The young people became real missionaries. Parents began to come, too. We had an adult class in the chapel, a kids' opening service in the garage, a youth class in the living room, a junior class in the kitchen, a primary class in the garage after opening service, and a beginner class in the basement. Talk about a beehive. We had it. Paul was a professional at organizing, and the Sunday school was especially dear to his heart.

Children began accepting Jesus as their personal Savior. They took the message home. One whole family found the Lord and are still serving Him today.

One day I was taking the streetcar to Darmstadt. A woman sitting next to me kept giving me angry glances. Finally, she turned directly toward me and snarled, "Aren't you Frau Williscroft?"

I wondered if I had offended her in some way, but tried to answer pleasantly and with a bit of humor.

"Yes, I am. Is that bad? You are looking so disturbed. I'm sorry if I have offended you."

She looked at me with a bit of a twinkle in her eyes and said, "Frau Williscroft, I don't know if I should love you or hate you. Before my children started going to that Sunday school, we could spend Sunday at Grandma's, go on an all-day picnic, or any number of fun things. Now, it doesn't matter what we suggest doing, a hue and cry goes up from our kids. They absolutely refuse to do anything or go anywhere until after Sunday school. It is funny in a way, but sometimes it makes us so mad we could shake them all good and wring your necks!" She spat out the last words, glaring at me angrily.

Somehow the whole thing struck me as so amusing that I burst out laughing. She stared at me a moment, then began laughing with me. We sat there in the streetcar and laughed and giggled like two schoolgirls. People turned, looking at us curiously.

When we managed to get hold of ourselves and talk, I told her she was a very privileged woman. The fact that her children were going to Sunday school and loving it was something to be thankful for. They were learning to know and love God, to avoid what is evil and to love the good. She and her husband would one day be very thankful for the Sunday school. She agreed and hugged me.

A few days later her husband came by and left a fifty-mark note for the children's work. Hurrah for Sunday schools!

Women's ministries have always been near to my heart. Many women attended the little Griesheim chapel. They were an unused power in the church. Why not organize them into an active force that God could use? They were thrilled and excited over this idea and gave their wholehearted support. We prayed for Germany, for Griesheim, and last, but not least, for the Bible School. They singled out people in town or in their own families for whom to pray. I gave them names and pictures of missionaries. They were to pray for them for a month. Then new names were given. We made prayer lists and prayed over them until the answer came. We did all the mending for the students, much to their joy. Mending was always a problem, due to a limited school staff and an even more limited budget.

The ladies were growing in the Lord and excited to see that God could use them. Paul was touched by the eager response of the women to every opportunity to serve. He called on them often to help in various ways. He also helped and encouraged me in my leadership position. We ladies didn't know it at first, but God had something special for us to do. He showed us in His time.

The chapel was so crowded that there wasn't even standing room. The air got bad, and we were troubled that people might stop coming if the situation worsened. I talked it over with the ladies and we decided to pray about this special problem for a week. At our meeting the following week, I felt I had an answer. Why don't we start a building fund? Apparently everyone felt the same way. They were a hundred percent for it.

I gave the gals little boxes to put on the table at meal times. Everyone in the family would try to drop something in the box, even if they only had a pfennig. We did this for a year. At year's end, on a Sunday morning, the ladies presented our German pastor, Cornelius Mohr, a check for a thousand marks to start a building fund.

The whole church became inspired over this start. They prayed, gave, and worked. A little man came by one day, stayed with us awhile, and worked for his keep. Paul noticed a native shrewdness about him. He got a sudden inspiration and sent the fellow out to look for an appropriate lot to start our church on. That little guy came back with the owner's signature to sell us the best lot in town. It was on the main street and near a streetcar stop. It was large enough for a building the size we would need, and some parking space. Best of all, it carried a price tag we could afford. Paul and I have always thanked God for tiny Herr Seidel and the lot God led him to.

The work began in earnest. A Christian architect drew up the blueprint of a building we could afford. It would also give us plenty of room to grow for years to come. One day the United States Army Corps of Engineers showed up with heavy earth-moving machines. They had the basement dug in a day. Men, women, young people, and children worked together. They carried heavy building blocks while a Christian bricklayer laid them. It was hard work, but nobody minded. They were working for the Lord and His church. That lightened the task. Students from *Berea* came to help whenever they had a spare minute. Paul, all the while, stood by, strong, steady, and encouraging. In some of the hard places, when we seemed to be at a standstill or faced a perplexing problem, Paul was there with his cheery, "We are going to make it, folks, we and God together."

Paul had a vision. He saw a beautiful church on that building site. It would stand as a beacon, drawing people to the light. It would meet a need in Griesheim. God would see to it that the work would be finished.

It took a long time. We built when the money was there. When it ran out we prayed and gave and held steady until we had enough to start building again. It was a slow, tedious process, but eventually a lovely church opened its doors to "whosoever will." Today this is one of the finest, most thriving churches in the State of *Hessen*. It had its ups and downs over the years, but God was faithful to the vision of that little group of refugee Christians who dared to step out on faith and build a monument to God's glory.

I visited this church a while back. It was recently renovated and looked fresh and new. Best of all, it was filled, balcony and below, with worshipping Christians, old and young. There were many university students among them and whole families I had never met before. As we praised and worshipped God together, the chorus kept singing in my heart, "Surely the presence of the Lord is in this place."

The Williscroft family in Griesheim bei Darmstadt, Germany,

※

In the late summer of 1961, one of the heartbreaks missionaries must face came to our family. It was time to send our firstborn home to college. He had decided on one of our denominational colleges. We could never forget the picture of that tall, manly, spiritual young man as he started through the passageway to his plane waving and smiling. With tear-dimmed eyes and tight throats we walked out of the Frankfurt airport. Why? Hundreds, maybe thousands of missionaries have sent their children home for college. We tried to comfort each other, but our hearts were aching.

The drive home was made in silence. Now and then a dry sob escaped as Paul drove over the familiar autobahn. He seemed utterly heartbroken. His only comment was, "I feel as though we are driving away from Bob's funeral."

The house seemed empty and lonely when we got home. Beverly was away at camp. Only Big Kitty, our large tiger cat, greeted us at the door, meowing mournfully. Bob was her friend and favorite. I went upstairs and started to tidy up his room just to be doing something.

Paul was in his office going over papers on his cluttered desk. There was something comforting and familiar about the routine.

Then the phone rang. Paul shouted up to me, "Honey, Honey, it's Bob!" I almost tumbled down the stairs in my haste to hear his voice again. His plane had a stopover in Amsterdam, so he took the opportunity to call us. That did us so much good we were able, for the moment, to dry our tears and get on with the business at hand. We learned, in the following weeks and months, to lean on God's sustaining grace as never before. He comforted us as a mother comforts her child. We could rest in Him, though deep inside, we couldn't quite get over the absence of our only son, our firstborn, our pride and joy.

Christmas time came and went. Oh, how we all missed Bob on this first Christmas without him. He spent the holidays with my brother, Walt Buck, and his family in Billings, Montana, where Walt was pastoring. Bob loved Billings.

He returned to college after Christmas, only to pack his things and drive back to Billings to attend the state college there. He let us know about it after he was settled in. We could tell from his letters that things were not right with him spiritually, and we prayed desperately night and day.

One day in May the letter came we hoped would never be written. It was a long letter, sad in parts, rebellious in others. He decided our way of life wasn't for him. He was an unbeliever, he declared. He felt he couldn't accept Christian truth anymore. He wrote on and on, trying to make his position clear and, possibly, trying to soften it a little for us. I am sure we aged ten years overnight.

We had to carry on our work, but the joy had gone out of everything. We couldn't laugh or smile. Every day was senseless drudgery. Our son was lost. That refrain rang in our ears night and day. How could we even want to go to heaven when our son wouldn't be there?

Spring passed into summer and summer into fall. Beverly graduated from high school in Frankfurt in June. As autumn arrived, she started school at *Berea*. They had been admitting girls for several years. She enjoyed it and school helped ease the pain she suffered over Bob. Autumn turned to winter. Christmas came and went.

Our hearts were still heavy over Bob. We had been in Germany almost six more years. We wanted to go home. We yearned to see our son.

Bob left college and joined the navy. His letters sounded unsettled and restless. We wanted to see him, talk to him, try to discover what was bothering him.

The work, both German and GI, had grown and together were just too much for us. Paul needed to make other arrangements to take care of both ministries, before we could even think of a furlough.

He got in touch with our mission, and they arranged to have a very fine and capable man, Richard Fulmer, come over to take charge of the servicemen's work. He, his wife, and three daughters arrived in Germany not long after Christmas. Everything was new and strange to them, but they adjusted wonderfully and soon fit right into the picture. The service people loved and accepted them readily. We felt comfortable now about leaving the servicemen's work.

Finding the right person to pick up the Christian Ed program wasn't easy. A lady missionary from another field had done this type of work and was willing to assist with our program. We were thankful to turn most of it over to her, with the exception of some small phases that Paul felt needed his personal attention. That was the situation as we boarded an Icelandic Airlines plane and once more crossed the ocean we had learned to know and love in its many moods.

It was late August. We wanted to get Beverly settled in Southern California College in time for classes. Preparing for the trip was a big job. We were all tired. It was wonderful to settle down in the big plane, forget all our cares, and relax to the hum of the huge turbo-jet engines. Good-bye Germany, until we meet again. *Auf wiedersehen.*

CHAPTER TWENTY-SIX

The flight was long. We enjoyed an interesting stopover in Iceland. There are so many hot springs that houses are warmed by them and they are the source of power for much of the industry. Huge greenhouses where tropical fruits are grown are heated from those marvelous hot springs. We thoroughly enjoyed the stopover and decided we'd do it again on the way back to Germany.

This was the most tiring, monotonous trip one could imagine. We missed the leisurely ocean voyages. We could rest and relax for five days or a week before the strenuous days of getting settled and starting deputation travel.

Not so now. We were tired when we started and more tired when we landed. It took us a long time to feel ready for travel again. Fortunately, overseas flights get shorter and shorter all the time. One can save time by flying. If preparations for the trip aren't too exacting, one feels almost ready to start itinerating upon arrival.

Beverly was excited to be in the States once more. She had fallen in love with everything here on our last furlough. Now, full of excitement, with sparkling eyes and pink cheeks, she joined us as we looked for Bob. He was supposed to be somewhere in Kennedy Airport.

We saw two ladies watching us with great interest. As soon as they could, they ran smiling up to us with open arms. To our joy, one of them was Dorothea Anderson, formerly from our church in Conrad, Montana. She was now working in New York for the Colgate family of toothpaste fame. Her friend, Evelyn Johnson, lived in upstate New York. She arranged for us to use her pretty little home while we were in that area. We could hardly believe it. Our Father God is so loving and faithful to His kids.

We soon saw Bob, dressed in his navy uniform, striding nonchalantly toward us. We all tried to act happy and cheerful, but it wasn't exactly a joyful reunion. Bob's whole personality had changed. He was edgy, defensive, self-centered. He seemed to feel the need of inserting expletives that were off limits in our home, between every other word. We had the impression he was trying to demonstrate his newfound freedom to do as he pleased. It was with heavy hearts that we gathered our luggage, picked up our car that had been shipped earlier, and headed for the borrowed house in upstate New York. Bob was on leave, so he went with us. We were glad for that. We hoped these days together would break the ice and at least a semblance of the old relationship could be restored.

Evelyn and Dorothea had their own car, so they drove up ahead of us to help get us settled in. The place was lovely. Evelyn even laid out certain records she thought Bob would enjoy, travel magazines and other reading material that would appeal to a young man. The cupboards were filled with edibles, as was the refrigerator. Everything was provided for our comfort and pleasure. I think even Bob was touched by the genuine Christian love displayed. The ladies soon took their leave and we were alone together as a family for the first time in many long months.

In this warm intimacy we found we were still family. We loved each other and all of us had much to share. Bob opened his heart and told of the lonely days and nights when he wrestled with himself over his beliefs. Could he go on pretending he was a Christian when he didn't believe anymore? He finally decided he could not. That's when he wrote us about it. The letter sounded harsh, because he probably wasn't sure how to tell us.

God's love and caring surely prompted a total stranger to turn her home over to us for two weeks. It was just what we needed to find each other again. Though Bob hadn't changed regarding his faith, we were comforted. We knew he needed more time, a lot more time.

We planned to arrive in Southern California early enough for Beverly to start college on opening day. Bob still had leave time, so he drove with us as far as Milwaukee. A young ex-serviceman friend whom we wished to see lived there. The few days with him were delightful. We enjoyed his lovely Christian family, and I think the enjoyment was mutual.

Bob had to leave us then and return to New London, where he was stationed. We hated the parting but were so thankful for the time together. I felt a part of my heart go with him. Paul was brave, but I could see how he struggled to show Bob a happy, loving face as we said our good-byes at the airport.

Southern California was brown and dry as it always is in late summer and early fall. It was so hot the heat was smothering. We longed to spend all day in a swimming pool. The hot weather was especially trying for Beverly. We had learned earlier that she had a congenital heart problem. In Germany, shortly before we left, she underwent tests at the Heidelberg University Clinic. Doctors there discovered that she had a large hole between the two upper heart ventricles and immediate surgery was advised.

When her doctor heard we were leaving for the States in a few weeks, he suggested having the surgery done in the UCLA Clinic, as they were more advanced in heart surgery. We all agreed. The German heart surgeon had trained at UCLA, so he put in a phone call. In five minutes arrangements were made for the following August. That's how busy they were. Beverly wasn't disturbed by the long wait. She was glad for a year's respite.

Paul and I wondered how we could bear the anxiety for so long. The German surgeon confided to us the seriousness of Beverly's condition. This type of congenital heart condition worsens as a child grows older. We could lose her at any time if she attempted anything too strenuous, overdid things, or lived under too much stress. Our hearts were heavy. We could do only one thing to find peace of mind: turn her completely over to God.

Registration day at SCC. The campus was swarming with students from everywhere. We ran into Bob Goodman, whom we'd known since the Goodman kids and the Williscroft kids played together at camp meeting years and years ago. We had seen him only months before, when he spent some time in Germany with the Air National Guard. He visited in our home and we enjoyed having him. He had decided on SCC, too. It was a wonderful reunion. He and Beverly had been good pals in Germany. It was a relief for her now to see a familiar face, especially such a jolly, happy one.

Bob Goodman and some other fellows rented an apartment near the college. He assured us there were some vacant ones. Why didn't we come and look them over? There was even a swimming pool. That was all we needed to hear. We checked them out, and in a matter of minutes rented a nice apartment.

Soon it became clear we were the only renters over thirty. Most of the others were students, but that didn't matter. We enjoyed the young folks and Beverly was in her element. I could spend whole days in the pool if I wanted to – wonderful, lazy days. It was like we were on vacation. For two weeks we really were. Then Paul felt it was time to start our deputation travels.

He started out alone, leaving me behind to make a home for Beverly. She was going through adjustment problems and culture shock. She couldn't relate to American kids and held herself aloof. She didn't understand the American dating game. To her, with her European background, you went out with a boy only when you were seriously interested in him. I tried to help her in this area, but I am from an earlier generation. We dated, but much more casually. In fact, I tended to agree with Beverly. What she didn't understand, though, was that a girl has the key in her hands. With humor and a friendly manner, she can steer an evening in the direction she wanted, without humiliating her escort. It took Beverly a long time to get a handle on this. In the meantime she suffered.

As the weeks passed, however, things improved. A lovely girl, also a missionary's daughter, took Beverly under her wing. She briefed her on the things she didn't understand. Beverly gradually gained self-confidence. She came out of her shell and began to have fun with the others.

Her daddy came home sometimes on Friday evenings when he was near enough. He took us with him to Sunday services where he would be ministering. Beverly was usually invited to sing in the meetings. She had a good voice and was majoring in music. It helped boost her self-esteem when people told her they were blessed through her song. We were both encouraged and uplifted through these little breaks from everyday life.

In late spring Bob wrote us he had met the girl of his dreams. She came from Germany and had lived in the States only a short time. She was the most beautiful, the most wonderful, the most perfect girl in the world. They planned to marry in the fall. We must meet her.

We wrote the kind of letter that any caring parents would write, pleading with him not to do anything hastily. He was young and inexperienced. Couldn't they wait awhile and get to know one another better? He was just getting started in the navy. He was in no position to support a wife.

Letters flew back and forth. We pled, exhorted, reasoned, all to no avail. He was determined to get married.

He paid us a short visit, enabling us to discuss the matter face to face. He was still adamant about getting married. We felt much better about his young lady when he shared with us that she encouraged him to visit us and talk things over.

After much prayer, we came to the conclusion it would be best just to accept the situation, love his choice of a life's partner, and leave the results with God. Bob went back to New London content over our attitude. Christine was probably relieved, too. We realized some things can't be changed. Such situations must be accepted, as the old prayer goes.

With Beverly's surgery coming up, we probably wouldn't be able to attend the wedding. We were really sorry about that. If all went well with Beverly, we planned to visit them in New London on our way back to Germany. In the meantime, a nice correspondence developed between Christine and us. We learned to love her and looked forward to knowing her personally.

Summer came, the summer of 1964. The summer break came for Beverly. Paul planned a long trip along the coast and through Idaho and Montana. It was mainly for previously arranged missionary services, but also to give Beverly and me a much-needed holiday. Beverly's surgery loomed before us. We knew it was still a precarious situation since heart operations were still relatively new at that time. The doctors in both Germany and in UCLA explained the procedure and warned us of the hazards. We prayed much for her healing and also for wisdom to make the right decisions. Now it was in God's Hands.

Beverly was excited over the trip. She would see relatives in Washington, Idaho, and Montana. She sang in the meetings, made new friends, had fun with her cousins, and thoroughly enjoyed herself. The missionary services were blessed and people told us they felt uplifted afterwards. We showed slides with a taped commentary of our students singing, the Sunday school conventions, the servicemen singing and praying at the rallies, and many more interesting things. I smiled when Paul announced he would now show a slide presentation of exactly seven and a half minutes and eight seconds. I noticed his annoyed little frown as a ripple of subdued laughter flowed through the congregation. The slides really did last just that long, but the announcement always sounded too exact.

The whole trip was wonderful. Beverly felt better than since coming to California. If only the dark shadow of the forthcoming operation weren't hovering over us, how happy we could be.

August, 1964. The reserved bed in UCLA was ready. We got the word on a Monday. Beverly should check in on Tuesday afternoon to be ready for surgery early Wednesday morning. She was so much better all summer we hoped God had performed a miracle on our daughter's heart. We hoped that for a long time now. Beverly did, too.

When we checked her in, we asked the doctor if he would examine her heart once more. He could understand that, as she seemed so improved. He did warn us, however, not to get our hopes too high. She probably looked and felt so well because of the absence of stress so common to college kids during the school year. He didn't know what an active summer lay behind us. He did test her heart again and X-rayed it, too. To our great disappointment, the hole in her heart was even larger, but God doesn't make mistakes. He knew exactly what He was doing.

The heart specialist in Germany had informed us that they lost one patient in twenty; in the States the death rate was one patient in a hundred. It is probably much less now. This knowledge did comfort us during those long, anxious hours.

We left Beverly at the hospital that evening, and drove home with heavy hearts. We prayed all night. Paul touched the Lord right away and was the very picture of peace and confidence. Not so with me. I went through a hard battle. How could I go on living if Beverly didn't survive the surgery? Life would be meaningless without her. She was our sunshine, our pride and joy. I literally wrestled with the Lord like Jacob of old.

He kept saying, "Will you just turn your precious daughter over to me? Give thanks for all the years you've had her to love and enjoy? Surrender her to me. Don't resist. Stop fighting. Trust me to do the right thing." The battle raged for hours.

Finally, as dawn was breaking, I sobbed a weak, "Yes Lord," lifting my hands in total surrender. "She is yours, to do with as you will. I thank you for giving her to us to love and treasure. Now I give her back to you. Your will be done, Father."

The long struggle was over. Peace came at last. We sing sometimes of perfect peace. Now I knew exactly what the term meant. Beverly was so completely in God's hands that I lost all jurisdiction over the matter. Whether she lived or died was all right with me. She wasn't my possession anymore. She was God's, and I could praise Him for being so wise and wonderful in all His ways.

We sat in the waiting room at UCLA, and God's peace rested upon us. The waiting room was full of people. All of them had a loved one undergoing some sort of serious surgery. Some were weeping softly; others were praying; some were staring blankly at nothing. All were frightened and bewildered.

I asked Paul if we possibly weren't normal. We were filled with a peace we never knew before. Troubled people around us asked why we were there. When they heard our teenage daughter was undergoing open-heart surgery, they did a double take and asked in amazement, "And you're just sitting there as relaxed as though you had no problem?"

We assured them we loved our daughter as much as any of them did their loved ones. We had put her in greater Hands than ours or the surgeons. They could only stare at us in total disbelief. We had beautiful opportunities to share our faith with many of them in the days that followed.

Hours went by – long, long hours. Every time a door opened, everybody turned expectantly. Despite our peaceful hearts, we turned like all the others. Had Beverly come through all right? Or did God, in his all-knowing wisdom, see fit to take her to Himself? The door suddenly swung open again. In the doorway stood our doctor, grinning from ear to ear. He beckoned us. We dashed to the door, almost tumbling over waiting people.

"How is she?" we both shrieked in one breath.

He patted us on the back and, still grinning, answered, "Wonderful! Just wonderful! You can see her for a moment. There she is, just being taken to intensive care."

We looked down the hall. A gurney was waiting. We hurried over. There lay our little girl, smiling weakly up at us. She was still strongly sedated, but she knew us. She seemed to be mouthing that everything was going to be all right.

The dreaded operation was over. Beverly had come through with flying colors. The doctor called her his miracle girl. He told us the danger point of open-heart surgery is when the patient is being taken off the heart-lung machine. A special electric shock is given to start the heart pumping on its own again. Sometimes the heart doesn't respond at this point and the patient dies. In Beverly's case, her heart never stopped. There was always a faint pulsating. He said it was really weird. At the moment when they should have given the electric shock, her heart just started beating normally again on its own. He called it a miracle. God was honored and glorified all over that great hospital because of this happening.

We knew now why God hadn't healed Beverly without surgery. He wanted to reveal himself to the skeptics and others in the UCLA Clinic. We had many opportunities to share our faith during the long hours of Beverly's convalescence. A Jewish woman who lost her sister there after heart surgery, and a Catholic lady, mother of Beverly's roommate, both rededicated their lives to the Lord in the hospital waiting room. We knelt together, regardless of those around us, and God touched their lives as we prayed.

CHAPTER TWENTY-SEVEN

All the way to the hospital to bring our darling home our hearts were singing. The operation was over. She was recuperating far beyond the doctor's and hospital staff's expectations. Though still weak, she experienced a sense of well-being she had never known before. Her heart was mended. She could breathe deeply without pain. It didn't matter anymore on which side she lay or slept. We felt deeply grateful to our Heavenly Father. He gave us our hoped-for miracle. It didn't come in the way we thought, but even more wonderfully. We stretched and grew in our Christian walk; many lives at the hospital were touched as they witnessed what God did for Beverly. Best of all, the doctor and his staff gave God the credit for the way the operation and recovery went.

The drive home with our dear daughter was one of the loveliest we ever knew. What a joy as we walked into our apartment. Heidi, Bev's kitty, lay on the bed with her newly acquired family. They were all purring a loving welcome. I don't think I ever saw Beverly happier to be home than at that moment. Paul and I tucked her into bed, as the drive home had tired her.

She couldn't sleep, though. It was so wonderful to have all the dear, familiar things around her, to know Mom and Dad were hovering nearby, to listen to the soft purring of Heidi and her kittens. The operation was over. She was alive, more alive than she had ever been in all her eighteen years. The sophomore year of college would begin in two weeks with all its challenges, friends, and fun. Life was good. Life was for living.

The two weeks before college opening day were filled with preparing Beverly's school wardrobe. Trying to keep our daughter as quiet as possible was a job. The doctor advised six weeks of rest before starting classes. Beverly would hear nothing of that. She insisted she felt better than ever before in her life. Rest was very important, however. Her heart, as well her whole system, was recovering from a tremendous strain. Rest was the medicine she needed now.

It was very frustrating when Beverly insisted she intended to be in college on opening day. I think one reason she was so set on being there at the start was because students donated the twenty-two pints of blood necessary for her surgery. This would be a good opportunity to thank them as a group.

On opening day Beverly felt "just wonderful." Her eyes were bright, her color good. She walked to help strengthen her legs and every day tried being a bit more active. It would be exciting to see all her friends again. She could hardly wait to get to the campus.

Beverly came home at noon simply radiant. Everyone was kind and attentive, her classes were interesting and challenging, her professors were "real neat," as she expressed it, and she looked forward to a great semester. I was glad I did not keep her from enjoying that special first day.

The fall months were full of activity for all of us. Paul was away most of the time, busy with deputational ministry in the churches. I stayed home to be with Beverly for the last time we would actually live together as a family. I never regretted that. It was hard for Paul to do all that traveling alone. It was not easy for me, either. I missed him every day. We wrote long letters to each other about everything that was going on in our respective areas. It was a red-letter day for each of us when one of us got a letter from the other.

Beverly was busy and happy with friends and college activities. She improved a little every day, in spite of a heavy study load. By mid-October she looked the picture of health. She told me often, she never knew before her surgery how it felt to be well. She thought everyone felt tired and dragged out just like she did. Now she exulted in her sense of well-being.

We both enjoyed the lovely California weather through October and November. Our thoughts were often of Paul traveling through North Dakota and Montana, where snow already had fallen. He couldn't even be home for Thanksgiving. We missed him more than ever at that special holiday time.

Beverly invited several students who couldn't make it home for Thanksgiving to be our guests. Everyone had a good time despite Paul's empty chair. We looked forward to Christmas, though, when our loved one planned to be with us.

It is amazing how quickly the days between Thanksgiving and Christmas go by for adults and how slowly they crawl for children. Christmas was upon us almost before we were ready for it. Beverly and I went shopping for that just-right present for her dad. We shopped every store in our area. We weren't sure just what we were looking for, but it must be useful, good looking, of excellent quality, and something that Paul wanted.

One day we went back to a store where we looked before. The first thing that met our eye was a beautiful man's robe. It was of the softest, finest wool in gentle tones of grey and soft red, both colors Paul loved. Only that one robe was left. It was exactly his size. Even though it was quite expensive, we decided we could pinch pennies somewhere else and give the man in our lives a gift he would enjoy for years to come.

Paul did just that. The robe was so soft and light it could fit easily into the smallest traveling bag. He was still using and enjoying it at the time of his death. It showed no signs of wear and the colors were as lovely as on that Christmas Eve when he so joyfully received it from his two girls.

Christmas was all one could desire. Olga Olsson, our fellow missionary from Germany, was also home on furlough and joined us for the holidays. The weather was like summer in Southern California. Roses were blooming, birds singing, the air balmy and warm. We took Olga to the beach to watch the waves roll in with surfers on the crests. We went on other short excursions together and had a lovely time. Our last trip together, before Olga began itinerating again, was to the New Year's Rose Parade in Pasadena. We left our apartment early and found a good place with a fine view of everything.

It was a happy week and a half for us all. Olga left January 2 to start her deputation. It was lonely without her, but we had little time to think about that. Our things had to be packed and ready to send back to Germany in a few days. The simplest way to ship them was by ocean freight from Long Beach. We decided not to take some of our most-treasured possessions back to Germany with us but to store them in the attic of our home in Union Gap.

We arranged to sublet our apartment to a young married couple from the college. They got it much below what we were paying, with the condition Beverly would keep her room as long as she needed or wanted it. These arrangements seemed good and practical. We were happy to have found a solution to Beverly's housing situation, as well as a place to leave our furniture.

The day for our departure to Germany came all too soon. Our goods were shipped, our good-byes said, our car sold, and we were on our way to the Los Angeles airport. A college friend of Beverly's agreed to take us in his car.

This was another sad drive. We just couldn't imagine leaving our baby alone to shift for herself and manage however she could. She was in college on a scholarship, but naturally she had other needs too. I was leaving a big part of myself behind. Life would never be the same for any of us.

It was evening when we boarded the plane, after a few tears, many hugs, and warm promises to write often. As we circled over the city with its millions of twinkling lights, we thought about our darling alone down there in that great, wicked city.

How would she fare? Was she mature enough to handle it? Would she remain true to the Savior who brought her so wonderfully through her heart ordeal?

We held hands as we silently prayed for God's protection, His keeping power, and His everlasting love to overshadow our precious daughter through the long years ahead. Our tears flowed freely now that we were alone, but we sensed God's presence with us. We dried our tears, committed our dear one again into the almighty Hands of our Father, and were comforted.

Another term of service in Germany lay ahead of us. Alone. What did it hold?

CHAPTER TWENTY-EIGHT

The flight to New York was smooth and pleasant. The past few days had been busy and hectic, trying to get everything done before our departure. The emotional trauma of leaving Beverly had also taken its toll. We felt weak and spent as the lights of Los Angeles faded from view. We finally relaxed and settled down for a long night flight. People about us chatted, laughed, played cards, and got acquainted. We dozed on, oblivious to everything.

The plane landed in New York during a blinding snowstorm. With the time difference, it was morning. We landed safely, deplaned, but found very soon there were no flights out of New York due to the weather.

We planned to fly from New York to New London, Connecticut, to spend a few days with Robert (he now answered to the beautiful name we gave him at birth) and Christine. We hadn't been able to attend their wedding in September because of Beverly's surgery. That had been a great letdown for them. We couldn't bear the thought of disappointing them again.

Paul inquired around, while I stayed with our luggage. He heard a train would be leaving New York early in the afternoon for New London; that is, if the weather cleared up a little. It did. A limousine was just leaving the airport for Grand Central Station. We managed to make it in time to get to the station and buy our tickets. A friendly policeman took us in tow through a back way and put us on the train just as it pulled out.

The few days with Robert and Christine were lovely. We liked Christine. We found her to be a pretty and practical German girl. She kept a nice home and was a good cook, besides selling fine women's wear in a fashionable lady's salon.

I think she was almost afraid to meet us. She hadn't known any missionaries and probably wondered what sort of specimens we would be.

These days together were a time of getting to know each other. They were over too soon. It was time to get back to the city. Paul needed to take care of a few things before we left the States. Our farewells were tinged with sadness, but Robert was in the navy and hoped sometime soon to make it to Germany. Christine's family was in Germany, too, so that was another incentive to come over when they could. Then we were off for the Big Apple again.

One matter that lay strongly on Paul's heart was to contact Dave Wilkerson. Dave was a very busy man, but his cordial welcome as Paul phoned him warmed our hearts. He invited us to come directly to Teen Challenge Headquarters. There we lunched with him and others of his fine team while Paul discussed what was on his heart.

He felt very definitely led by the Lord to publish Dave's famous best seller, *The Cross and the Switchblade,* in German. Dave was excited over the possibility, as together they worked out all the details. I could see Paul was itching to get to Germany and start things moving.

Before we left, Dave introduced us to some precious young people who had gone through the Teen Challenge program. They were former drug addicts, street fighters, prostitutes, and had done almost everything Satan tempts young people with. They kicked drugs and alcohol cold turkey, while dedicated workers prayed with them, read them the Bible, loved, and encouraged them. Wonderful miracles of complete deliverance happened. Those radiant young men and women were living witnesses of the mighty power of God. Teen Challenge today is a great international Christian rehabilitation program with one of the highest success records of any rehabilitation program anywhere.

We left Teen Challenge with a new zeal to work with youth. Paul's eagerness to get *The Cross and the Switchblade* started in German was contagious. I, too, was tingling with excitement. I thought of what this book meant to youth in America, both to those in trouble and to those challenged to do something about it.

Paul and I had one yearning prayer at that moment: "Oh, God, help us with the publishing of this book in German! Make it a best seller. Bless it to German youth, as you have blessed it here in the States."

Our Icelandic flight was scheduled to take off at midnight. We took our leave of Dave and his wonderful co-workers. They assured us of their prayers for the success of our German edition of *The Cross and the Switchblade*. It was quite late. The hours at Teen Challenge flew by so fast we couldn't believe only an hour and a half was left before our flight. With a trip on the subway and a bus, we made it to the airport with little time to spare.

CHAPTER TWENTY-NINE

The winter flight with Icelandic Airlines was really special for that time of year. Our stopover in Iceland was enjoyable. We missed having Beverly with us. She had been so excited about Iceland on our trip back to the States. Still, Paul and I found pleasure in being alone together. For a long time we had been unable to do things with just each other. We decided to take a sight-seeing trip, but when we went down to the hotel lobby to join the group, we found we were the only ones ready to brave the elements. The bus was canceled, but a taxi was arranged for us, and off we went to see the sights.

The driver was a member of the Assembly of God church in Reykjavik, the largest city in Iceland. He took us to meet the pastor, who immediately invited Paul to speak at the service scheduled for that evening.

We spent the rest of the winter day looking at geysers in out-of-the-way places, wandering through greenhouses heated by natural hot-water springs. Bananas, pineapple, and other exotic tropical fruits are grown in abundance in these hothouses. Another interesting diversion was looking at all the beautiful woolens sold in the air-terminal store. They were quite expensive, but very nice.

The service that evening was warm, informal, and packed with young people. We loved that and felt right in our element. Paul talked to the kids from his heart, sharing about Teen Challenge and what God is doing today for and through young people. He challenged them to give their all to Jesus. They flocked to the altar when the invitation was given. We had a wonderful time of prayer, praise, and commitment together. It was a beautiful evening we remembered for a long time.

Early the next morning we boarded our plane and flew off through a murky overcast. Next stop, Luxemburg. From there, Jack Hetzel, a fine ex-serviceman then working with service people himself, planned to meet and bring us home. It was a several-hour flight to Luxemburg, but the weather was fair with a brisk tail wind, so we arrived earlier than planned. Jack was waiting for us at the terminal, a warm grin lighting his face.

He loaded our luggage in his car, and we were off for Germany, about a three-hour drive to our home in Griesheim. The Hetzels had occupied it during the last days of our furlough and were still there. I was so excited I could hardly wait.

I knew Paul was anxious to get home because of the book. I wanted that, too, but I think I was lonesome for the old house where we had lived so happily as a family. It was plain, old-fashioned homesickness.

Our excitement increased as we drove off the *Autobahn* and through the old cobbled streets of Griesheim. We were like a couple of kids.

One of us would shout, "Look! There's the depot. It hasn't changed one bit."

Then the other would point excitedly at something else that looked dear and familiar, crying, "Just look at that! There's the old streetcar terminal. Isn't it exciting." Those common, everyday objects were all a bit of home. We even loved the dirty, slushy, cobblestone streets. We were home again.

Finally we drove down our street, *Hofmann Strasse*. There stood the old house, looking even more dilapidated than we remembered it. Some of the windows were broken and stuffed with old rags or papers to help keep out the winter blasts. It needed painting. Some of the stucco had fallen off, too, and the yard looked neglected. We couldn't believe our eyes. Jack explained the situation in answer to our questioning looks. In order to keep the house, rent was required while we were away. Our colleagues had, in all good faith, sublet it to an American military family. They were either not interested in keeping it up, or possibly, did not know what to do. In any event, to quote our neighbors, "It looked like a slum." The Hetzels were just living there until we arrived, as a stopgap measure. They were trying to make do, fixing what they could and leaving the rest for us to decide when we got there. Neighbors told us we should have seen the house before the Hetzels moved in.

We were shocked and upset that people could be so careless, but with the help of students and friends we soon got the place pretty well renovated. Later in the summer our landlord painted the house. The old place looked clean and homelike again, and we were happy.

Other unfortunate things had transpired during our absence that caused us much heartache. The blossoming little pioneer work in Griesheim had gone through hard times with the building program, and there were other problems. Paul was the motivation behind everything. When he was gone, there wasn't the proper supervision, guidance, or encouragement. The Sunday school was down, too. Some of the best workers were now in Bible School. The children missed them, and there was no one to help and encourage them when their parents were not interested. Even the Christian Education Program for Germany was going through a crisis.

We were heartsick. It is so easy, in situations like that, to look around for someone to blame. That helps nobody, though. Paul just tried to pick up the pieces and start from there. Slowly things began to get better, and one new and exciting thing began to develop.

Paul worked with *Leuchter Verlag* (the publishing endeavor he had started back in Stuttgart so long ago) to print David Wilkerson's best-seller *The Cross and the Switchblade*. A university student in Griesheim consented to translate it into German with the help of Hildegard Zornow. Hildegard translated all our Sunday school quarterlies over the years and did a fine job. She understood translating and liked doing it. I'm not sure at this point just who did more on getting the book ready for printing, but it was beautifully done. Paul was more than gratified when it became a best seller in Germany, too.

Many testimonial letters came to us, and to the *Verlag*, of how reading the book changed people's lives. One especially heartwarming letter came from a young man who would have nothing to do with God or religion. His mother was a devout Christian who constantly prayed and believed God for the salvation of her son. One evening while the young man was waiting for a crony to pick him up for a night of revelry, he picked up a book lying on the coffee table. His mother had left *The Cross and the Switchblade* there, with a prayer that her son might read it.

He became interested. He couldn't put it down. He sent his friend away with a lame excuse and continued reading. When his mother arrived home late in the evening, she found her son on his knees by the couch, the book before him. He was sobbing as though his heart would break. His mother knelt beside him, her heart pounding for joy and thankfulness. When they rose from their knees in the wee small hours of the morning, Mom had a new son. He was a full-fledged member of God's wonderful family.

There was much more in the letter. He told of his joy in the Lord. He loved the church his mother attended and went with her there. He was sharing his newfound faith with his friends and fellow workers. What a triumph for the Lord. That was just one of many similar letters. The book was a success. God was honoring and using it.

Not long after the book came out, a charismatic sisterhood in Darmstadt, The Sisters of Mary, invited Dave Wilkerson to Darmstadt to minister to youth. They offered the use of their large chapel.

Their advertising was outstanding. People were alerted to something special through large placards everywhere with only three six-inch words: DAVY IS COMING! Time and place were below in smaller letters. It was interesting to watch people in streetcars, trains, before shop windows, or anywhere else where placards were posted. They would look at the poster and ask aloud, "Davy? Who is he? A film star, a singer, some other kind of celebrity?"

David Wilkerson came. People flocked to the Sisters of Mary chapel to see and hear him. The crowds were mainly young people, but many older ones came, too. I will never forget those evenings.

Young people gave their lives to Christ. Dave spoke right into their hearts. They were moved. They wept and sobbed as they laid down their drugs, cigarettes, and other things that kept them in bondage. Paul showed Dave's book, presenting it in such a way that everybody wanted a copy. It was a thrilling time.

Paul always felt that getting out *The Cross and the Switchblade* was one of the highlights of his ministry in Germany. He also considered it one of the most blessed and productive projects he had attempted up to that time.

One exciting result of this great book was that it came out during the first wave of the *Jesus People* movement in Germany. It played a prominent role in reaching and strengthening young people caught up in this ever-widening stream of youth seeking reality.

Later the movie of the same name came to cinemas all over Germany. It made a huge impact and created new interest for the book. It is still, after all these years, one of the most popular books sold from *Leuchter Verlag*.

When we returned to Germany at that time, early in 1965, the little church in Griesheim was almost ready to dedicate the lower floor. Paul was so glad he could be a part of that. The lower auditorium was adequate for services and the Sunday-school rooms were finished enough to use. It was a great milestone for the little group to move into their own building. There was still much to do, but everybody helped when possible.

When there were funds, we built. When they ran out, we stopped and prayed more money in. Then the work moved forward again. It was a great day for Paul and all the congregation when the sanctuary finally was dedicated. A nearby gardener and florist donated green shrubs and blooming flowers to decorate it. There was still much to be done before the little church could be called finished, but we could use most of it. That sufficed for the moment.

The dedication was lovely. People came from all the surrounding churches. The place was full, including the large balcony. Special music, testimonials, tributes to those who had helped so much, a word from the mayor and a dedication address from the German leader of the movement all contributed to a very special afternoon.

Paul training Christian workers in Germany

The people were finally in their building. Now it was time to start growing. Paul's assistant in the Christian Education Program, Dieter Mantey, started a boys' group. He led them very satisfactorily in a program of crafts, Bible, games, and fellowship. Before long he had most of the boys in our neighborhood coming to his group. We were all excited about it. Some of the girls from the Bible School helped me with a Missionette program. We started it mainly with girls from the neighborhood. The girls loved it. We sent to the States for the equipment we needed. The Missionettes in Germany was launched. Girls brought their friends. These friends, in turn, brought their friends. The work grew. Girls gave their lives to the Lord. They shared Jesus at school and at play. We made blue skirts, which they wore with white jerseys. In crafts class they made themselves Missionette badges. Everybody proudly wore her outfit to Missionette meetings. Other girls were attracted by the pretty outfits and the work kept growing.

Slumber parties in our house were wonderful times of learning and fun. Trips to the Frankfurter Zoo, where literature for children, wrapped like sticks of candy, were passed out, inspired the girls to share their faith. Field trips to museums and other cultural centers helped broaden the horizons of these young missionaries. The young ladies from the Bible School were learning by doing, along with their young charges. It was a great time in Griesheim.

CHAPTER THIRTY

In the summer of 1966 we were busy with tent meetings, children's meetings, and other activities, besides Paul's usual tight schedule with the Christian Ed program. My area of involvement was with children. In a well-attended tent meeting, I was busy helping in the children's afternoon, when a sudden strange weakness came over me. I managed to struggle through the afternoon, but staggered home afterwards.

Paul was shocked when I came in. My face was grey and a cold sweat covered my forehead, dribbling down over my cheeks. I dropped wearily into a chair, gasping, "Oh, I'm so sick!"

Paul sponged my face and made me a cup of tea. That helped and I managed to fix supper. I felt well enough to go to the children's meeting but was very tired when I got home. This went on for several days. Paul was worried, but a night's sleep usually put me on my feet again. We both thought I was probably overdoing it and weren't unduly anxious.

On a Sunday afternoon Paul had a meeting somewhere, but insisted I stay home and rest. I hated for him to go alone, but I didn't resist his urging. I had never felt so tired in my life.

After Paul left I went out to our back garden and settled down in a lawn chair for a long rest. Soon I was fast asleep.

Something startled me awake. A glance at my watch reminded me Paul would soon be home and would want a snack before the evening service. I stood up and found I was completely disoriented. I could barely find my stumbling way into the house. Paul found me, a huddled heap, in a corner of the couch.

He did all he could for me before church, assuring me as he reluctantly left, "We are going to the hospital tomorrow. This has gone on long enough. I'll get things going at church and come right back. I'll try and get hold of the doctor tonight and arrange for a thorough examination tomorrow."

The week in the hospital was a nightmare. One test followed another. The days went by. I grew weaker. The probing, the X-rays, and over and over again, the looking into my stomach. What were they doing to me? I couldn't stand much more.

"Please come with me to my private office, Missionary Williscroft. I must speak with you today." Our doctor and friend studied Paul's face. His eyes were sad and filled with compassion. "I'm so sorry! I have bad news for you. Please sit down. Your wife has an advanced case of stomach cancer. We must operate immediately. It could save her life, but I can promise nothing. This has been coming on for some time. Has she gone through a time of severe shock or stress in the past year? That could have started this, or perhaps hastened the advance of cancer already in an early stage."

His clear blue eyes looked deep into Paul's as though trying to read his thoughts. Paul couldn't answer right away. He was in a daze. The doctor's words came from far away. He felt he must be dreaming. This couldn't be happening to us.

Dimly the memory of my agony on our return to Germany a year and six months previously crossed his mind. Much of our work, that we thought to be in good order when we left Germany, had fallen apart and lay in shambles at our feet. He remembered my tears and prayers and my effort not to blame or condemn. Yes, the doctor laid his finger on the cause of my problem.

The doctor waited quietly for Paul to assimilate his words. Now and then he laid a gentle hand on his shoulder.

At last, as from a great distance, Paul forced himself to say three words, "Are you sure?"

"Absolutely! There is no doubt about it," was the doctor's solemn answer.

Paul was stunned. He couldn't move or speak for a few minutes. He sat with bowed head, his face in his hands. The doctor probably thought he was weeping. He wasn't! He was praying. Then a thought popped into his mind. He lifted his head and looked at the doctor.

"I want to ask a favor of you, Herr Doctor. My wife and I believe in prayer. I would like to take her home for just one week. I will have friends and loved ones hold a prayer vigil for her all week. If she isn't better by then, I will bring her back and you can go ahead with the surgery."

The doctor was astonished. Missionary Williscroft sounded assured and confident in spite of the awful news he had just received. How could he refuse that kind of faith? With tears in his eyes, he reached for Paul's hand. Paul took it as he rose to his feet, looking expectantly at the doctor.

"All right, Herr Williscroft. You may do that. I wish you luck. I'll call for the nurses to prepare your wife for leaving." Then he added, almost to himself, "One week won't matter much now, anyway."

So Paul brought me home. It was a dark, rainy Saturday. I was weak and ill. I think all the many tests were as much the problem as my illness. I had, as yet, been told nothing of my condition.

I sensed from Paul's stricken face, which he tried to conceal, that I must be quite sick. I determined not to ask questions, though. I would just wait until he was ready to tell me. He knew me well enough to understand I would want to know the truth, whatever it might be.

We sat a few minutes at the kitchen table. He made a pot of tea and some hot buttered toast. I wasn't hungry, nor was he, but we made a pretence of enjoying the snack. I sipped the tea in silence while he watched me.

Then he reached over and took my hand. As gently as possible he told me the doctor's verdict and his own counterproposal. His eyes were dark with the pain he felt, but there was triumph in his voice as he pressed my two hands in both of his and almost shouted, "Honey, we are going to lick this devilish thing! You'll see. God is greater than anything Satan can attempt. Do you agree?"

I did, but all I wanted at that moment was to lie down, close my eyes, and forget everything.

Paul wired for Beverly to join us and help in any way she could. He knew having her there would be better than a tonic for me. She joined us in just a few days.

She grieved for her mother, but always in my presence she wore a sunny smile. Her songs and music soothed and comforted me. I thanked God for her and that she could be there. After Paul alerted friends, family, and some of our supporting churches about my need and the prayer vigil they were starting in Germany, he began his own prayer program.

He shut himself in his office and prayed, hour after hour, day after day. He came out only to check on me, encourage Beverly, and take a bit of nourishment. Then he was on his knees again, or leaning back in his arm chair, his heart lifted in prayer.

This went on for a week. I could feel I was failing fast, in spite of all the prayers. I was too sick to take an interest in anything. I wanted to be with Jesus.

The prayer vigil began on the Saturday afternoon when we got home from the hospital. On Wednesday our dear missionary friends, the Walker Halls from Hong Kong, came by to greet us on their way home. They were saddened to see me so ill. I barely knew they were there.

Then Mrs. Hall laid her hand gently on my abdomen. She prayed softly, "Jesus, touch Gladys. I know it isn't time for her to go yet. Paul needs her. Their children need her. Thank you, Lord, for your healing power that is just the same today as it ever was. Thank you that you are healing Gladys. Amen."

They slipped quietly away. I hardly noticed their departure. I lay for awhile in a drowsy half sleep. Thoughts kept coming and going through my mind.

I'm so weak, but what is the matter with me? I don't want to die! I want to live. I will live. I will get well and serve the Lord as never before.

Slowly I put one foot out of bed, then the other. Weakness and dizziness enveloped me. Sitting on the edge of the bed, I noticed the clock. My husband would be coming from his prayer time and Beverly from a job in Darmstadt.

I wonder if I could manage to get to the kitchen. It would be fun to fix them a nice little supper. I'm going to try.

Carefully I stood up. Clutching a door knob here, a piece of furniture there, I made my way to the kitchen. I was weak, but felt stronger and better as I moved about. When my loved ones came in, they stared in astonishment to see the table prettily set and Mother, in a fresh housecoat, smiling at them from the kitchen door.

That was the beginning of a gradual improvement in my condition. We celebrated that evening, cautiously but joyfully. I had been literally surrounded with prayer since Saturday. The Halls' visit and her prayer somehow seemed to clinch the matter. A new desire to live was born in me. Each day I felt a little stronger and could do a wee bit more. Best of all, I was so freshly in love with Jesus, my family, the whole world, that living was a pure joy.

We went back to the hospital on Saturday, the day I was to undergo surgery if there were no change. We walked into the doctor's office. He stared at me as though he were looking at a ghost. Reaching out both hands to us with a look of awe, he murmured, almost in a whisper, "Frau Williscroft! You are better, aren't you? We are going to have to take more X-rays and tests before we even think of surgery now."

Paul smiled his little knowing smile. I'm sure he knew all the time what God could do. His faith never wavered or left room for doubt. I'm confident I am here today because of Paul.

I was sent to the lab for the X-rays. When they were finished and I was dressing in my cabin, I heard one lab technician call to his colleague. "This can't be the same patient we X-rayed last week. Just look at this picture compared with the old one. This stomach is as clean and healthy as a newborn baby's."

I thought, I wonder if they are discussing my Xrays! I'm sure they are. Oh, Father in Heaven, thank you, thank you.

As soon as I was ready, I hurried upstairs to the doctor's office where he and Paul were expectantly waiting. The doctor held the set of new X-rays in his hand. There were tears in his eyes, but a smile played on his lips. He extended his slim, sensitive hand to me.

"Congratulations, Frau Williscroft! You are a well woman!" We shook hands all round. Our hearts were too full for words. The doctor, too, could only shake his head in amazement.

Later, when we sent to the hospital for those health records for admittance to a different hospital, we had an opportunity to examine them. Our doctor, who has since passed away, had written:

> Patient's condition diagnosed as cancer of the stomach. Confirmed by several physician colleagues. Patient suddenly went into complete remission before surgery could be performed. Divine intervention? So it seems.

Translated into English, it sounds more doubtful than the original German, but the embryo of faith in the divine is nevertheless to be assumed from the good doctor's report.

My strength slowly but steadily improved. I began to enjoy life again. Friends and loved ones seemed more dear than ever. Our missionary activities took on a new challenge for me. I loved working side by side with Paul in a new and sweeter way. Life became truly a precious gift of God, to be expended wisely and well. Our love for each other was deeper and richer than before my illness. Paul cherished me as a gift to treasure, having so nearly lost me. I appreciated the deep faith, devotion, and humility that was such a part of his character. I knew I owed my new lease on life to these qualities in him. I loved and respected him as never before. This new commitment to God and each other catapulted us into a new dimension of service for the Lord.

CHAPTER THIRTY-ONE

One of the highlights of our work in Europe was a visit to Osijek, Yugoslavia, in the winter of 1967. Paul was long interested in the Eastern European lands. He had made a few short exploratory trips to several of the countries. He wanted to talk with leaders and learn what the needs were and what could be done to help.

The response was always the same. "We need Bibles. Could you get us Bibles?" Another need they felt keenly was for good Bible teaching aids. Many of the church leaders in lands he visited were interested in a strong Bible teaching program for children. This type of program was almost unknown in these lands. There was no teaching material for either adults or children.

Paul was thrilled when he received the invitation to hold a Sunday school conference combined with a how-to seminar in Osijek.

I was included in the invitation, so one cold January day we set out for Yugoslavia in our SpeedtheLight Mercedes. It was a long drive from the Frankfurt area where we lived to the part of Yugoslavia where we were going. We drove through a beautiful part of Austria with its snow-clad hills and mountains.

At Bad Gastein, a lovely Austrian winter resort, we put the car on a quaint little train that took us right through the mountain. It was wonderful to avoid driving over the mountain on icy, snowy roads. We spent the night at a cozy inn in Southern Austria after we came out of the tunnel and were back on the road again.

We started early on a bright, cold morning. Rooftops, trees, and fences glistened in the morning sunlight. The sky was a deep azure. Little puffs of steam drifted upward from the mouths of people on their way to work or school. It was a glorious drive through a winter wonderland. We "ohhhed" and "ahhhed," we laughed and almost wept over the sheer beauty of it all.

Then we saw a narrow road winding up a hill. A sign reading "Yugoslavia" pointed in that direction.

Could we possibly make it up that steep, winding, slippery road? We started out with a prayer on our lips. Up, up, up. Take it easy, Paul. Our wheels are spinning. Watch it. There comes a huge truck slithering down the mountain. Is it out of control? God help us. It's sliding over to our side of the road. Look! Oh, Honey, there's a pullout. Thank God! Thank you. Thank you.

The truck continued its precarious way down the mountain, and we sat petrified in our pullout. We paused for a few moments of quiet prayer. It was good to catch our breath and take a short inventory of the road ahead. It looked even steeper and the snow was deeper. Again our united prayers were raised to our Father who had cared for us so faithfully only moments before.

The car moved easily out of the safety zone and we were on our way once more. To Paul's joy, the added snow on the road made it less slippery. We reached the top of the mountain without further difficulty.

On the summit was the Yugoslav customs house, a welcome sight. The car was filled with materials we would need to show and demonstrate in the convention and seminar. We were not sure if they would make it through customs or not. Among them was a large rag doll about the size of a two-year-old, which I used in teaching preschool children. The officials came out and pointed to one of the suitcases, demanding, "Open it!" We did. There was the doll.

The scowling official grabbed it at once. "What is this?" he roared, holding it out to Paul. I watched, fascinated, praying as usual. What would Paul do or say? Would we lose our materials even before we had an opportunity to use them in this country?

Paul looked the stern official straight in the eye, smiled gently, and answered cheerily, "It's a doll."

The man looked at him a moment, quite taken aback. He grinned sheepishly and, without further ado, waved us on our way. It was so simple and comical, we giggled all the way down the mountain.

We were ravenously hungry by this time. There was a restaurant of sorts in a little town at the foot of the mountain. It wasn't clean and the food was fatty, but to quote a German saying, *Hunger ist der beste koch.* (Hunger is the best cook.) It didn't taste too bad, and soon we were on our way again.

We stopped in Zagreb for a while, visiting the pastor and inquiring the way to Osijek. It was still miles further. Evening shadows were falling and we were tired, but we decided to drive on. The convention was to begin the next day and we wanted to be on hand.

It was a long, long drive through the night over strange roads. We sang and planned and talked to keep ourselves awake. Hour after hour we drove. At last we saw the twinkling lights of a town in the distance. Then a road sign appeared reading, "Osijek."

Paul training Christian workers in Yugoslavia

We found the church without much trouble. The good pastor had waited up for us. We received a warm welcome. It was wonderful to be at our destination. After a happy visit and a bite to eat, we were taken to our hotel. Tomorrow our first real effort for the Lord in Yugoslavia would begin. We needed to be rested. We prayed together, thanking God for His keeping power on our long journey and for His blessing and anointing for the days ahead.

The church was well filled when we arrived the next morning. Interested people came from all over Yugoslavia. Many of them were doing their best to teach children without help or training.

They were excited over the teaching course. They learned how to use pictures from calendars, magazines, and other sources for illustrating stories, songs, memory verses, and other things. They loved it. We also taught storytelling, use of the flannel board, illustrating truth with everyday objects, and how to lead a child to Christ. We had our puppets along and gave a short course on puppetry. Paul did a magnificent job of showing the need for laying a strong foundation in the church through children's work. He presented these eager, enthusiastic learners with firm Biblical grounds for the reaching, teaching, and disciplining of children.

The interested listeners sat from nine in the morning until six in the evening on hard wooden benches. There was a lunch break at noon and a light supper break after the last teaching session. Then people began to gather for the evening service.

I don't know how they all packed in, but somehow they did. Paul preached every evening and again the worshipers drank it all in. Their faces were often haggard from the burdens of life. The hands they raised in praise and prayer were gnarled and toilworn, but their eyes were alight with love for God and for His servant who came to teach them.

We were especially drawn to one little boy. He came every morning and stayed until after the evening service. He sat as still as a mouse on the hard bench, listening enraptured to the illustrated stories, the new songs, and all the practical things presented for teachers, not little children.

Those days in Osijek showed us clearly how great was the need for teaching in that land. As we came to the closing day, one dear young man read a poem he had written expressing the sentiment of all who attended the course. It was beautiful, even through interpretation. All the love and appreciation they felt for the days together were poured out in that poem. Paul and I wept unashamedly as our interpreter put it into English.

We loved them all. It was very hard to say good-bye. We were comforted by the thought that we had another training course in Yugoslavia before our return to Germany. With tears and waving handkerchiefs, we left them standing forlornly on the sidewalk before the church.

Pastor Volf, from Novi Sad on the Danube, was our interpreter both in Osijek and in Belgrade, where we headed after leaving Osijek. He was one of the best interpreters we had in any of the Eastern European lands we visited.

We needed to drive through Novi Sad on our way to Belgrade. Pastor Volf was happy for the stopover, as he had missed his family while in Osijek. Now he could enjoy a short visit with them. We were tired and glad for this short pause in our activities. A good supper, warm fellowship, and a clean bed were exactly what we needed. Mrs. Volf was as dear as her husband. Their son and daughter were beautiful young people. The boy was about twelve then; the daughter, a teenager of fifteen or sixteen. We enjoyed them both. When we left for Belgrade, Mrs. Volf came with us. It was lovely having her. She didn't speak English or German nor did we speak Serbian, but with eyes, head, hands, and heart, we managed to make ourselves understood. We had a wonderful time together.

We stayed in a high-rise hotel in downtown Belgrade. We were eleven or twelve stories high with a wonderful view over the city. We took our meals in the hotel, too, and found food and service excellent. We could have been in Germany or even in the States.

The church in Belgrade was small, shabby, and tucked away in a back street. The people lacked the interest we had found in Osijek, probably because most of them were older and had never heard the words "Christian Education." They attended faithfully, though, and day by day attendance and interest picked up.

Evening services were especially meaningful to these dear people. Paul had a special gift for leading people into heartfelt worship. The congregation gradually began to enter more into communion with the Lord. It was a time of spiritual renewal for everybody. The dear Volfs shared with us how much these evenings meant to them. So did all the others. Even though the training course was somewhat less than we had hoped, the evening services more than made up for it.

It was very cold in this part of Yugoslavia in January. Streets were icy and the snow piled high. Sometimes in the morning fog was so dense we could barely see the star on the hood of our Mercedes.

On one such Sunday morning we were driving with Pastor Volf to a service in another city. Paul was creeping along a two-lane highway behind a big blue bus. It was crawling cautiously through the fog while the driver tried to follow the road. We came to a portion of highway that looked wider than usual. Paul thought maybe he just might be able to pass the bus here. He signaled, then carefully moved out into the left lane.

Horrors! Coming right toward us was another car. We were about to have a head-on collision. We began to pray with all our might. Paul swerved to the right as close to the bus as he dared to go. We scraped the bus. It swayed a tiny bit to the right. Next thing we knew we were ahead of the bus and the oncoming car missed us by about a quarter of an inch. We could breathe easily again and had our own little praise service right there in the car.

The blue paint from the bus remained on our car for a long time. It was a continual reminder of God's love and care for His children.

Our next trip to Yugoslavia was in the early spring. The ground was still white with snow, but the roads were clear and we arrived in Subotica in northeastern Yugoslavia without mishap.

This is a Hungarian area. Before World War II it belonged to Hungary. As we understood the story, the border was moved back after the war. To their dismay, all the Hungarians there suddenly found themselves citizens of Yugoslavia.

They slowly adjusted. They are gracious, talented people. The women and girls are unusually attractive and feminine. They are noted for their beautiful needlework, some of the finest in the world. The men are dark and handsome, and are famous for their music and poetry.

Hungarians are a high-strung, sensitive people who feel deeply about things. They are warmhearted and hospitable, too. Their depth and sensitivity are carried over into the spiritual lives of Christians there. It was a joy to work among them.

Paul and I had met Pastor and Mrs. Sabo when we were in Novi Sad with the Volfs. Pastor Sabo had made the long winter trip just to meet us and invite us to his church for a teacher training course. He already had a little Sunday school that was started by a lovely and talented young lady, Elizabeth Radnic. She went to Germany to learn the language and then to attend Bible School there. She is now Mrs. Ditmar Mittelstaedt. Her husband directs the International Correspondence Institute (ICI) program in Germany. Elizabeth publishes one of the finest Christian women's magazines I know of. The Lord laid a burden on her heart for the women of Germany. This outstanding magazine is the result.

The seminar in Subotica was very special to us. The response was phenomenal. Hungarian Christians from all over the area came day after day and night after night. They were ready learners, quick and intelligent, and eager to help their children. Everyone brought notebooks and pens. They sat hour after hour, listening, absorbing, studying displays, taking notes. They were a joy to teach.

Workshops were offered where they could make things to use with the children. We never saw neater work than what some of these people did.

Again Paul preached in the evenings. He noticed some of the weaknesses in the lives of Christians due to a lack of teaching. He discussed them with Pastor Sabo and taught the whole church in the evening hours. They absorbed it like sponges. It was truly a great time.

Everything was taught in German. Pastor Sabo interpreted for Paul, his wife for me. Everything takes twice as long with this method, but no one seemed to mind. The Sabos became some of our dearest friends. Over the years we saw their children grow up, marry, and attend Bible School.

Their son, Victor, is now in the work of the Lord in that area. He has a precious little wife and three lovely children. Paul loved him like a son and did all he could to help him in his ministry.

The church in Subotica took our teaching to heart. They reorganized the Sunday school, starting different classes for different ages. Before, all the children were taught together. Teachers took their classes seriously. They spent hours preparing visuals of all kinds, fixing up nooks and corners to serve as class areas, visiting the children, and much, much more. One of the men in the church was a printer. He started a church paper, a Sunday-school paper, and put out other printed materials. It was exciting to see what these people could do when they really got turned on.

The following summer, when Elizabeth finished her first year of Bible School, she and Paul worked out a Kids Camp for her church children. Many unchurched kids came, too. Paul and I were invited to come and help them. The camp was held in a little country church not far from Subotica. The boys slept in the church and the girls were in an old tent.

The evening rally and the morning Bible work were all held outdoors. It had rained in that area for weeks. The church people were getting anxious. How could they have an outdoor camp if the rain didn't stop? They prayed and trusted day after day. Dear Elizabeth never doubted. She had a beautiful, childlike faith that could move mountains. Still the rain poured down. Why didn't God do something? Where was He?

Two or three days before camp was to begin, the rain stopped, the sun shone warm and bright, and the muddy grounds dried. The people rejoiced. God was faithful. He did not fail them.

Camp lasted two weeks, and there was only one thunder shower. That was in the afternoon. The children gathered in the girls tent and played games or heard stories. The evenings were warm and pleasant for the rally.

We arrived late in the afternoon of the first day, and were met by a bevy of boys and girls hugging us and dancing about us like elves. Such joy and excitement. They got to come to camp. They would be here for two whole weeks. Uncle and Aunty Williscroft were there.

They would hear stories and sing and play games. How lucky could they get?

We found our quarters, freshened up, and ate a light supper under the trees with the children. A gong sounded. It was time for the rally. There was a scamper to get the front benches. They were rough and backless, but who cared about such minor things? They were more excited than opera goers in their tuxedos and formal gowns, looking for plush seats.

Finally everyone was seated. Elizabeth raised her hand for silence. One could see how much the children loved and respected her. Immediately the babble subsided. The children sat still as mice as she prayed for God's blessing on the camp. Then one of the workers led in singing children's songs. The children sang with all their hearts. A few naked light bulbs were strung among the trees. That gave all the bugs in the vicinity a hearty welcome to join the crowd.

When it was time for the story, the children sat in total silence, eyes and ears open. Mouths, too. They slapped away at mosquitoes, never taking their eyes off me as I spoke. They were a rapt little audience. Every word had to be translated into Hungarian. They gazed at me as I talked, than turned their eyes in absorbed fascination to the interpreter.

When the story was finished, the children were asked to stand for prayer. Before Paul could pray one word, the whole camp began to weep and sob. They cried out for God to forgive them and make them His children. It was such a move of God as none of us there ever experienced. No human charisma or magnetism influenced this outpouring. It was from God alone. We heard little children speaking in an unknown tongue, tears streaming down their cheeks, their little hands lifted to heaven, their faces radiant.

No one could ever say these children were just mimicking their elders. Many of them were never in the church, just in Sunday school. Others were from completely unchurched families. Many were from Communist homes. None of us leading the camp had influenced them, as it was the first evening. They were not in any class or under any minister yet, as all of us had just come. This was truly an act of God. All those long days and weeks that the dear Christians spent praying, while the rain poured down, were not in vain. That was the best camp we ever worked with. Most of those children are serving God today. Some are in the ministry, others are Christian workers in various other capacities. No one who attended that camp will ever forget it. It will forever remain indelibly stamped on our hearts and minds.

That was the beginning of what later developed into a strong camping program for Yugoslavia. In the Hungarian area, Paul organized teen camps and youth camps. Then a good campsite opened up in another part of Yugoslavia. Kid's camps, teen camps, youth camps, and many other activities are carried on there. It became a center of blessing for Yugoslavia. Dedicated young people and men and women in churches all over Yugoslavia gave their lives to the Lord in these camps. God has put His seal of blessing upon this endeavor. We thank Him and all the dear ones in that great country who have worked so tirelessly with us over the years.

Paul seemed to have a special talent for spotting potential leadership in the young people he contacted. Then he would move heaven and earth to interest others in them. He arranged for several young people to go to one or another of our Assembly colleges in the States to further their education and broaden their horizons.

Best known of these is probably Peter Kusmic. We first met him at a conference and seminar in Zagreb. He was a teenager in high school. One day after a session, he approached us and asked about young people in the United States. His questions were thoughtful and heart-searching. He started like this: "You can do so much for the Lord in your country, can't you? There is so much freedom to witness and share Jesus with people. I suppose the church young people spend a lot of time out witnessing, passing out Christian literature, sharing Jesus at school, or going from house to house to tell people about Jesus – maybe all kinds of other things, too. Please tell me about it."

We could hardly say, "Oh, no, I'm sorry to say our kids are too busy with sports, studies, jobs, and dates to have much time for these things you mentioned." Paul and I looked at him a minute.

Possibly he saw the sadness in our faces, for he didn't pursue the matter. Instead he started talking about something else. But we never forgot that wistful question from a young man who did not have freedom to do those things.

One thing that interested Peter was Bible School. He longed to study the Word when he finished high school, but it seemed impossible. Paul urged him to plan on Bible School and he would do all he could to arrange something.

I'm sure Peter prayed a lot about it, and we did, too. A missionary friend, originally from Romania, Steve Goulash, also felt burdened for Eastern Europe. He learned to know Peter and helped him with his Bible School expenses.

Peter did come to Germany, improving his German as he studied. He was one of the best students we ever had there. After Bible School, Paul and Steve helped him go to Southern California College. He graduated with the highest marks of anyone ever graduating from SCC. He won a scholarship to Wheaton and then to Harvard.

We were very proud of Peter. Now he is president of the Biblical and Theological Institute in Osijek. God is using this fine, talented young man in many lands today, including the United States. Paul always had a special place in his heart for Peter.

Until the split-up of the country and the beginning of hostilities, God had been moving in Yugoslavia as never before. Peter Kusmic wrote that there are more Muslims in Yugoslavia than in any other European country, about four million and growing. A work was being done among them, but not by outsiders. Yugoslavian missionaries were doing it and God was blessing, Peter reported. I smiled when he wrote how he would like to establish a Paul and Gladys Christian Education Department in their Bible School. I can see how Paul's eyes would twinkle if he heard that. It would be a beautiful tribute to a humble man to whom God was everything.

With the advent of the awful conflict in that part of the world, we simply do not know what has happened, but I trust that the Lord will keep his loving protective hand over his people.

CHAPTER THIRTY-TWO

Paul rejoiced over what God was doing in Yugoslavia, but for him, that was just a start. What about the great Soviet Union with all its satellites? What was happening in all the countries of Eastern Europe with their teaming millions? Christians lived in all those lands, but how did they fare under Communism? What was happening to the children of these Christians who were denied any kind of Christian training? In most of those nations, the majority of the Christian community had no Bibles or Christian literature of any kind. There were no Sunday schools, youth groups, or other ways of reaching and teaching the young. Christians were generally treated as second-class citizens, often being cruelly discriminated against. In some places they were relegated to the lowliest jobs. Their children were bullied at school and often denied entrance into institutes of higher learning.

As Paul's heart reached out to Eastern Europe, God opened many doors of service. He took long, tedious journeys into one land after another, talking with Christian leaders, learning their problems and heartaches. How could he help? What could he do to meet their needs? These were always his first words after listening to their problems.

Paul and Gladys in Yugoslavia

Almost without exception, the urgent cry was for Bibles. "Just bring us Bibles! How can we teach and help our people without Bibles?" Usually they didn't even mention other needs. Paul observed, however, the thin faces, the shabby clothes, the almost impossible housing conditions of many. It broke his heart. He always returned to Germany fired up to set the wheels in motion to help the courageous Christians of Eastern Europe.

Paul in Budapest, Hungary

As you travel with us through one communist country after another, of necessity, names of some places and people must remain anonymous. Things have changed, but there still is great potential danger for those who have risked everything for God. Every country is different, but still similar. Some have been a bit more lenient in certain areas, while others have deprived their people of almost every freedom. With the advent of glasnost and the overthrow of communist rule almost everywhere, there is much more liberty in Eastern Europe. Visas to Western countries are easy to obtain. Doors are open for trade with the West. Guests from the West are not harassed as before, but are often welcomed.

Best of all, those who have risked so much over the years to bring in Bibles and other Christian literature can rejoice. Bibles can now be brought legally into all of these countries. With the collapse of the Soviet Union, the worship of God has blossomed like a flower in a desert that has received adequate water after a long drought. The future of the Gospel message in Mother Russia and in the former Soviet Union satellites is looking much brighter.

✳

We were approaching the bleak Czechoslovakian border on a late afternoon of a dreary winter day. Dark clouds and pouring rain enhanced the desolate feeling of the place. To our horror, before us a long line of cars inched its way toward the inspection area. A number of harsh customs agents were moving along the column of cars, kicking tires and flashing lights and mirrors beneath the vehicles, hunting for contraband. Occupants of cars were ordered out. They waited, shivering in the rain, while the car trunk, floors, under seats, or any other possible hiding place were thoroughly searched.

Our hearts sank. We were slowly, but surely, approaching the inspection area. What would happen to us? We were completely innocent of wrong doing, yet we felt like criminals. Why? Just because we had things in the car that could help make life a little brighter and fuller for dear Christians living in that land?

Paul turned to us white-faced, whispering, "Pray, everybody! Believe God for a miracle! Everything depends on it!" And we prayed.

The customs officials reached our car. What next? Paul quickly opened the door and jumped out into the rain. Our car had a German license so the official greeted us pleasantly in German.

Paul smilingly returned the greeting, also in German. "Open the trunk," the official ordered, not unkindly.

Paul quietly obeyed.

"Open that suitcase." Another commanded, but still quite amicable.

We kept on praying, still holding our breath. Paul pulled out the designated piece of luggage. He opened it, revealing nothing but our neatly folded clothing. The man mauled through our things a moment, motioned for Paul to close the suitcase, and, with an inscrutable expression on his face, waved us on.

Were we dreaming? Did the official really mean for us to drive on, just like that? We looked at one another in utter bewilderment.

Suddenly everybody snapped back to life. With one voice we urged Paul, "Drive on. The man means for us to get going! Oh, hurry, hurry, before he changes his mind."

As in a daze, Paul started the car and moved apprehensively away from the border. No one could fully comprehend that the inspection was over and we made it. As we pulled away, I glanced back to see if the inspection had actually slacked off. The customs men continued down the line of waiting cars, lights and mirrors flashing as they conducted their thorough search. We had indeed witnessed a miracle. We drove on, praising the Lord and rejoicing in His goodness. Our questionable cargo reached its destination safely, bringing great joy with it.

※

Six months before Paul went to be with the Lord, we were on our very last trip through Czechoslovakia, on our way to Poland for seminars and evangelistic meetings. For some time Poland had been one of the most open countries in Eastern Europe, and we loved to minister there.

We made an error in judgment driving through Czechoslovakia. Officials there had a reputation for being unfriendly and rude. Foreign visitors were looked upon with suspicion. They often suffered indignities at the hands of the police or other leaders with whom they were unfortunate enough to tangle with.

We took with us a few little treats for a family in Prague. They were a gift from friends in Germany. We didn't know the family, but were looking forward to a short visit with them and a pleasant break in our long journey.

We arrived in Prague and found the address without difficulty. The house was a typical highrise. We parked in the area provided, walked up a number of flights of stairs and soon found the family we were looking for. They were a dear young couple with a baby. We loved them at first glance, and they seemed to feel the same about us. Their pastor was also visiting the family.

The pretty little wife, baby on arm, made us coffee. We were just starting to sip it when a loud banging sounded outside the door. Before our host could answer it, two secret police shoved the door open and barged in. We sat petrified with astonishment and fear.

"Who does that German car in the lot belong to?" bellowed one of the intruders.

Paul stood up and nodded, indicating himself.

"You are under arrest," snarled the second man. "Follow us. You men must come, too," indicating our host and the pastor. "We are taking you all to prison."

They would tell us nothing more. We followed the police in our car. The other two followed in theirs. We were all mystified and badly shaken. It almost broke my heart to see that dear little mother kiss her husband good-bye, pressing her little one to her breast, as we followed the police down the stairs.

At the prison we were taken to separate rooms for questioning. I don't know exactly how long we were there, but it was hours. No one came to question me. I sat alone praying that God would give the men wisdom to answer well. These secret agents love to confuse their victims. They might tell each individual that all the others have confessed, so they had better do the same promptly; or Paul might be threatened that harm will come to his wife if he doesn't confess or told to confess if he hopes to see her again.

It was closing time at the prison. The janitor came to my room and gestured for me to leave. He jangled a huge bunch of keys before my eyes. I tried to tell him I had to wait for the others. He just shook his head impatiently. Walking behind me with keys waving, he finally got me out the door and onto the street while I protested helplessly all the way out. I was so indignant, I was ready to do anything.

I stood there, gulping in the fresh air and trying to form some sort of strategy. I was free. I didn't know why, nor did I have any idea where the others were. I was apparently the only one of us in a position to do anything. I looked around. A streetcar was jangling down the track in my direction.

"I'll get on," I decided. "Maybe I can find the American Consulate."

Then it dawned on me I had only German currency in my purse. I feared it was too risky to try and change any. Only banks can legally do that there. People do try to change their money for western currency right out on the streets, but for me to try anything illegal when I was already in trouble could be disastrous. That took care of the streetcar idea.

While wondering what to do next, a man approached me. He asked in broken German, "You Mrs. Williscroft?" My heart skipped a beat. Maybe he came with news of the others. I answered with a nod. He continued. "You man, Williscroft, come soon." I was beside myself with joy and relief.

"Where is he? Oh, where is he?" I cried. "What have you done with him? Where are the others? Can you take me to them, please?"

He beckoned me to follow him. I was uneasy, but went with him. He pointed to a far end of the prison that I hadn't seen before. Gesturing, he tried to tell me this was the main part of the foreboding looking place. My heart sank. Had Paul, or one of the others, in some way answered questions in a manner that had incriminated them? Were they already incarcerated in this dreadful place?

We arrived at the steps of the prison section where Paul was supposed to be. The man grinned as he announced, "Other men free. They go home. You man here. I go get. You wait. No come in. No go way. That bad. Too bad."

I wasn't about to go away. I just might go in, though, if we didn't get some action soon. The man disappeared into the building.

I waited. I waited some more. The minutes ticked by, then half an hour, three quarters of an hour. I'd waited long enough. It was late in the evening. I was going into the prison. I'd had it!

Pushing open the heavy oaken doors I walked in. A heavy brute of a man sat behind a barred window. He glared at me as I approached him. I asked in English, "Where is my husband?" He just shrugged. *Maybe he doesn't understand English,* I thought. I tried German. "Where is my husband, Paul Williscroft? You have him here somewhere. I want him in this room within five minutes. Do you understand?"

Again came the nonchalant shrug and a leering grin. I could see he really had understood. A sort of holy anger came over me. I glared back at him as I almost shouted, "If Paul Williscroft isn't here in five minutes, I will go to the American Consul. You will be sorry, I can assure you."

To my relief, the fellow got slowly to his feet, reached for the phone, and talked heatedly to someone for several minutes. It sounded like quite an argument. Then he slammed the phone back in its place and sat down. *It didn't work*, I thought, as he made no further move to communicate with me. I felt sick and hopeless. Standing by the barred window, wondering what to do next, I saw a door in the back part of the room open. There stood Paul accompanied by two guards. They took their leave in good German tradition with a hearty handshake. Then they kissed my hand, a Czechoslovakian custom, and escorted us cordially to the door.

It was a miracle; my own private miracle. God had made a way for me to get out of my interrogation room. He showed me just what to do next. I obeyed, though by nature I am a gentle person. I would normally not take the initiative, especially in a dangerous situation like this. God knew what He was doing and arranged everything to help His faithful missionary out of a sensitive situation.

Paul told me what happened as we drove to our hotel. He was questioned for many hours. They used trick questions to try and trap him into saying something that could condemn him. It seemed that a Western agent had crossed the border at the same time as we, and was headed for Prague. The secret police lost the agent somewhere between the border and the city, but we showed up in Prague about the time they were expecting this agent. The people we visited were under surveillance for religious reasons. They often had visitors from the West, too. That, alone, was enough to put them under suspicion. The Prague secret police detachment made the obvious assumption that Paul was the agent their colleagues had lost. It was marvelous how the Holy Spirit put the right answers on Paul's lips. It happened again and again during the long afternoon and into the evening.

Paul said he started asking the police questions, finally. Why was it wrong to be religious? Don't they profess to have religious freedom there? Why aren't people allowed to have guests from the West? Is that a crime? On and on he went with his interrogation, until the officials got so confused and nervous they didn't know anymore how to answer.

Then Paul witnessed about Jesus and what He can do. He shared his own conversion and encouraged them to try Jesus. I guess they believed in him, even though they were not ready to believe in Jesus. It was then that they sent the man to find me. They weren't quite ready to let Paul go, though. That was when I bluffed the doorman and the police decided it was best to release him. They didn't want to get mixed up with the American Consul.

Free at last. We got settled in our hotel room but decided it would be wise not to talk about what had happened. Hotel rooms there really did have ears. The hotel was under guard all night because of us, but we were free to leave after breakfast the next morning. We were thankful to drive away, but our hearts ached for all those people held captive in their own land. They couldn't be released to thankfully drive away like we were doing. We prayed for them more earnestly as we started out for Poland, where people still have the right to be Christians.

✳

Penetrating the Iron Curtain was hardly an easy task anywhere or at any time, but Paul seemed never able to withstand the urge to get into one more country. One special place he loved to visit is Hungary, a beautiful country with cultured and attractive people. We learned to know some of them when Paul arranged to have a group of young people from Hungary attend a youth camp in neighboring Yugoslavia, which was more lenient at that time. As a result of these kids sharing their experiences with pastors and church leaders, Paul received an invitation to visit one of the larger churches Hungary. They were eager for a seminar on organizing camps, Sunday schools, and teacher training sessions – an ambitious program in a land where these activities were discouraged, if not actually forbidden.

Bible School class in Budapest, Hungary

The sessions were to be held in a large church in the center of Budapest. It was a marvelous experience. Young people and older ones came from all over the country. They slipped in quietly through a back door, by ones and twos. They stayed inside the building the whole day, trying to be as inconspicuous as possible. We lectured and showed visuals on how to reach and win boys and girls for Christ. We never taught a more eager and fascinated crowd. They took notes, they visited workshops where they could do hands-on preparation of materials. They shared with us their lack of even the most basic materials for their children's work. As we took our leave late in the evening, their tears mingled with ours as they tried to express what this day had meant to them. Then they crept silently out the way they came in, quickened and inspired to fulfill their mission for the Lord better than ever before.

✻

In all Communist lands before the overthrow of the old regimes, children's work was considered to be exclusively the task of The Party. Sunday schools were forbidden in most churches and in some East Block lands it was actually against the law for children to attend church at all. We could never forget one time in Romania where the parents rode to church with us in our car, leaving the children at home. They sadly waved good-bye as we drove off.

"Why didn't you bring the children? We could have squeezed them in," Paul asked our host.

"Well, it's like this," he responded. "In Romania it's against the law to take a child under eighteen to church. Some parents do smuggle their youngsters in with them, but if they are caught, their children could be taken from them and put in a home where they are taught to be Communists. We don't feel we could risk that. We do our best, even without a Bible or any kind of teaching materials, to bring our little ones up to love and honor God. Please stand with us in prayer about this." We entered the packed church with a heavy heart.

✳

One day a letter came from David Wilkerson. He mentioned a Spirit-filled Catholic priest living on the outskirts of Budapest. This priest had read the English version of *The Cross and the Switchblade*. He wanted to know more about these deeper experiences and how he could get the book printed in his language. Dave wanted us to try and contact this priest the next time we were in Budapest. All he could give us to help locate him was a rather inadequate address, but Paul agreed to try.

The time came when we did make a trip to Hungary. We were in Budapest for a seminar on children's work scheduled for the following day. We got settled in our hotel on the edge of town. We were tired from the long day's drive, but Paul couldn't eat or sleep until he accomplished his mission.

It was late in the evening. A wet fog was creeping over the city. Paul asked at the desk just where in that vast metropolis this address might be located. The clerk wasn't exactly sure, but he directed us clear out to the very opposite end of town. He assured us that, somewhere out there we would find our man.

We started out, praying as we drove. On and on through the deepening fog we made our unsure way. Finally, as we tried to follow the directions given at the desk, we came upon a street with the name Dave had given us. Then the fog closed in. We couldn't see the houses or even the street before us. We prayed again as we tried to peer through the gloom.

To our astonishment a form loomed up in the mists beckoning us on. We followed until he gestured toward the right side of the road. Then, as quickly as he appeared, he vanished into the fog.

We strained our eyes trying to see our benefactor. The fog lifted a little, allowing us a better glimpse of our surroundings. There was no sign of anyone on the road before us, but to our right was a house. No number was visible. The place looked dark and deserted. Paul felt God had led us this far, so why not try to arouse somebody?

He knocked at the front door. No response. After trying again without success, he began to feel around in the darkness with his foot. Just when he was ready to give up, his foot touched a narrow path leading around to the back of the house. He followed it, and to his joy saw a faint light in a window. He gave a couple of resounding knocks on the weather-beaten back door, calling me to join him. It soon opened. An elderly woman stood in the doorway, her old eyes squinting into the darkness, trying to see who could be there.

Paul introduced us and asked about Father so and so. He had to shout into her ear as she was quite hard of hearing. Then her face lit up as she understood.

She led us into a pleasant room, though shabby and worn from long usage. She silently motioned us to a seat on the couch. Her German was very limited and with her hearing problem she could hardly understand a word we said. With many gestures, interspersed with bits and pieces of broken German, she finally got through to us that the priest would be home for supper in about half an hour. Then she bustled off to prepare a meal for us all.

Paul and I relaxed on the couch and tried to put the pieces of our strange adventure together. Who was that person who led us to this house? How did he know where we wanted to go? Why did he vanish so quickly? In His own mysterious way did God reach out to meet the needs of a lonely priest hundreds of miles to the east of us? We would soon know.

And the sweet old lady, was she his mother, his grandmother? Maybe she was his housekeeper or an elderly family servant retained after the family fortunes dwindled away under Communism.

Footsteps sounded outside. The door opened to admit a slender, dark-eyed young man in the garb of a priest. He looked wide-eyed at us. He had evidently noticed our German car outside and was puzzled to know who could be visiting him from there.

We both stood up to greet him. Paul smiled warmly as he explained. "We bring you greetings from David Wilkerson. He is a friend of ours and wrote me about you. We are Paul and Gladys Williscroft, Americans, living and working for the Lord in West Germany." Then we both held out our hands to him.

The young priest, eyes shining, made one leap across the room. Ignoring our outstretched hands, he gathered us both in his arms, repeating, "Praise the Lord. Praise the Lord. How I've longed and prayed for this. I've been hungry to know what God is doing in other parts of the world. God has sent you to me. Thank you. Thank you, Father God." He spoke in perfect English.

After a hugging good time, he led us back to the couch, checked in the kitchen to see when supper would be ready and drew up a chair near us. He was eager to hear all about what God was doing in the Catholic renewal in America.

Then he told us what was happening in Hungary, which is almost entirely Roman Catholic. He had been filled with the Holy Spirit through reading in English about the move among Catholics in the States. He shared his experience with friends, also priests. They began to seek the Lord and many more received the baptism in the Holy Spirit. Some of their superiors heard what was happening and began to wait on God, too. At the time we were there, some of the top leaders of the Catholic community were waiting on the Lord for an outpouring of the Spirit upon the whole church. It was inspiring to listen to this precious man of God tell in glowing words of the Holy Spirit's moving in his country.

While we listened, engrossed, to all the exciting things the priest was sharing, the elderly woman appeared, announcing our meal was ready. We gathered around the table, realizing suddenly how hungry we were.

The meal was simple, but so spiced with lively conversation it seemed like a banquet. Paul talked about ways we might be able to help with getting *The Cross and the Switchblade* translated and published in that land. Our new friend agreed to see what he could do from his side of the Iron Curtain.

The kindly lady took part in the conversation as best she could. We learned, then, that she was the priest's long-time housekeeper. She treated him with the love of a mother and the deference of a parishioner. He assured us he simply could not carry on his parish work without her. She blushed with embarrassment and pleasure at this expression of appreciation. We all tried to hide our smiles. What a homey, pleasant evening it was.

Then Paul glanced at his watch. It was midnight. How could an evening fly by so quickly? We sprang to our feet, apologizing for staying so late. Our ecclesiastical host grinned impishly, eyes twinkling, as he remarked from the side of his mouth, "Yes, yes, I've always heard that you Americans never know when to leave. True, yes?"

Everybody had a good laugh. Forming a circle, with arms about each other, Paul committed this dear brother in Christ, his household and parish into God's hands. We drove off into the night with the sense of satisfaction one feels when a mission is accomplished.

Plans for the book hit many snags, as such attempts always did under the existing government. It took a long time to get it off the ground. We hadn't heard yet at the time of Paul's death just how the book was progressing. My heart is still in this project, and I believe God will work it out. Perhaps the book has been published since I've been back in the States. This was the hope and dream of that dear priest. I don't know if he is still living. People with such projects can often disappear without a trace. He will always live in my memory as a precious and humble servant of the Lord Jesus. Whether on earth or in heaven, he will never be forgotten.

✳

Paul was ministering in a Czechoslovakia where evangelicals were especially frowned upon. Their activities were closely monitored. Every move came under strictest surveillance. Paul knew this and tried to be very discrete in everything he said and did for the protection of that struggling congregation.

After a morning service in a small church in a large city, a young man drew Paul aside and quietly whispered, "There is a home meeting in a farmhouse out in the country. They would love to have you minister to them this afternoon. The time is three o'clock. I should mention that this is an unregistered group. It could be risky. I would be glad to ride out with you if you'd like. I could show the way and help you park as inconspicuously as possible." He turned and walked nonchalantly away, giving Paul time to think it over.

We picked up the young fellow at the designated place that afternoon. He guided us through the city traffic and into the countryside. On and on we drove. At last our guide directed us into the driveway of a quaint farm home off the main highway. We parked behind a barn. People arrived in groups of two or three. Most of them lived in the area and walked. Some took a bus from town as far as it went and walked the rest of the way. They gathered in several rooms, leaving doors open so everybody could hear.

It was a wonderful service. They sang lustily with all their hearts. People gave short testimonials of how God cared for them, healed them, or protected them during the week from dangers they would rather not mention. Often the tears rolled down their tired, worn faces as they thanked God for His goodness to them. Their prayers were deep expressions of thanksgiving, praise, and worship. They forgot the clock, the farm chores, the evening meal. They were in God's presence!

The sun was setting when Paul finally stood to speak. They had been huddled together on improvised seats for hours. They should have been tired and ready to go home. Instead, things were just starting for these spiritually hungry people. They were not just grandmas and grandpas, either. A third or more of the group were young people, teenagers or a bit over, and a number of children. Paul brought a simple message on the love of God, weaving through it the goodness and sovereignty of our great Father God and what He is doing all over the world today. The listeners sat spellbound. It was exciting to hear that people were being reached by the thousands in great crusades in many parts of the world. It was thrilling to know it was possible for people in some countries to gather in masses like that to listen to the gospel message. They laughed and cried for joy. They stood up and clapped spontaneously, their smiles and tears mingling. I could feel with these people. They were probably thinking, *If only it could be like that here!* but utterly without covetousness or envy. They were amazing! In spite of all the needs, restrictions, wretchedness, and the poverty that was their lot, they could rejoice over what God was doing for other people in other lands.

A young fellow was stationed as a lookout where he could observe the road from both directions. Suddenly the quiet of the Sunday evening and the thread of the inspiring sermon were interrupted by the loud clatter of some heavy vehicle pulling into the yard. A deadly hush fell over the people. Mothers clutched their babies closer to their breasts. Strong young men formed a circle around Paul and the women and children, while the older men gathered just inside the ring formed by the younger ones. This was a tactic used by most of the unregistered groups in Eastern Europe and the Soviet Union. This gave the pastor, together with the women and children, a chance to escape, while the secret police are being held at bay by the men, young and old.

This strategy was very important. If the pastor were arrested, he could have been imprisoned, often for years. The laymen were usually let off with a fine, either personal or which the church had to pay. Sometimes, they were roughed up and beaten by the police.

Everybody sat, still as mice, lips moving in silent prayer. I glanced at Paul as he stood with bowed head, arms stretched out toward the people as though in blessing. There was no fear written on his face, only love and compassion for this brave little flock.

The trance was suddenly broken as the watchman called out, "All's well!" His voice trembling with relief. He stepped inside to let us know what had happened.

A neighboring farmer was having trouble with his truck. Our host was a friendly fellow and also something of a mechanic. The neighbor brought the truck over to see if he could help fix it. The lookout assured him the matter would be taken care of, so he left his truck there and walked home.

The men quietly took their seats; the women gently laid their babies back on their arms; the children smiled up at their mothers with love and relief on their rosy faces. They all looked expectantly at Paul, waiting for him to finish the exciting message. I peeked at him out of the corner of my eye, wondering how he would manage. He wasn't a person who could, right off the cuff, handle such a startling interruption with poise. I really felt uneasy for him. Would he manage it?

With a smile, he picked up right where he left off and brought his message to a glorious conclusion.

It was late, but the people stayed to praise and rejoice that nothing bad had happened. We were led to a little back room where bread, tea, and sausage were put out for us. It was their best, and they wanted to share it. Some stood around us to watch. The women loved to touch my blouse or my hair. They loved and patted me and a few wept on my neck as they begged us to come again. We could hardly drive away. They pressed closely around the car as though to keep us there.

We were weeping as we finally drove on through the dark countryside. Our guide told us they often have scares like the one today. Most of them were false alarms, but through them the group learned to plan for the real thing when it happened. As we drove along, he told us many things about the persecution, the discrimination, and the many hardships they suffered for their faith. He wasn't bitter, just factual in his sharing.

Like the apostles of old, these Christians actually felt honored to endure hardship for Jesus' sake. Paul and I felt privileged to be associated with these gallant soldiers of the cross. We returned to Germany determined to pray more earnestly for our brothers and sisters in Eastern Europe.

CHAPTER THIRTY-THREE

Eastern Europe is a many-faceted panorama of traditions, customs, peoples, climates, and problems. No two nations are alike. Religion is one thing some of them have in common: Roman Catholicism. Others are Russian Orthodox and some are home to Muslims, especially Bulgaria and what used to be Yugoslavia.

Bulgaria has a large Muslim community, though there are many of Orthodox background, too. East Germany has a large Lutheran majority.

Paul was neither eloquent nor particularly gifted as a speaker, but his vision and burning heart enabled him to touch Eastern Europe as few others have.

It was a cold, rainy spring. All over Eastern Europe farmers were in despair. Fields that should have been planted weeks before lay under water. Disastrous floods completely devastated Romania, leaving many homeless. There was some loss of life, and whole villages were cut off from food and other much-needed supplies. In some towns, people could only get around by boat. The situation worsened until there were dangerous food shortages all over the land. The Communist government, never known for its efficiency at best, finally felt compelled to ask for help from the countries west of their borders.

The response was immediate, and help was sent from all over Western Europe. The German group with whom Paul was associated was one of the first to swing into action. They sent out a call for relief to all of our churches in Germany. Promptly tons of goods arrived at the center. Young men from the Bible School in Germany volunteered to drive the truckloads of food, clothing, blankets, and medicines to their destination. Packed in with the other things were hundreds of Bibles, New Testaments, and other Christian literature. Christians in the East Block had constantly been pleading for these things. They trickled in periodically, but transporting the supplies had always been a risky undertaking. The Christian materials that got in were only a tokens compared to the crying need of the churches there.

The thrilling tales that came back with our returning truck drivers are more exciting than fiction. Two of our fellows always went in each truck, the driver and a helper. One truck was headed for one of the depots where all goods were to be unloaded on a dark, rainy, late afternoon. An ominous feeling was in the air. The men looked at each other. What would happen when they got to the depot? Would the officials be so happy for all the material things that they just might overlook the Bibles and other Christian materials?

Suddenly a police officer waved the men down. He wanted to show them the left turn they needed to take to get to the depot, so squeezed in the cab beside the passenger. A policeman was the last person needed in the truck right then.

Our boys were praying for guidance before the uninvited guest made his abrupt appearance. Now they took hold of God in earnest as the drippy spring evening began to close in on them. Just before it got too dark to read the road signs well they came to a crossroads. One road turned left. "Here, here!" shouted the official in his language, gesturing frantically to a sign pointing left.

That's when it happened. As though an unseen hand took the wheel, and an invisible foot pressed the brake, the bus slowed almost to a stop. The boy in the passenger seat gave the official a gentle push.

The next thing the poor guy knew, he was standing in the rain at the crossroads, while the truck vanished around the curve to the right. Shortly they found the church where they really wanted to deposit their load. No words can describe the joy and relief of the Christians when the trucks were able to avoid the Communist depots and arrive safely at the predetermined destinations.

A second great flood swept over Romania, a flood of literally thousands of Bibles and New Testaments pouring into that thirsty land. Many trucks sent by Christians in the West carried only the normal relief goods and deposited them in the government-controlled depots, but the special trucks added uncounted blessings to this land.

*

On another occasion, we got over the Romanian border, but just barely, after a long hassle and a wait for hours before we got our passports back. A passport is the most valuable possession traveling abroad in western lands. It was doubly so in Eastern Europe, and especially so in Romania. Some people there would give almost anything in the world to get their hands on an American passport. We were happy finally to have those precious documents safely in our hands again.

We were all tired and hungry. We looked at Paul to see if he had any place in mind where we could eat. He grinned a very naughty little grin and beckoned us to come with him back to the car. We piled in, and down the rutted, uncared-for street he drove. Before long he stopped at a not-too-bad looking building, and we all went trouping in.

Inside it looked as forlorn as outside. It was crowded with people sitting at none-too-clean tables, smoking and drinking a dark grain coffee. We suspected they were trying to find a little cheer through this pastime. A long-faced waiter showed us to a table. Paul asked in German for a menu. The man shook his head, "No menu."

In broken German he let us know that the meal that day was potatoes, pork, and a vegetable. It didn't sound too bad. The plates were piled high with plain boiled potatoes with no butter, gravy, or the like. Accompanying the mountain of potatoes was a very tiny piece of fat pork and the biggest sour pickle I had ever seen – our vegetable.

We were on our way to visit some dear Christians. Maybe they had even less. This was a good meal for this poor and very badly managed country, so "*guten appetit!*"

We drove on to the once-lovely old capital city, Bucharest. The streets were broad and lined with magnificent old trees. The buildings along the streets were often of marble blocks, but they were so blackened with time and neglect that their identity was unrecognizable.

Paul had the name and address of a family in this city and hoped he could find them. I still don't know how he did it, but after a long sightseeing trip all over the city, we stopped before what had once been a fine old house. Now it looked run down and neglected.

Bucharest was plastered with Communist propaganda. Everywhere the blood-red hammer and sickle were displayed. Great red posters extolling the glories of Communism decorated every building, overpass, or anywhere else they could be posted. People on the streets looked grim and unhappy. Smiles were rare. We wondered what the family's attitude toward us would be.

Paul left us in the car while he went to check things out. He wanted our arrival to be as inconspicuous as possible. During our long wait we took stock of our surroundings.

Then we saw him, a small man in plain clothes and dark glasses, loitering nonchalantly across the street. We couldn't see his eyes, of course, but we knew he never took them off either the car or the house.

A door slammed. Paul strode determinedly to the car. Without a word he drove off, tires screeching. A strange dread filled our hearts. The strained expression on Paul's face warned us not to talk. We drove around several corners, then up some hills, down some more streets, and into what looked like a completely different neighborhood.

Twilight spread across the sky. Paul opened the doors, beckoning us to get out. With finger on lips, he led the way down one street and around a corner to another. After a short walk we turned into a dark, dingy courtyard. We sensed that no word must be spoken until Paul gave the signal.

We came to a heavy, ancient door. Paul reached into his pocket and produced a huge key. He turned it cautiously in the rusty lock. We sighed with relief when it opened noiselessly. We walked in silence up one flight of stairs. On the landing we paused a moment as Paul checked things out. We climbed another flight and still another, not daring to make a sound. Very dim, naked light bulbs hung from the dark ceilings. We went up two more flights.

Just as we reached the landing, one of us couldn't hold it in any longer and sneezed, loud and vibrating. It echoed through the murky stairwell. We stood petrified, waiting for some awful thing to happen. The seconds passed. No door opened. No one appeared to have noticed. Paul grinned a little as he raised one finger to show we had only one more flight of stairs to climb.

We remembered all the escalators we had carelessly used, all the elevators we had taken for granted, as we wearily toil up that last flight of stairs. Now we were at the right floor. Paul knocked at a door. It was cautiously opened.

There stood a handsome, elderly gentleman with a halo of snowy hair. With his finger on his lips, he led us quickly and quietly into a large entrance hall. Still motioning for silence, he took us through the dim hall into a warm, cheery living room. The mother and her two grown daughters greeted us with warm hugs and kisses as they took our wraps and waved us to inviting old armchairs. The father, one of the pioneers of the full gospel in that country, greeted us with stately dignity and inborn graciousness. We listened with awe and deep respect as he told of persecution and discrimination, even before Communism, because they were evangelicals.

We heard about the many imprisonments he endured since Communism took over. Months and months were spent in dark, dank cells. His wife raised her three beautiful little daughters almost entirely alone. He would be released for a while and then sent to prison again because of his steadfast activities for the Lord. The wife and daughters wept as he shared these testings and trials with us.

We were surprised to see sofa cushions tucked around and on top of the telephone. They told us that was because the phone was bugged. The cushions muffled our conversation, making it more difficult for anyone listening to understand us.

We had to shout at our host, as he was very deaf. He told of being beaten over his head, face, and ears. His nose was broken, his eyesight impaired, and his ears so badly damaged that deafness set in. It grew gradually worse as the years passed.

None of them complained or acted bitter toward their tormentors. Just the opposite. They prayed for them every day. In our prayers with the family, we were shamed as we listened to their loving intercession for those who had made their lives so harsh and difficult. We thought of the petty little things that get us down and vowed, with God's help, to be different.

It had been a fascinating evening, but all of us were dead tired. Our day was long and filled with many experiences and impressions. This family was so delightful, though, we felt we could stay up all night listening to them. Our gracious hostess had other ideas. She had left for the kitchen some time ago, and now she returned and ushered us to the dining room where a simple but attractive supper awaited us.

We did ample justice to the meal, hungrier than we realized. We shared again, and in this happy atmosphere, we learned the details of our arrival.

Paul had entered the house through the front door. Our hosts recognized the man hanging around across the street as a plainclothes secret policeman. They showed Paul from a back window how to dodge him and the henchmen who were likely waiting out of sight. From that vantage point they showed Paul the route that would lose the watcher and bring him back to the other side of the block where there were no watchers. By then it was dark enough to avoid being seen. Had we spoken in the hall, our language would have betrayed us. The sneeze wasn't so dangerous. A resident of the house could have sneezed.

We had a precious few moments of prayer before we said good night. Our dear pastor host thanked God for the guests in his home. Weeping, he sobbed, "Guest in house, God in house!" He tenderly thanked God for bringing us safely over the miles to their home, then committed us all into the loving hands of The Father.

CHAPTER THIRTY-FOUR

There is much to tell about every country in Eastern Europe. God has done exciting things in most of these lands, but much of the triumph was accompanied by persecution, discrimination, and heartbreak.

Romania is a Balkan land of rare beauty--high mountains, green valleys, rushing mountain streams- – and a decadent, but still lovely capital city. God is moving in fantastic ways in this nation. During the final two decades of Communist rule, there were hundreds of churches all over the country. Not old cathedrals, which served as museums, but vibrant, living, evangelical churches. Some had their own buildings, but most were in rented halls or whatever sort of facility was available to them.

We never visited a congregation in Romania where all the people could get into the building. Very often there were as many people, or more, standing on the outside as were on the inside. Many on the inside were standing, too. Many worshipers came two hours early to find standing room only.

Services were long, often continuing for five or six hours. These services were filled with singing, which was wonderful despite the fact that most of them didn't even own a real songbook. They simply bought a school composition book and copied the songs from the leader or someone else fortunate enough to own a printed songbook. They prayed and testified. They enthusiastically listened to three or four speakers and the great messages they brought. They could not easily imagine a shorter meeting.

Foreigners were always asked to present a greeting. The pastor would explain that a greeting can last a half hour or so. It had to be interpreted, of course, which would extend it to an hour. The longer, the better. Join me on a visit.

✳

On a sunny Sunday morning in midsummer, Paul rose early, breakfasted in the hotel dining room, and set out to locate the church. He left us at the hotel to have a more leisurely breakfast, planning to come for us later. We wandered around the lobby looking at anything of interest. When Paul arrived, he had a big smile for us.

As we drove to church, Paul told about finding it. He noticed crowds of people all going in the same direction. Stopping a man, he asked if he spoke German. He did, so Paul asked about the church.

"Oh, you just follow that crowd. They are all on their way to church. I am, too." Then, with a wistful look toward our car, he hesitantly asked if he might ride with Paul. Of course he could. So they drove on until they came upon many people all pressing into a large old building. Paul had difficulty getting anywhere near the place because of the throng. He let the man out and came back for us.

We enjoyed looking the city over as we drove. It was once a fine metropolis, but now appeared neglected and forlorn, like cities all over Eastern Europe. Still, there was a dignified atmosphere about it that attracted us. We parked about a block away from the church so as not to attract too much attention.

There was a small, fenced-in courtyard around the building. It was jammed with people. Most were standing. A few brought little three-legged stools, like milking stools of long ago. There were mothers with babies; little children running around as best they could in the shuffle; men and boys, leaning on each other for support during the long service. We pressed our way through the crowd. They looked us over curiously as though we might have dropped down from another planet. We smiled at the babies and children, hugged some of the women, and shook hands with a few of the men as we worked our way into the building.

The pastor was expecting us. He sent a man to usher us to the front. It really took shoving and pushing to work our way up. Our escort did most of that for us. Some of the people on the backless front benches stood and offered us their seats. We hated to take them, but since the people were so gracious, how could we not accept? Just before we sat down, we turned and looked out over the audience. A sea of faces looked expectantly back! Old and young, men and women, young people and children. It was wall-to-wall people.

The windows were all wide open. We could see the crowds in the courtyard milling about. The summer sun beat down on them relentlessly, but they had come to church, and here they would stay.

We listened to the singing with pure delight. Many of the songs were the same old hymns we loved, translated into their language. A large choir sang a number of beautiful songs from their improvised hymnals. Most of their own music was in minor keys, and the sweet, plaintive melodies brought tears to our eyes and a lump to our throats. They had suffered so much for their faith. Many had endured long prison terms, beatings, and other atrocities. Lines of pain and sorrow were evident, but hope and faith shined through. We felt honored to be their guests.

A couple of hours passed as we sang and prayed. Paul finally brought his greeting, a word of hope and encouragement. The people wept openly as they listened. They needed that kind of message.

Quietly the pastor took Paul by the shoulder and gently pushed him toward the door, beckoning us to follow. People made way for us, smiling and nodding as though we were old friends. Some of them caught our hands, beaming through the tears still glistening on their cheeks.

We looked at each other questioningly. What was happening? Where were we going? Why did we leave such a good meeting before it was over? We soon found out. Two other churches in the city wanted us to visit them and bring greetings.

We drove to the first. It was almost a twin to the one we had just left. A crowded courtyard...wall-to-wall people inside...the press through the crowded sanctuary to the front. Again we loved the singing, the prayers, the testimonies, even though we couldn't understand a word. Paul's greeting touched hearts, just as before. The smiles and the tears, and sometimes even clapping, indicated just how much the sermon meant to these people. It was all wonderful and, somehow, sweet and natural. To our surprise, we felt right at home among them. They are truly our brothers and sisters. Even the long services in a language we didn't understand fail to bore us. It was the unmistakable moving of the Holy Spirit that we sensed there.

Our host pastor beckoned us on again. Another open-hearted crowd was waiting. This church building was smaller, but overflowing like the other two. The welcome was as friendly, the atmosphere as warm.

This time all of us said a word. Speaking through an interpreter is quite an experience. You feel like you are being interrupted instead of interpreted. The normal thing is to find yourself running on ahead before the interpreter has finished. You stop then, embarrassed, knowing the people haven't understood a word you've said.

We enjoyed sharing with these open, hungry people. They were our kind of folks in spite of their shabby clothes and strange language. We left our third church service of the morning to find it was almost three o'clock. We were tired and hungry, but we wouldn't have missed this blessed day for anything.

We went with pastor number one to a large and rather nice restaurant. The other two pastors were waiting for us there. With them was the leader of our denomination in that country. They had planned with the restaurant to honor their visitors from afar with a banquet. It was a beautiful meal and time of fellowship. They shared many heart-stirring things with us. We were even more grateful for the freedoms we enjoy in our beloved homeland.

✳

One of the great needs always mentioned by the leader and his pastors was for church buildings, but in Romania permits to build were often denied. After many unsuccessful attempts to get a permit, congregations often commenced building anyway. The men of the church ordered building materials privately for themselves, then gave them to the church as a gift. They donated building stones, cement, lumber, and other supplies. All the men then got together to build at night, any way they could, as fast as they could, to complete the building before the construction attracted official notice. If it could be finished to a certain point before it was discovered, they could keep it. If not, demolition crews would come with bulldozers and knock it flat. When this happened, the church people were devastated. All the money and work was lost.

Often these buildings were financed by money from Sweden or West Germany. One congregation we knew of acquired a large, barnlike structure that long served as their church. Through donations from outside and what they could rake together, they finally collected enough money to start building. Still no permit was forthcoming. They simply removed furniture, walls, and everything else from the structure until it was only a shell. Then they proceeded to build the new church right inside the old one. They worked practically day and night. No one bothered them or seemed to notice what was going on. When the building inside the barn was finished, the men just tore down the shell to unveil their sparkling new house of worship. It was as though it sprang up overnight.

There was great rejoicing among the members. The officials left them alone and the church has blossomed.

Today there is still a great move of God in Romania. The churches are full to overflowing. If possible, they are more crowded than before. New people are constantly coming into the churches and giving their lives to Christ. Many professionals are among them: doctors, lawyers, teachers, scientists, and others. Before the democratic revolution this was an enormous step for these people. Many lost their positions. Christian teachers, for example, were not allowed to practice their profession. In fact, Christian young people were not even permitted to study education.

Conditions have changed dramatically. The freedom that Paul and his brethren only dreamed of finally has arrived. Paul would have loved to see this happen, but his own efforts were instrumental in keeping things alive until it was possible.

Paul gave much time, devotion, and caring to this part of the world. The journey was long and arduous. The food did not always agree with him. Government officials thwarted him at every turn. Much had to be done covertly. Strain and tension were hard on him. He often lay awake at night praying and planning how he could do the most good for the most people with the least hindrance from the powers that be.

One problem was baptisms. Baptism was strictly forbidden for anyone under eighteen. Young people were coming to the Lord in great numbers. They rejoiced in their salvation. When they learned about baptism, they wanted to take this next step of obedience to the Lord, but many of them were under eighteen.

Many clandestine baptismals were held, sometimes in a pond or river in the woods late at night, other times in someone's large bathtub, in the dead of night. They were taking great risks, but they felt it was more important to obey God than man. They didn't always make it. Someone would betray them or they would be discovered in other ways. Discovery meant huge fines for the church, even imprisonment for the pastor, but they carried on bravely in spite of every obstacle.

Often when Paul and I visited Romania, he would be asked to officiate at one of these secret baptisms. He dared not take me with him. An American woman would have attracted too much attention; it would have been too dangerous. The only safe thing for him to do was to park me in our hotel and go off alone into the night. I would wait there all by myself in a strange city among hostile people who spoke a foreign language.

I could visualize Paul in some dark forest by a lake or river, baptizing people at the risk of their freedom and possibly his. Prayer was my solace as the long hours went by. I jumped at every sound. When sleep did come, it would be fitful, filled with tormenting dreams.

Sometimes it was almost morning when Paul finally crept wearily into bed. Usually I was still awake when he came. It was so good to have him back unharmed, I cried for joy. He couldn't tell me anything until we were safe in the car. Romanian hotel rooms were often bugged. It was never wise to discuss anything while still there.

The stories he would tell as we drove along were as exciting as a James Bond novel. One stands out especially. The candidates for baptism met in someone's home far out in the country, where a meal was served to all. Then the long walk in total darkness and absolute silence, out to a spot by a river, deep in the woods. Lookouts were be stationed all around to watch for intruders. The people sang a few songs, almost under their breath.

Those to be baptized were given a few moments of instruction. They were dressed in long white robes. Paul said most of them were young and looked like angels. Then it was time for the baptisms to begin. Paul got into his garb and led the candidates into the water. The national pastor followed.

Just as the ceremony was about to begin, the sound of voices came from further down the river. The lookout snapped to attention, peering through the darkness, trying to see what was going on. They couldn't see enough to tell if it was safe, so the ceremony came to an abrupt halt while some of the men slipped through the woods to see if they could find out what was happening.

Everybody waited in the darkness with baited breath, longing for the men to return. Suddenly footsteps sounded in the darkness. The people seemed to shrink together. They held hands as silent prayers were breathed. Dark figures crept into the tiny clearing. They came nearer. The people all breathed a great sigh of relief. It was their own men. They assured the group that everything was all right. The voices were from some young men having a drinking party. They were totally unaware of this group.

With thankful hearts, the people slipped back into the river, and the ceremony began again. There were no more delays or interruptions. The young people were all baptized, rejoicing in this step of obedience they were privileged to take.

The happy group hurried back to the farmhouse, where a warm meal was prepared for everybody. It was a triumphant night for them all. Bone tired and still shivering from the cold water, Paul wished the dear Christians good night, got in his car, and drove back to the hotel.

This story was repeated often, with only slight variations. Today, with democracy restored, these beautiful people can, at last, worship God as they wish. It is a dream come true, something Paul spent a lifetime working toward.

CHAPTER THIRTY-FIVE

One of our favorite Eastern European lands is Poland. I have already told of our visits to Poland as starry-eyed young missionaries. We never forgot Poland and always hoped to visit this land of spunky, friendly people again sometime. That time finally came in 1970.

Paul planned this trip without an invitation. He wasn't in touch with any of the church leaders, but he knew about one or two of them. He had also heard about a Bible School in Warsaw serving evangelicals. He hoped to visit there while in Poland. This trip, however, was to be our vacation.

We drove over the border. The officials were courteous and friendly. They spoke good German and gave us a practical brochure showing places of interest, hotels, campgrounds, and many other things to make our trip easy and pleasant. Naturally, our first destination was Gdansk – the old city of Danzig. It was a long drive from the border where we enter the country. We drove over low hills, through green forests, and by serene lakes. We enjoyed the interesting hamlets and villages we passed through.

Very soon we spotted a street market just like the ones we remembered from long ago. Chickens, ducks, and geese were hung up by hooks, still in full feather. I had never seen so many varieties of gorgeous flowers all in one spot. Also vegetables, meats, sausages, and fruit of all kinds were available for those who had the money. They seemed very inexpensive compared to prices we were accustomed to. The dollar bought a lot of Polish *zloty*; they jingled in our pockets like toy money. It was fun loading up on fruit, good Polish sausage, straw hats, and anything else we fancied.

We drove through many places we knew before World War II. They looked different now. We hardly recognized them. At last the beautiful Baltic Sea lay before us, shimmering in the late afternoon sunshine. We were thrilled. We drove on through Zoppet, an old seaside resort where we whiled away many a happy hour in days gone by. There we stopped and walked together down the boardwalk. We strolled along the beach looking for the pretty amber pebbles that wash ashore. Nothing there had changed much, except that now Polish people enjoyed the sun and sea. The Germans who survived had left after the war.

The drive along the shore to Oliva, a pretty little resort town, was familiar and nostalgic. Paul and I had spent many lazy Saturday afternoons there during the summers. Old memories washed over us, bringing a feeling of nostalgia we couldn't resist.

Before we arrived in Danzig itself, we decided to look for the old Bible School. We found it run-down and dilapidated. Probably no one used it anymore. Paul went to the door, which was opened by a very ancient woman. She spoke only Polish, and we couldn't get much information from her. Then we drove through the city to our old apartment. The main part of town looked much as it did before. It was totally destroyed but has since been restored. We were happy to see those grand old Hansa houses looking very nearly as we remembered them.

We tried to find our old street and apartment house, but landmarks were gone. The old houses we knew had disappeared. Cheap new housing had replaced them. At last we found the street. The name was the same, but was now spelled and pronounced in Polish.

No wonder we had such a hard time finding it. By this time we were tired and hungry and decided to go to the old Rathskeller. Paul and I had loved to eat there when we lived in Danzig. It looked very much the same now and had the usual fine cuisine. The food was distinctly Polish and tasted delicious.

Paul knew about a youth retreat center somewhere near Danzig that would be a delightful place to visit. Paul made a phone call. They were open, and they had a youth retreat in session and would consider it a favor if Paul would come and minister to them. They invited us to stay overnight. Paul gladly accepted the warm invitation, and we were off to the youth center.

The leader had given Paul good directions. We found the place without difficulty. It was located in a lovely wooded spot near a lake. This pleasant stay was a treat for us and our guests. Paul had always loved young people and was right in his element there. His warm faith and words of encouragement challenged his hearers.

Some of the kids rededicated their lives to the Lord. Others accepted Jesus as their personal Savior. Afterwards Paul opened the session for questions. Like young people the world over, these teenagers were full of questions. Paul and the leader tried to answer them, or to encourage the kids to think their own questions through. They enjoyed that and came up with some excellent answers.

The morning flew by. We enjoyed lunch and good fellowship with counselors, leaders, and especially with campers. Everyone came out to the car as we prepared to leave. Smiling faces, handshakes and hugs, one last prayer, and we were off for Warsaw and the Bible School there.

Warsaw still showed the ravages of war. We saw demolished buildings, but more often we saw vacant lots where the rubble had been cleared away. As we visited students and leaders at the school, we learned much about Poland's suffering during the war. She fought valiantly, but her best was not enough. The enemy was too much for her, numerically and in war readiness. Poland was conquered, but she went down fighting. She was still resisting a tyrannical puppet government during that visit. The whole world now knows and applauds the spunky Polish people who dared to stand up for their rights, in spite of internal and external objections.

Our brief familiarization trip to Poland rekindled Paul's interest in that country that we had visited and loved as fledgling missionaries. He had a dream. Someday he was going back to Poland. He wanted to initiate a teaching program for churches there. The leaders he spoke with regretted the lack of solid Bible teaching in their churches. Couldn't Paul do something? This need, and the leaders' recognition of it, kept tugging at his heart. He was a busy man with the programs in Germany and other German-speaking lands. He was also deeply involved in the Eastern European lands where he was already working. Could he possibly take on anything more?

Several busy years went by. Poland was temporarily put on hold. Paul knew God's timing was always right. When He was ready, He would make it known.

One day a German missionary to Eastern Europe brought back a message for Paul. It was from Pastor Suski in Poland. Could Missionary Williscroft come to the city of Cieszyn? It was just over the Czechoslovakian-Polish border. They wanted a seminar on Christian Education in their church. They would appreciate teaching during the day and evangelistic meetings in the evening. Interested people from all over Poland planned to attend. Pastor Suski assured Paul they were eagerly awaiting his reply.

God's timing was perfect. The dates suggested by Pastor Suski came at a time when Paul could best get away for a week.

Early one sunny morning we loaded the car with Sunday-school material in English. Poland is partial to the English language. Most young people learn it in school. It isn't hard to find people who can translate easily and well. We brought songs, stories, quarterlies, flannel-board pictures and lessons, puppets, pictures, object lessons, and workshop materials.

We had to drive through Czechoslovakia to avoid the long, roundabout way through East Germany. We got a transit visa, which allowed us forty-eight hours in the country. This wasn't the easiest East Bloc country to visit or even drive through. We did make a short stop in Prague to greet some Christians we knew. It was like a homecoming. Their joy made our day. We continued on to the small city of Tesin on the Polish border.

There we risked stopping again to visit dear Christians. It was Saturday night. They begged us to stay over and minister to their group on Sunday. We were not expected in Poland until Sunday evening, so gladly granted their request. We would still be within our visa time limit.

It was a precious Sunday. The people were thrilled to have visitors, but I think they blessed us more than we blessed them. I can still see those earnest, eager faces looking up at us, their hearts in their eyes.

When the Christians heard we were having a teacher training seminar in Poland, they begged for one in Tesin sometime in the near future. Paul was later able to arrange for such a weekend. God's ways are not our ways, though. He called Paul to Himself before that seminar could be realized. I have thought of these loving, gentle people often, and I pray that God will eventually move to let them have the training course they wanted so much.

The seminar in Cieszyn, Poland, was a rich and meaningful week for the many who came. Classes were carried on all day, with short breaks sandwiched between teaching periods. A hearty meal at noon and a light supper before the evening service were graciously provided by the church ladies. The workshops were an appealing attraction for those who already worked with children and for others who wanted to learn how to do it. This was an informal time when workers could share experiences, work together on projects, and plan how they would incorporate the new ideas into existing church programs. We stayed close by to guide, encourage, and answer questions.

The evening meetings were the crowning hours of the day. People came from all over the surrounding area. Another church in town sponsored a rehabilitation center for drug and alcohol abusers. They brought their people every night. God did some mighty things among them.

One young man looked hopeless – bloodshot eyes, bloated face, trembling hands, dirty and unkempt. He rushed forward when Paul gave an invitation to accept Christ as Savior and Lord. No one went to pray with him. Paul was busy helping and counseling the many who came to talk with him.

I finally decided I'd try to see what could be done for the poor fellow. He knelt alone, shoulders shaking with sobs, eyes red from weeping. Feeling the gentle nudge of the Holy Spirit, I laid my hand on his shaking shoulders and prayed, first in English, then in a soft prayer language.

The man stopped crying and began to pray. I thought he was speaking Polish. I stayed with him and prayed on. Someone from the center came and listened as he prayed. I asked in what language he was praying. This person answered with a puzzled look, "I don't know. He isn't speaking Polish. I didn't know he spoke another language. He is a very simple, uneducated boy."

Then Pastor Suski came by. He listened a moment, then turned to me, eyes shining, and said, "Gladys, he is speaking in tongues."

God knew the needs of a lost young man. He saved him and filled him with His Holy Spirit in one wonderful operation. When he finally managed to stand, he was so happy he had to hug everybody around him.

Next evening a fine looking young man came, shook hands, and gave me a big hug. I must have looked surprised. As far as I knew, I had never laid eyes on this man before. He could see my puzzled expression. He beckoned someone over who could speak English or German. That individual interpreted for him.

"Don't you remember me? I am the young fellow you prayed with last night. I still can't grasp it. I am a brand-new man. I feel different, the world looks different. I am truly happy for the first time in my life. I love everybody. I don't even crave drugs or alcohol anymore."

The people from the rehabilitation center were electrified. This must be the missing factor in their program. They were loving, caring, and compassionate. They were tireless in their efforts to help their patients recover. In spite of everything they did, the results were minimal. These troubled people needed more than human goodwill, knowledge, or skill could accomplish. They needed a living relationship with an almighty God. The leaders and their patients never missed a meeting during the rest of the series. Nothing as dramatic as that first conversion occurred, but lives were changed and the leaders themselves received new faith and courage to work together with God in their center.

The whole week was one of blessing and spiritual growth for the church. Paul had a gift of leading congregations into worship. Corporal worship was not generally practiced in this group of believers. Paul encouraged them in the beautiful reality of worship in spirit and in truth.

During that wonderful week many were filled with the Holy Spirit in the worship times. Pastor Suski was deeply moved as he went to pray for his young son and heard him praising the Lord in a prayer language before his father even got to him. The Suskis became some of our dearest friends during that week together. Our friendship has continued over the years. It was Pastor Suski who, at Paul's funeral, tearfully challenged me to write this book.

We returned to Poland many times after that. New doors opened all over the country. We held Christian Education seminars in many places. Paul ministered in several youth camps with exciting results. We held a marriage enrichment seminar in one area. Another fine missionary, Paul Weresh, worked with us.

Many marriages were helped, but the most outstanding was a young wife whose husband was a government official. He was very much against her faith. We spoke at the seminar about spouses being thankful for each other and expressing it. The husband was not present, but the wife decided to try it.

We were in that area a year or two later for meetings. A lovely young woman came to me after the service. An English-speaking friend came with her to interpret. The young woman threw her arms around me as she told me, with the help of her interpreter, what had happened. She was the young wife whose husband opposed her Christian faith. She had listened to the lectures. When I mentioned being thankful for our spouses, she suddenly saw herself for the ungrateful, fault-finding, critical wife she was. She hated herself. When she got home she went to her husband and, sobbing, asked his forgiveness. He was so astonished and touched that all he could do was hold her tight and let her sob it out on his shoulder.

He gave his life to the Lord shortly after. Today he is a Spirit-filled Christian and a leader in the church. He is in charge of a large building program for the fine new church the congregation is putting up. Marriage seminars were one of the most fruitful ministries in the last years of our missionary service.

Poland is being visited today with a wonderful spirit of revival. In the Catholic church, leaders are pleading for Bibles for their parishioners. There is an insatiable hunger to read God's word among Catholics and Protestants alike. Churches have a problem getting enough Bibles to supply the demand. It doesn't seem to matter who preaches. People come to see, stay to hear, and remain after the service to pray and give their lives to Christ.

New churches are being built all over Poland to meet the need of growing congregations. Pastor Suski is just finishing a lovely new building.

It was always a mystery to us how the church people raised the money they needed for these large projects. None of them were wealthy; some were quite poor. Of course they often got help from abroad, but pastors told us it was the sacrificial giving of their people that made a building program possible. That was Poland, though. Even during times of food shortages and nearfamine conditions, people seemed somehow to scrounge up a meal. How much more were they motivated to find ways of getting badly needed churches built. They are a plucky, resourceful folk. It was a privilege to work with them.

CHAPTER THIRTY-SIX

October of 1986 started out as one of those blue and gold months that are typical of this time of year in most of Central Europe. Paul had been invited to Poland as guest speaker in the fall conference of our denomination. Pastor Orzechowski of Hamburg had also been invited and planned to arrive a few days later. It was a good conference. Paul ministered the Word the first day or two. God's presence was very real in those meetings. The third day Paul suddenly became violently ill. He was rushed to his quarters, and Pastor Orzechowski took over the pulpit for the rest of the conference.

Paul was so ill the doctor feared for his life. The conference guests prayed earnestly for him. The family where he was quartered ministered tirelessly to his needs, praying day and night for his recovery. The doctor was a dedicated Christian and attended Paul with loving concern. He tried everything but couldn't seem to find the source of the trouble. It could have been his heart. It could also have been a stroke, or even some serious disease.

When it seemed almost hopeless, Paul suddenly began to improve. Even the doctor attributed this turn to the Lord and gave Him all the glory.

The whole conference and all the friends rejoiced. After another day or two, Paul felt ready to travel and wanted to go home. The doctor and other friends protested, but Paul's schedule was heavy. Work waited for him at home, and he finally persuaded the doctor to let him go. Pastor Orzechowski drove Paul's car while Paul rested, warm and cozy, in the reclining passenger seat. A friend from Hamburg who had accompanied Orzechowski to Poland drove the car back to Erzhausen.

Early Monday morning I was awakened by the loud jangling of the telephone. It was from the Bible School. A call had come from Pastor Orzechowski, telling of Paul's illness. He had informed the office that they would arrive in Erzhausen in about an hour. I should call his clinic and inform them of his illness and alert them to have everything ready to receive him for a complete checkup and any necessary tests in about an hour.

I was devastated. I just couldn't grasp it. Paul had seemed quite well when he left. Whatever had happened? He was seldom ill. A dark cloud suddenly blotted out my sunshine. When the car drove up to the door, I put on a smile and rushed out to greet Paul and Pastor Orzechowski.

Everything that happened from that point on is a blur in my memory. Ditmar Mittelstaedt drove us to the clinic, as I recall. He was such a tower of strength. Pastor Orzechowski and his friend drove on to Hamburg. Ditmar and I waited a long time in the clinic. When Paul came out of the doctor's office, he looked weak and ill. Ditmar picked up some prescriptions the doctor had given and drove us home.

Paul spent a few days in bed. A dear Bible student who is a registered nurse came over as often as she could and was a comfort and help to both of us. The tests from the clinic showed that Paul had very high blood pressure, his heart was skipping beats, his cholesterol level was high, and he showed evidence of a slight stroke. The days in bed, the loving care we all showered on him and the medication he was taking helped him. He was soon up and back at his desk.

Things seemed almost back to normal. Still it wasn't the same. Paul tired too easily. He suffered headaches often, something new for him. He had little appetite and was losing weight. He rarely complained, but I could see he wasn't well, and I was anxious about him.

I began to realize how serious Paul's condition was when we held several seminars in November and December and on into the new year. He forgot vital parts of his teaching. He often repeated himself. Sometimes I noticed a slight slur in his speech.

One lovely, snowy day Paul took me for a little drive through the winter wonderland of a German woods. We found a pretty place to park and just chatted for a while. Then he took my two hands in his and began to talk about the future. I was frightened when he began with these words, "If the Lord lets me live another two years I plan to do thus and so for the work in Eastern Europe. I want to make arrangements for the Christian Education program in Germany, too, so it will go on smoothly if I should ever have to drop out suddenly. I hope to have everything so well planned and organized that my successor could pick right up where I left off."

He went on to share with me just how he planned to do this. I was so shaken by his obvious assumption that he might not have long to live that I could hardly take in all that he told me. I felt like I must be having a bad dream. I asked him hesitantly if he felt he might not have much more time to live. He laughed and hugged me, calling me his little worry wart. He assured me he felt all right but thought it wise to have things taken care of so there would be a smooth transition in the event that something should happen. He said his recent serious illness had made him think about these things. I felt better, but wasn't wholly satisfied with his explanation.

The lovely Advent season arrived. These four Sundays before Christmas Day are celebrated almost everywhere in Western Europe, but especially in Germany. It was originally a time of preparing the heart for celebrating the birth of Jesus. This is still true in most churches – theoretically in some, from the heart in others. A wreath with four candles is the center of every home and church. There are other decorations, too, but the wreath reigns as queen until Christmas Eve, when the tree takes over. Each Sunday a candle is lit. Family and friends gather around a festive table in the afternoon, listening to Advent music, talking and munching on Christmas goodies between sips of rich, delicious German coffee.

This was a time Paul and I especially loved. To my joy, he felt quite well, so I invited friends on Sunday afternoons. Paul seemed almost like his old, happy self.

Two Sundays stand out in my memory. On one we had my orthopedic doctor and his pleasant wife with us. They are loving, sensitive people. Both are interested in spiritual things. We wiled away the hours sharing thoughts and experiences, exploring one another's minds, comparing books we had read and music we loved. It was a beautiful afternoon. I was glad we had invited them. It was a highlight of the season for Paul.

The next Advent Sunday a dear German lady visited us. She had learned to know the Lord in a servicemen's rally in Stuttgart that Paul had started years ago. We hadn't seen her for years. Her visit was a joy for both of us, but it was like a shot in the arm for Paul. She had been only a girl when she gave her heart to Jesus. Now, to see her living for her Savior in spite of hard trials was very rewarding.

Our Christmas was special, too. We were with the Mittelstaedts and Aunty Decker, our dear, elderly missionary. We spent Christmas Eve in our home and Christmas Day with Ditmar and Elizabeth in their charming duplex. We loved those precious young missionaries, and it made our Christmas perfect to have them with us. I have no recollection of what we ate or did. I just remember how happy we all were that last Christmas together.

Paul kept up with his work quite well during January, though he tired easily and ate poorly. I prepared all his favorite dishes, but he just couldn't do them justice. He went to his office every day, never complaining, trying to act as natural as possible. Nobody, not even I, realized how he was pushing himself. I did notice that he was losing weight, but I attributed that to his loss of appetite. He seemed to be driving himself to get everything finished before some undetermined deadline. Others may have noticed it, too, but Paul was always such a hustler that no one thought much about it.

January melted into February. It was a mild, rainy month with a few sunny days in between. In the middle of February we held two or three seminars for children's workers. The last two were a night-mare for us. Paul's speech was more slurred than usual. His voice was weak and thin. He kept forgetting things he wanted to say and often repeated himself. I agonized through the whole of our last seminar. It was in Bremen. We were among friends who would surely notice the change in Paul and wonder what had happened. I tried to think how I could broach the subject to him without hurting him.

I wanted to suggest a few months in the States where he could rest and relax. I thought we could perhaps find good medical help, as well as seeking prayer support from our missions department and our supporting churches. While I was still pondering what to do, the Lord stepped in and tenderly settled the matter. It was not what we would have chosen, but God knows what is good and right for His children. He doesn't make mistakes.

February 24th dawned mild and sunny. That is Beverly's birthday, so we lingered at the breakfast table discussing when would be a good time to call her with our birthday greetings. We decided, with the time difference, that five o'clock in the evening would be about right. It was a day of fasting and prayer at the Bible School, so we planned to go. I insisted on Paul eating a little breakfast. God would understand if he didn't fast.

We were so happy for the beautiful, mild weather in February. It was a lovely drive through the fields. They had that fresh look that grass has after the snow is gone and gentle rain has fallen on it for a few days. Even now, when I smell the fresh, early spring grass, I feel again the sweetness of that short drive. We came out of the country-side into the village streets. Children were laughing and playing on their way to school. Shops were opening, people were leisurely going about their business, enjoying the bright morning. We were glad to be alive and part of everything.

When we arrived at the Bible School, Paul went up to his office to get his assistants started for the day. I can still hear his cheery greeting to friends he met as he hurried along.

I decided to go to the chapel, where Paul would join me as soon as he could. A guest speaker from South Africa whom God had greatly used there to help and encourage Christians in their prayer lives was speaking. Paul joined me, and we drank in the rich, spiritual feast being served us. As we knelt, we felt we were literally in the presence of the Lord. We spent the whole morning praying, worshiping, and bringing our requests with thanksgiving to our Father.

At the noon break we drove home, talking all the way about the wonderful message and the blessed time of prayer. We felt spiritually refreshed.

Upon our arrival home, we decided not to eat lunch but to have a snack before we went back to the school. Paul always took a short rest after lunch. He was tired and glad to lie down for awhile. I decided to rest too, until he got up. I must have dozed off, for suddenly I awoke with a start and glanced at my watch. It was three o'clock. Paul should have been up long before this.

I knocked softly on the bedroom door. No response. My heart beat faster. What could be wrong? I wanted to go in but dreaded what I might find. Was he too ill to speak? Had he fainted? Did he have a stroke? I knocked again, louder this time, then resolutely pushed the door open and walked in.

God had stepped into that room before me and escorted His beloved missionary home.

I called the doctor and Ditmar. While waiting for them, I gave him mouth-to-mouth resuscitation, praying as I worked. I didn't cry. I couldn't. I was beyond that. A strange numbness had taken possession of me. Then the doctor and Ditmar arrived.

The doctor saw what I was doing and gently drew me away.

"Herr Williscroft doesn't need any help now, Frau Williscroft. He is with Jesus," he said softly, after examining him.

Stunned, I sat by the bedside rubbing Paul's cold hands, trying to warm them. I was in shock but refused the proffered tranquilizer. I wanted to keep alert, but at the same time felt this couldn't be happening to *us*.

Soon the house was full of people. The undertaker and his helpers, friends who came to comfort and be with me in my sorrow, neighbors who noticed that all was not well at the Williscroft home. Elizabeth and Ditmar were a great comfort. They stepped in and took care of everything. Ditmar completed the paperwork required by German authorities for a foreigner. Elizabeth arranged for food, care of the house, and countless other details.

At five o'clock I called Beverly as planned and wished her a happy birthday. After a little chat, I had to give her the sad news of her daddy's death. She burst into hysterical sobs for a moment, then pulled herself together as much as she was able and listened while I told her what had happened. I tried to comfort her in spite of my own sorrow. It helped us both to make some necessary plans. She would call my son immediately, then try to book an early morning flight to Frankfurt. We then made arrangements to get in touch with my family. We were both feeling better when we hung up.

I called one of Paul's brothers next. We sorrowed a few moments together, then I reminded him that Paul was at home with the Lord he loved. Shouldn't we rejoice with him? He called his brother, John. I know it was hard for them. Death is so final if one does not have a living faith.

Beverly arrived quite early the next morning. Robert and Christine came as soon as they could get away. There was much to do: funeral arrangements, sending notice of Paul's death to European and American friends, Paul's papers to digest and sort.

God did a beautiful thing in me during all this hectic time. I felt as though I were wrapped in a soft, down comforter that insulated me from anything that could disturb, upset, or hurt. I was surrounded by the warm, loving presence of God. Others who have gone through the grieving process have experienced the same insulation and presence of God. I learned to know my heavenly Father in a new dimension during those dark days. I know now that there is no situation so hopeless and despairing that God will not be with us and make a way to bring us through.

The days before the funeral were filled with activities. We closed Paul's accounts and took care of many other business details. Ditmar had informed our mission of Paul's death. Our field representative, Jerry Parsely, was in India and called from there. He visited me as soon as he could. That was a real comfort. Cards, telegrams, and letters came from all over Europe and the United States. Paul's secretary answered as many as she could. Many of them I would answer later.

The day of the funeral dawned dark, rainy, and cold. Guests came from Eastern and Western Europe, the United States, and the American community in Germany. Paul was laid out in a side room with a large glass window, through which guests could view. Guests streamed into the funeral chapel, stopping on the way for a last glimpse of their friend and brother. He appeared to be sleeping peacefully, with just the shadow of a smile. Surrounded by soft organ music, I sat in the place reserved for family, with my children and with Christine's mother, sister, and nephew. We drew strength and comfort from one another.

Beautiful floral tributes were tastefully displayed on the platform, on the floor in front of the platform, and on and around the casket. I never did know how many there were. The chapel filled to overflowing. We had been in Erzhausen for many years, so were well known. Some of the business people closed their shops to attend the funeral. Others sent flowers and cards expressing their sympathy.

The Bible School choir sang so beautifully I wept; the obituary was read; there were more lovely vocal contributions, one a singing and guitar group of teenagers from teen camp that touched me to the core. Richard Krueger, *Berea Bible School* president, paid Paul a wonderful tribute, relating his pioneering achievements and all his other accomplishments during nearly forty years in Europe. Even I was surprised. Paul did only what he felt needed doing. He never considered it special. He pioneered many projects, turning them over to gifted nationals who carried them on.

Bob Krist, the Assembly of God Service Personnel Representative, gave a kind word about Paul, too. Representatives from several Eastern European countries conveyed tearfully what Paul had meant to them and their compatriots over the years. They told of churches that wouldn't exist today were it not for Paul. They talked of the vision for reaching children that was born in their hearts because of him.

As it went on and on, something happened. We lost a measure of our sorrow. We knew Paul still lived through the contributions he had made in both Eastern and Western Europe. Unobtrusively, lovingly, and selflessly he influenced the lives of others. "He, being dead yet speaketh."

Pastor Reinhold Ulonska, General Superintendent in Germany, brought the main message. He eulogized Paul as his good friend and former teacher, but he didn't stop there. He challenged the people to give their all to the Master, to rise up and fight against the powers of darkness, remembering that we are more than conquerors with Jesus at our side. One by one the old heroes of the faith go on to their reward, but they throw the torch to us who live, to hold high and go on to glorious victory.

Paul's funeral became a celebration. We celebrated the victory of a man of God, who, like another Paul, had fought a good fight, had finished his course, had kept the faith.

EPILOGUE

Paul was laid to rest in the village cemetery in Erzhausen. This was a wish he had expressed many times. The best years of his life had been there. He loved the Bible School, the teachers, and students. Germany was his home. The townspeople knew and respected him. His barber asked me, before I left Germany, if he could have the honor of caring for Paul's grave. His eyes were filled with tears. I felt a warm affection for this dear German man. I knew he could not have paid my husband a higher tribute.

The funeral was over. The people went home, hearts filled with the awe of a burial that should have been sad, but was not. The townspeople talked about it for a long time. They had never experienced anything like it.

The representatives from Eastern Europe lingered a few days in Erzhausen. Pastor Suski visited me to talk over what could be done to continue Paul's Polish work. We talked and prayed as he shared his dreams for his town and for the new church he was building. What would happen now?

"We will trust God to work it out. He has it all in His hands," he said at last.

As he rose to leave, he looked me straight in the eye and asked in a strong, challenging tone, "Gladys, why don't you write a book about your husband?"

I stared at him in disbelief. I couldn't write a book. I had never written anything for publication in my life, except for a few articles in our church paper.

"I'm sorry, Pastor Suski. I am not a writer. I would love to do it if I could, but I just can't. Please don't ask me again."

Pastor Suski looked at me with determination in his eyes. "Oh, yes, you can! Paul has a story that needs to be told. No one can do that but you. Pray about it. Trust God to write it, using your brain, your love, and your hands. I believe God wants you to tackle this challenge and finish it for His glory. Your husband was a leader, a pioneer, a trailblazer. His story will remain buried with him unless you write it. His is a story that can challenge and bless multitudes. Many of us will be praying for you. You *have* to write that book, Gladys."

I had been looking down, hardly daring to face him. I glanced up uncertainty for a moment, with a sense of inadequacy. Pastor Suski's tear-stained face was a study in earnestness, determination, and sorrow. He had a vision. He knew what God wanted, and he knew I must do it. In that moment I also knew.

I reached for his hand, as I brokenly answered, "All right, with God's help and your prayers, I'll do my best. I'll write it."

Thank you, dear Pastor Suski, for your insistence and encouragement.

Paul and Gladys Williscroft
toward the end of Paul's life

Please Post a Review for
Mission Possible

Authors rely on reviews, so I really appreciate your posting a review on Amazon and Goodreads. To post a review, scan the pertinent QR code below and follow the prompts. You will be prompted to log onto the platform. If you are not a member, you will need to sign up. It's free. Amazon will require a minimum $50 purchase volume during the past twelve months. Goodreads has no requirement. Thank you very much for going through this effort!

Scan to review on Amazon

Scan to review on Goodreads